Conversations with Salman Rushdie

Literary Conversations Series

Peggy Whitman Prenshaw
General Editor

Photo credit: ©1999 Nancy Crampton

Conversations
with Salman Rushdie

Edited by
Michael Reder

University Press of Mississippi
Jackson

Books by Salman Rushdie

Grimus. London: Victor Gollancz, 1975; Woodstock, New York: Overlook, 1979.
Midnight's Children. London: Jonathan Cape; New York: Knopf, 1981.
Shame. London: Jonathan Cape; New York: Knopf, 1983.
The Jaguar Smile: A Nicaraguan Journey. London: Pan; New York: Elizabeth Sifton/Viking, 1987.
The Satanic Verses. London: Viking/Penguin, 1988; New York: Viking, 1989.
Is Nothing Sacred? London: Granta, 1990.
In Good Faith. London: Granta, 1990.
Haroun and the Sea of Stories. London and New York: Granta/Viking, 1990.
Imaginary Homelands: Essays and Criticism 1981–1991. London and New York: Granta/ Viking, 1991.
The Wizard of Oz (essay and short story). London: British Film Institute, 1992.
East, West: Stories. London: Jonathan Cape; New York: Pantheon, 1994.
The Vintage Book of Indian Writing in English, 1947–1997 (Edited with Elizabeth West). London: Vintage, 1997; published in USA as *Mirrorwork: 50 Years of Indian Writing, 1947–1997.* New York: Henry Holt, 1997.
The Moor's Last Sigh. London: Jonathan Cape; New York: Pantheon, 1995.
The Ground Beneath Her Feet. London: Jonathan Cape; New York: Henry Holt, 1999.

www.upress.state.ms.us

Copyright © 2000 by University Press of Mississippi
All rights reserved
Manufactured in the United States of America

08 07 06 05 04 03 02 01 00   4 3 2 1
∞
Library of Congress Cataloging-in-Publication Data

Rushdie, Salman.
  Conversations with Salman Rushdie / edited by Michael Reder.
    p. cm. — (Literary conversations series)
  Includes index.
  ISBN 1-57806-184-9 (cloth : alk. paper) — ISBN 1-57806-185-7 (paper : alk. paper)
  1. Rushdie, Salman—Interviews.   2. Authors, English—20th century—Interviews.
3. Islam and literature—History—20th century.   4. Censorship—History—20th
Century.   5. Fiction—Authorship.   I. Reder, Michael.   II. Title.   III. Series.
PR6068.U757 Z465   2000
823'.914—dc21
  [B]   99-057120

British Library Cataloging-in-Publication Data available

Contents

Introduction

Salman Rushdie is one of the most famous and arguably the most important novelist writing in English today. This fame has come at a price beyond the obvious toll on the normalcy of his life: his writing, like the author himself, is often terribly misjudged by people who, although familiar with his name and situation, have never read a word he has written. Most people are unaware of the breadth of Rushdie's writing and thinking; he is known as Salman Rushdie the novelist, a writer of contemporary (and always controversial) fiction. But there are many other Rushdies: the travel writer, the crafter of short stories, the filmmaker, the "children's" storywriter, the essayist and reviewer, and the unflinching commentator upon contemporary culture, particularly upon issues of race and inequality. His impact on contemporary writing as a whole cannot be underestimated; his writing has influenced an entire generation of authors, those that now help comprise the "empire writing back," the new British and postcolonial literary canon.

In these interviews, Rushdie offers insight into all of his books, from his first novel *Grimus* to his recent, best-selling *The Ground Beneath Her Feet.* Rushdie participated in numerous interviews even before the controversy surrounding his novel, *The Satanic Verses,* and many of his most insightful interviews appeared in smaller publications spread throughout the globe: not only in England and the United States, but also in India, Canada, and Europe. This collection brings together the best—and some of the rarest—of the over 100 interviews that Rushdie has given throughout his career. Often autobiographical in nature, they deal extensively with Rushdie's creative process, his views on art and politics, and his life both before and after the *fatwa.* Of interest to both the specialist and to a more general audience, this book covers a wide range of topics. Some of the interviews are academic, in which Rushdie speaks in detail about his work; many are political in nature, when he discusses contemporary politics or the relationship between the artist and the state; most are also of general interest, as he often addresses world politics, his life in hiding, and contemporary culture. Above all, these interviews reveal a man with a powerful mind, a wry sense of humor, and a compelling commitment to social justice.

Articulate, witty, and learned, these interviews also make clear that wherever Rushdie goes, whatever he writes, controversy seems to follow. Rushdie does not necessarily seek out controversy: controversy seems inseparable from the politically charged situations and issues on which he feels compelled to write. He takes risks in his writing, pushing both the novelistic form and language itself to their limits. In the 1982 title essay of his collection *Imaginary Homelands,* Rushdie discusses the need for such risks: "[T]he real risks of any artist are taken in the work, in pushing the work to the limits of what is possible, in the attempt to increase the sum of what it is possible to think. Books become good when they go to this edge and risk falling over it—when they endanger the artist by reason of what he has, or has not, *artistically* dared" (*Granta* 15). Controversy, indeed, seems written into Rushdie's fiction. Rushdie states that "the speaking of suppressed truths is one of the great possibilities of the novel, and it is perhaps the main reason why the novel becomes the most dangerous of art forms in all countries where people, governments, are trying to distort the truth. The novel requires no stage, no film crew, no gallery to hang in. It can be made by one person in a room and read, secretly if necessary, by another individual in another room. This makes written words the hardest messages to ban. In my own writing, I have tried to bring things out from under various carpets, and I suppose that I may go on doing so."[1] There is no doubt that Rushdie takes the power of literature seriously: "I think that there is nothing wrong with the idea that fiction is a matter of life and death. Look at the history of literature. Look at what happened in the Soviet Union. Look at what's happening in China, in Africa, and across the Muslim World. It's not just me. Fiction has always been treated this way. It does matter and it's often very bad for writers that it does. But that just comes with the territory."[2]

For Rushdie, politics and the novel go hand-in-hand because the act of writing creates alternative versions of reality. In the title essay in *Imaginary Homelands,* Rushdie states: "I must say first of all that description is itself a political act. . . . So it is clear that redescribing a world is the necessary first step towards changing it. And particularly at times when the State takes reality into its own hands, and sets about distorting it, altering the past to fit its present needs, then the making of the alternative realities of art, including the novel of memory, becomes politicized." (*Granta* 13–14). It is perhaps for this reason that Rushdie moves easily between the worlds of art and politics. For instance, in his interview with Salil Tripathi the conversation flows easily from a discussion of the Indian novel, to a dialogue about race relations in

England, and on to Rushdie's comments about world political leaders and his opinion of Britain's treatment of Indira Gandhi during her state visit.

In addition to being a gifted crafter of words and worlds, Rushdie is also an accomplished literary and political theorist, making him the postcolonial novelist *nonpareil.* He, like his work, embodies many of the tensions and seeming contradictions of the modern diasporic individual. Rushdie's multiple allegiances and identities make him a citizen of many countries, both real and imaginary. Rushdie tells Michael T. Kaufman in *The New York Times Book Review:* "I don't think that migration, the process of being uprooted, necessarily leads to rootlessness. What it can lead to is a kind of multiple rooting. It's not the traditional identity crisis of not knowing where you come from. The problem is that you come from too many places. The problems are of excess rather than of absence. That's certainly the feeling I have."[3]

As these interviews also reveal, Rushdie is articulate about the art of writing. He talks about struggling with unwieldy drafts, about honing difficult dialogue, and about writing his first love scene. He tells David Brooks "I have all the standard views about writing, which is that it's lonely and you sit in a room and it's hell and sweat and it takes a long time and you despair and so forth, but also it's better than having a job." Rushdie also offers insight into the composing of his novels. For instance, we learn that the original draft of *Midnight's Children* was not narrated by Saleem and was twice the length of the final version (Durix; Haffenden). Rushdie comments on the history of the novel, the recent shift to postmodernist or magical realist fiction: "[T]he 1960s represented a kind of shift in people's perceptions. The simplest of these was the perception that reality was no longer something on which everyone could agree, which it *had* been at the time of the great age of the realist novel. For realism to convince, there must be a fairly broad agreement between the author and the reader about the nature of the world that is being described. I think that for Dickens, George Eliot and others, that would by and large be true. But now we don't have that kind of consensus about the world" (Brooks). Perhaps Rushdie's comment upon the delight of his craft is best revealed in this playful remark: "It seemed to me that the thing that was attractive about fiction was that it is a kind of formalised lying" (Brooks). Of course, this statement, like much of Rushdie's work, cannot be taken simply at face value; Rushdie's "fictions" provide access to the often inexpressible truths about humanity and history.

Rushdie seems to have an uncanny knack for foreshadowing his literary future. For instance, in a 1982 interview with Jean-Pierre Durix concerning

Midnight's Children, while he was still writing what would become *Shame,* Rushdie ends the interview with the following, off-hand remark: "I am very interested in writing about the idea of migration and the effect it has on individuals and groups. And somewhere, I think, there's an enormous novel waiting to be written, unfortunately . . ."; the interview trails off and ends, yet provides a flash of the novel that will be *The Satanic Verses,* a book that would forever change Rushdie's life. Yet, Rushdie's writing has always been controversial. Indira Gandhi sued Rushdie for defamation of character for his portrayal of "the Widow" in *Midnight's Children.* Almost immediately upon its release, *Shame* was banned in Pakistan. In early 1984, four years before the publication of *The Satanic Verses,* interviewer David Brooks asks a hauntingly prophetic question: "There have been times, rereading *Shame* and *Midnight's Children,* when I've actually winced, thinking of what the things you were saying must have been doing to your own life, because you're proscribing whole areas of possible existence for yourself by attacking in the way that you do certain of the people that you do. I was wondering what effect in fact these things have had on your own life, your own freedom or options?" Even with these previous brushes with controversy, no one could have foreseen the turn Rushdie's life would take soon after the publication of *The Satanic Verses.*

In February of 1989, when the Ayatollah Khomeini issued a *fatwa,* a religious edict, calling for Rushdie's death, Rushdie's life changed forever. In 1990, Rushdie comments about his new life in hiding: "One of the most extraordinary things about human events is that the unthinkable becomes thinkable."[4] One cannot help but feel that Rushdie somehow was silenced by this event, by both the absurdity and the gravity of his situation. The threat upon his life made Rushdie a household name, and increased his fame tenfold. Yet, as the English author Martin Amis is said to have told Rushdie after he went into hiding, it is as if Rushdie had "disappeared into the front page" (Rose). Rushdie, living under the protection of the British secret service, was no longer seen in public, yet his name was the topic of news across the world. In some strange way, the message of Rushdie's work was also lost, or at least temporarily mislaid, by all of the hoopla surrounding his controversial novel.

If Rushdie did in some way "disappear," he has managed to fight back with both honesty and tenacity. He has never really been silenced, for he has gone on writing and speaking: "If there's an attempt to silence a writer, the best thing a writer can do is not be silenced. If somebody is trying to stifle your voice, you should try and make sure it speaks louder than before" (Dhillon). Somehow Rushdie has endured his situation, and has continued to write and publish his essays and his best-selling fiction for an ever-widening audience. Rushdie, a great admirer of Günter Grass, speaks of the influence that Grass's *The Tin Drum* had on Rushdie's own attitudes about writing: "This is what Grass's great novel said to me in its drumbeats: Go for broke. Always try and do too much. Dispense with safety nets. Take a deep breath before you begin talking. Aim for the stars. Keep grinning. Be bloody-minded. Argue with the world. And never forget that writing is as close as we get to keeping a hold on the thousand and one things—childhood, certainties, cities, doubts, dreams, instants, phrases, parents, loves—that go on slipping, like sand, through our fingers."[5] Rushdie is compelled to write, it would seem, by writing's sheer power to resist and somehow overcome the limits of being human, even the power of time itself. For Rushdie, the creation of text relates closely to the creation of self, of history, and of reality itself.

Rushdie has no other choice but to keep on writing, to keep describing the world. He comments upon the controversy surrounding *The Satanic Verses:* "Literature is a war of descriptions, and one of the sad things about the Muslim world is that there has been a narrowing of descriptions since the great period of the Islamic Renaissance. By and large, the literal has triumphed. Islam in theory is a religion without priesthood—in its theology it has no room for priests. And yet it now has this fanatically powerful clerisy. I think it's important that these people should not be the only people who have power over the descriptions."[6] Perhaps *The Satanic Verses* can be read as Rushdie's attempt to widen, to reopen the world of descriptions: not only within Islam, but also within contemporary England, which has often marginalized and demonized its immigrant population.[7]

Rushdie himself has been a victim of a "narrowing" of descriptions. First-time readers of Rushdie are often surprised at both his sense of humor and his passionate political commitment. In her interview with Rushdie, Terry Gross notes that the main character in Rushdie's novel *The Ground Beneath Her Feet,* the rock and roll star named Ormus, disappears, propelling him into the headlines and towards greater fame. When Gross suggests that Ormus's situation is analogous to Rushdie's own fame, Rushdie at first seems genuinely surprised by the connection. Then he agrees, and continues: "It is very odd how an absence of a well-known person creates a receptacle into which people can pour all of their ideas about that person."[8] Rushdie has suffered a similar fate during his *in absentia* fame. When Rushdie became front-page news the world over, along with his sudden notoriety came preconceived ideas about his personal life and his work. The number of people who have opinions about Rushdie and his work far exceeds the number of people who have actually read anything that Rushdie has written. In my experience, people unfamiliar with Rushdie's work assume he is too clever for his own good, a troublemaker who tried to ruffle some feathers but got in over his head when he angered a religious leader: they have painted a picture of the missing Rushdie as a fame-seeker and mere caricaturist. In reality, Rushdie is both funnier and more serious than his non-readers believe. His writing is deeply comedic and ironic; he is able to find humor—and therefore the resilience of humanity—in the conflicts between good and evil, understanding and ignorance, pain and happiness, history and the individual. Rushdie is not so much a troublemaker as a tender, albeit brutally honest, chronicler of humanity.

For those people who will never meet Rushdie in person, these interviews offer insight into the person behind his writing. What I like most about these interviews is what I like most about Rushdie's writing in general: that in them, Rushdie is allowed to speak for himself. Some of the recurring themes in these interviews include Rushdie's literary influences, immigration, the relationships between fantasy and realism, history and narration, literature and culture. As with most writers, Rushdie's life informs much of his fiction, and thus many of these interviews, particularly those early ones concentrating on *Midnight's Children,* contain autobiographical information.

Although Rushdie interviews are not rare and many have appeared on major networks or in major international newspapers, high-quality interviews, ones in which the interviewers are well-informed about Rushdie's writings and political situation, are more difficult to come by. I have chosen interviews that I feel to be the most in-depth, literate, and wide-ranging. As with any collection of this type, some repetition is inevitable. The interviews are reprinted in their entirety with minimal editing; as is the tradition of the Literary Conversations Series, titles of books have been italicized, and typographical errors and mistakes in transcription have been silently corrected.

I want to thank many people without whose work and support I would never have been able to complete this collection: Kathy Diehr Pitcher, Brooke Steinle, Doreen Vaillancourt, Douglas Pierce, Joanna Sweeney, and Dan Pincus all helped with research, including tracking down permissions. Thanks to Theresa Ammirati, Brooke Gessay, and Shane Gong for help with the proofs and index. Chaman Sahni and Stephen Clingman introduced me to Rushdie's work. Norm Weinstein never allows me to think conventionally. Carmel Bedford of the International Rushdie Defence Committee has been generous with her help and support. Baylor University provided me with a President's Research Fellowship. I want to thank the many librarians who helped contribute to this project, particularly those at Boise State University, Baylor University, and Connecticut College, most notably Steve Bustamante, Melody Hamilton, and Beth Hansen.

I am very thankful to Professor Amritjit Singh for his support of this project and for his help in tracking down difficult-to-obtain interviews. I am greatly indebted to all of the people behind the scenes who make sure the world's media run smoothly, the many editors, researchers, and permission coordinators, including Janine Dyre and Vicky Mitchell (BBC), Sally Sweet (Routledge), Sonya Singleton and Elaine Dawson *(Guardian/Observer),* Nicholas Clee *(Bookseller),* Sophie Harrison *(Granta),* Anne Collett and Anna Rutherford *(Kunapipi),* Robyn Goldman (WHYY), Shelley Hoffmann (Charlie Rose), Claire Lloyd (Blackwell), Kirby Wiggins (NPR), Bob Sharrard (City Lights), Raymond Shapiro *(New York Review of Books),* Stacey Purpura *(Newsweek),* Vivek Sharma (Syndications Today), Cliff Garboden *(Boston Phoenix).* Finally, thanks to Anthony Roland, who has assembled an excellent collection of video interviews with contemporary authors and artists that are available to the public.

This book would not have been possible without the contributions of all the people who have interviewed Rushdie, particularly those who facilitated the use of their interviews, including Salil Tripathi, Dina Vakil, Blake Morrison, David Brooks, and John Clement Ball.

I want to thank my editors, Anne Stascavage and Seetha Srinivasan, without whose threats I would never have finished this project.

I appreciate the continuing support of my colleagues, particularly Theresa Ammirati, Deborah Carlin, Reggie Flood, Bindu Malieckal, Josna Rege, and Marjorie Salvadon.

Finally, I would like to thank Andrea and Noah, whose smiles and giggles make my life worth living. This book is dedicated to my parents, Marjorie and David Bryant, Bernard and Elizabeth Reder, and John and Lucy Rossi.

MR

Notes

1. Interview in "A Dangerous Art Form" in *Third World Book Review,* volume 1, 1984:10.
2. From the *Salon* interview. <http://www.salon.com/06/features/interview.html>
3. "Author From 3 Countries," *The New York Times Book Review,* 13 November 1983: 23.
4. Interview with Gerald Marzorati, *The New York Times Magazine,* 4 November 1990: 32.
5. "Günter Grass," *Imaginary Homelands,* 277.
6. Interview with James Wood, *The Guardian,* 21 September 1991: 23.
7. For greater insight into the genesis of *The Satanic Verses,* I recommend "Salman Rushdie talks to the London Consortium about *The Satanic Verses,* Colin Mac-Cabe et. al., in *Critical Quarterly* 38.2 (Summer 1996): 51–70. In this in-depth interview, Rushdie speaks in detail about the many complex issues in the novel.
8. "Fresh Air," 21 April 1999.

Chronology

1947   Salman Ahmed Rushdie is born in Bombay on 19 June to Anis Ahmed Rushdie and Negin (nee Butt) Rushdie; he is the eldest child of this prosperous and liberal Muslim family.

1961   Goes to England to attend Rugby School.

1962   Family moves to England and later become citizens.

1965   Rushdie enrolls in King's College, Cambridge; parents move to Karachi, Pakistan.

1968   Receives his M.A. in History with honors from King's College, Cambridge. Joins family in Karachi and works in television production and publishing.

1969   Returns to London, where he acts and works in television, advertising, and publishing.

1970   Meets Clarissa Luard, whom he marries in 1976 (child, Zafar, b. 1979; divorced 1987). Begins to write two novels, both unpublished.

1975   *Grimus* is published. Works with emigrants in Camden. Visits India to conduct research for next book.

1981   *Midnight's Children* is published. Wins the Booker Prize for fiction, the James Tait Black Prize, and a prize from the English Speaking Union.

1983   *Shame* is published. Short-listed for the Booker. Wins the French *Prix du Meilleur Livre Estranger* for postmodernist fiction. Becomes fellow of Royal Society for Literature.

1984   Travels with Bruce Chatwin in Australia.

1985   Produces *The Painter and the Pest* for television.

1986   Travels to Nicaragua and lives with the Sandinistas.

1987   Publishes the non-fiction *The Jaguar Smile: A Nicaraguan Journey.* Meets Marianne Wiggins, whom he marries in 1988 (divorced 1993).

1988   Produces *The Riddle of Midnight,* a documentary for Channel Four television.

1988   26 September. Viking/Penguin (UK) publishes *The Satanic Verses;* wins Whitbread Prize.

1988   In October British Muslims protest in Bradford. *The Satanic Verses* is publicly burned. In India, after protests by Muslims, the book is banned by order of India's Minister of Home Affairs.

1989   14 February. The Ayatollah Khomeini, religious leader of Iran, issues
        a judicial decree (a *fatwa*) denouncing Rushdie and his publishers and
        calling for his death. Rushdie and his wife, Marianne Wiggins, go
        into hiding under the protection of the British government.
1990   In response to the *fatwa* publishes *Is Nothing Sacred?* and *In Good
        Faith.*
1990   Publishes *Haroun and the Sea of Stories.*
1991   Publishes *Imaginary Homelands: Essays and Criticism, 1981–1991.*
1991   December Surprise appearance at Columbia University forum on free
        speech.
1992   Publishes *The Wizard of Oz,* an essay and story for the British Film
        Institute's series on classic films.
1992   March Goes to Washington, D.C. to meet with US Senators, who are
        pressured by the White House to cancel meeting; US President Bush
        refuses a meeting.
1993   *Midnight's Children* awarded "Booker of Bookers" for the best
        Booker Prize-winning novel in 25-year history of the Booker.
1993   November Visits Cambridge, Massachusetts and is made an honorary
        visiting professor of humanities at MIT. Meets with US President
        Clinton.
1994   Publishes *East, West: Stories,* a collection of short fiction spanning
        his writing career. Meets Elizabeth West, whom he marries in 1997
        (child, Milan, b. 1997).
1995   Publishes *The Moor's Last Sigh.* Short-listed for the Booker. Wins
        Whitbread Prize for Fiction. Makes first announced public reading in
        Oxford, England.
1997   Edits (with Elizabeth West) *The Vintage Book of Indian Writing,
        1947–1997* (published in US as *Mirrorwork: 50 Years of Indian Writ-
        ing, 1947–1997*).
1998   In March Iranian government releases official statement that they op-
        pose the *fatwa;* several days later, however, a fundamentalist Islamic
        group renews the call for his death.
1999   Publishes *The Ground Beneath Her Feet.* Openly promotes book at
        public readings and signings.

Conversations with Salman Rushdie

Contemporary Authors Interview: Salman Rushdie

Jean W. Ross / 1982

From *Contemporary Authors.* Vol. 111. Detroit: Gale, 1984. 414–17. Copyright © The Gale Group. Reprinted by permission of The Gale Group.

CA interviewed Salman Rushdie by phone on 1 June 1982, at his home in London.

CA: *You said before the announcement that* Midnight's Children *had won the 1981 Booker McConnell Prize, "Winning might not be good for my soul but it would be good for my ego." What has winning the prize done for you?*

Rushdie: It's had the most extraordinary effect, of a kind that the Booker Prize hasn't ever had before. It's only in the last couple of years that this huge aura has grown up around it. The year before me, when William Golding won it, was the first year there had been a lot of noise surrounding the prize, and this year it seems to have been even bigger than last year. So the immediate result was to turn my book into a great commercial success, which it certainly hadn't been up to that point. So it has obviously made a financial transformation in my life which I hadn't counted on.

Apart from that, for about two months after winning the prize I found it almost impossible to do any work—not because of the prize itself, but because of the endless telephone calls and things that surrounded it. And it's had a peculiar long-term effect, because it seems to have halved my writing speed. I don't know quite why that is. What everybody tells me is that it's because I'm worried about following that winner. I'm not conscious of thinking that, but it's true that I used to get through three or four pages in a day, even if I then rewrote them, which I usually did, but now I produce only about two and am rather pleased at that.

CA: *Reviewers have compared your writing to that of Sterne, Joyce, Marquez, Naipaul, Kundera, Conrad, Grass. How do you feel about such comparisons?*

Rushdie: I won't deny that it's flattering. It's very pleasant to be mentioned in the same company as those people, because that kind of comic,

1

satirical tradition is the one I've always admired and certainly the one to which I would like to think *Midnight's Children* belongs. And there are other writers in that tradition who weren't mentioned as direct influences on the book but whom I admire very much, like Gogol and Kafka and Calvino.

But one of the things I tried hard to do in *Midnight's Children,* probably one of the hardest things to do in the structure of the book, was to create images or symbols which have different resonances for Indian readers and Western readers. For example, Saleem's nose. In America and England people writing about the nose and its comic uses put it into the tradition of *Tristram Shandy* and Gogol and *Cyrano de Bergerac,* and they're quite right. Those were not unconscious references. But there were also purely Indian references, which Western critics tended not to pick up. The nose is a comic version of the trunk of the elephant-headed god Ganesh, to whom Saleem compares himself a few times.

Ganesh is interesting first of all because he's a comic figure, a god with an elephant's head, and he has the big nose. He's also the patron deity of literature. And he's the god who, according to legend, sat down at the feet of India's Homer, the poet Valmiki, and copied down the *Ramayana.* Ganesh was the child of the gods Shiva and Parvati, who pop up in my book in other ways. Shiva thought Parvati had been fooling around, you see, and that the child wasn't his, so when Ganesh was born, Shiva lost his temper and cut off Ganesh's head. Then he repented and rushed around heaven looking for a head to stick back on the torso. The first one that came to hand was an elephant's, so he stuck that on, and that's why there's an elephant-headed god. Saleem's biography is also full of doubts about his parentage—it's a murky thing. That was another useful connection. So the book isn't derived entirely from Western sources, but probably equally from Eastern ones. And one of the things I enjoyed about it was making it in such a way that it would have those dual reverberations in it.

CA: *When did you know you wanted to be a writer?*

Rushdie: My parents tell me that I knew I wanted to be a writer when I was about five. I was a bookworm when I was a child; it got to the point where people stopped asking me what I wanted for my birthday and gave me books. I certainly had a disembodied desire to be a writer when I was at university; I didn't ever have an ambition to be anything else. But that was a long time before I actually had a book to write or anything like that. It was just a sort of abstract want.

I wrote my first novel, which wasn't published, in 1971. It also had an Indian setting, but it was very bad. I've still got the typescript and I look at it to horrify myself. It was real junk and very, very derivative of things like the French *nouveau roman,* which I was interested in at the time, though I'm not now. After *Grimus* was published in 1975, I wrote a whole draft of another novel that I ditched because I didn't think it was working. But I did cannibalize quite a lot of elements from that for *Midnight's Children.* For instance, Saleem, the narrator, did appear in a minor role in that other draft and struck me as being one of the few interesting things about it. One or two other things like the Widows' Hostel cropped up in there. So it wasn't entirely wasted time.

CA: *The Brass Monkey, Saleem's little sister in* Midnight's Children, *is an enchanting character. Have many readers commented on her?*

Rushdie: Yes. In fact, large numbers of people assume she's based on my sister. Actually, she's one of the most fictional characters in the entire book. I have three sisters, and none of them is like her.

CA: *None of them ever set people's shoes on fire?*

Rushdie: That's the bit which, because it's so outrageous, people assume really must have happened. It didn't happen; I just made it up.

CA: *What about the tough little American girl, Evie Burns, with her hair "made of scarecrow straw" and teeth that "lived in a metal cage"?*

Rushdie: She comes close to being somebody I knew, though she's not one person. You see, probably the most autobiographical things in the book are the places. Saleem's house is the house I grew up in and have a photograph on my wall here. The school that he goes to is my school. Those things are certainly based on my childhood. And in the area where he lived there were a large number of European families as well as Indian families, and three or four very tomboyish girls. The one who probably was most Evie Burns wasn't in fact American; she was Australian. But then there were a couple of English girls and a couple of American girls, and Evie Burns is a mixture and an exaggeration of the worst features of all of them.

CA: *You worked in advertising until shortly after* Midnight's Children *was published. Are you glad to have given it up now?*

Rushdie: Yes, it's the best thing that's happened, in a way. Basically, I did it in order to finance the writing of the book, two or three days a week. I've not said too many rude things about advertising; it seems churlish to bite the hand that fed me for so long. Actually it was a serious pain in the neck most of the time, though it had some marginal uses. For instance, it did teach me the discipline of sitting down in the morning and writing—not pacing around waiting for the muse to descend, but just sitting down and doing a day's work and then stopping. And that's a very useful routine to have got into. I might have got into it anyway, but certainly working like that obliged me to do it. The other thing it teaches you is not to waste words because you don't have them to waste. It seems peculiar, given the length of *Midnight's Children,* to say that I've benefited from learning how to compress things, but the first draft of the novel was about twice the final length. A lot of the work in it was condensing.

CA: *Do you write every day?*
Rushdie: Yes. I get twitchy if I don't write every day.

CA: *All day long, usually?*
Rushdie: No. I've discovered that it's fairly stupid to try to write for more than about four hours, or a maximum of five hours a day. If I do, then I find I throw away the stuff I do towards the end because it just stops being any good. I'm not very good at working early in the morning, though I wish I was. I envy those people like Hemingway who write about getting up at six and having done their day's work by half-past eleven and having the rest of the day to get drunk and go to the boxing ring and the racetrack and the cafe. I start work about half-past ten in the morning, and I usually finish about three o'clock, half-past three, something like that.

CA: Grimus *got you listed in the* Encyclopedia of Science Fiction. *Did you intend it as science fiction?*
Rushdie: I was never really sure. I personally think it doesn't fit very easily into any category. I noticed that when it came out in hardback in England it wasn't classified as science fiction. But when the paperback came out in England they *did* classify it as science fiction. And now that they've reissued the paperback in the wake of the Booker Prize, they once again *don't* call it science fiction. So the publishers have had difficulty in making up their minds, too. I don't think it's *science* fiction, anyway, because there's no science in it. It's a fantasy novel, really, and I suppose that the *Encyclopedia of Science Fiction* operates on the broadest possible definition that it can manage. I know, for instance, that they have Thomas Pynchon in that encyclopedia, and I wouldn't consider Thomas Pynchon to be a science fiction writer.

CA: *Do you get a lot of mail from readers?*

Rushdie: Yes. It slowed down, but now that the paperback of *Midnight's Children* is out, it's started up again. I get less from America than from here, because obviously since it won the Booker Prize it's now much better known here than there. I get a very small proportion of crank mail, and quite a lot of very, very interesting letters.

I'll tell you the funniest letter I got—well, the letter wasn't funny, but the implications were. You know the bits in the book about the pickle factory? They were vaguely based on the fact that in Bombay, when I was a child, there was a very good pickle factory called Fern's Pickles. And on all the labels of the Fern's Pickles you would see a little rubric along the bottom which said, "Made from the original recipes of Mrs. N. Fernandes." And Mrs. N. Fernandes became a kind of myth figure for me. I imagined this little old lady sitting in a corner making these wonderful pickles and sending her recipes to the factory and getting rich and famous. I suppose what happens to Mary Pereira in the book is an expression of that fantasy of mine. I was interviewed here on television about the book, and I told them that as far as I knew, Mrs. Fernandes was this little old lady who had sold her formulas to the pickle factory. The day after the television program went on the air I got a letter from an English lady who'd spent most of her younger days in India, and she said that she and her husband had lived very near the pickle factory. They'd gone to visit it one day and discovered that Mrs. Fernandes was a very fat, bald old man. I was so furious. I wish the letter had arrived two days earlier; then I wouldn't have made a fool of myself on television.

CA: *Many good writers have had two countries, as you have. How do you think it has affected your writing?*

Rushdie: I find it very, very valuable, because in a sense I'm both inside and outside both the cultures. There are ways in which I'm no longer Indian. There are ways in which I've never been English. I still speak Indian languages, still feel at home when I go there, and actually I feel quite at home here. It's curious; it gives you—what shall I say—stereoscopic vision, so that you can simultaneously look at two societies from both the inside and the outside. And I think the tensions in that are quite useful; they strike sparks. I find quite attractive those writers who have faced similar problems, like Nabokov and Conrad. I don't think either of them has particularly influenced me, but I find it interesting to see how they handled the same thing.

CA: *How long have you lived in England?*

Rushdie: I got sent here to school in 1961, when I was fourteen. I didn't really make the decision to settle here until after I'd left university, which was in the latter part of 1968. During the school and university years I was going back and forth visiting my family for holidays—they were in India originally and then moved to Pakistan—and I didn't really think that I had "moved" to England at that time; I was simply here being educated. I went back to Pakistan after leaving Cambridge without any particular plans to return here and just discovered that I was not enjoying myself at all. At that stage Pakistan was the country I'd spent the least time in of the three, and I thought of it then only as the place where my parents lived. The choice between Pakistan and England, I suspect, was always likely to come down in favor of England simply because I knew it better then. Now I feel quite close to Pakistan and involved in it because I've spent more time there, but at the time I made the decision about where to live, I knew England much better than Pakistan.

CA: *Did you live exclusively in Bombay until you were sent to school in England?*
Rushdie: Yes. Until I was fourteen I'd never left India, except for two short visits to Pakistan.

CA: Midnight's Children *gives the reader a very real sense of Bombay.*
Rushdie: I'm glad, because that was probably the original motivation for the book, long before I knew its plot or anything else. I just wanted to write about the city at that time, when it really was a very extraordinary city. It's rather less extraordinary and coarser and more vulgar now, I think. But Bombay in the fifties and sixties was a remarkable city, and I remembered a lot of it. In a way my memory was frozen at the time that I left, so it was as though the city which no longer existed continued to exist inside my head. I thought I'd better write it down before I forgot.

CA: *Movies and moviemaking also figure strongly in the novel. Do you think movies have influenced your writing a great deal?*
Rushdie: I am very interested in movies, and I think they probably have influenced the writing quite a lot. Bombay, as the book makes clear, is very much a movie city, apart from anything else, so you grow up there with the feeling of being in a film capital. And I did have relatives who were involved in the movies, although not quite in the way the characters in the book are, so I've had movies in my blood from an early age.
And I think there's one thing particularly which the development of film

since the New Wave has done for audiences and even for readers: It has made people much more sophisticated about accepting what might once have been thought to be very strange techniques. For instance, if you want to intercut two scenes in prose now, people know what you're doing and don't think of it as being confusing. The whole experience of montage technique, split screens, dissolves, and so on, has become a film language which translates quite easily into fiction and gives you an extra vocabulary that traditionally has not been part of the vocabulary of literature. And I think I used that quite a bit.

CA: *Have you done any writing for movies or television?*

Rushdie: Once when I was about twenty I wrote a forty-five-minute television play that got produced in an acting school where I knew some people who were doing the actors' course. They had video equipment, and they recorded this play. But mercifully, I've lost the script! There's no trace of it anywhere.

CA: *Would you like to write for movies or television?*

Rushdie: I think so. The trouble is I also have books to write, and if I did do television or plays or anything else, I think they would have to be done in between books and when I didn't have a major project on the boil because I think of them as being secondary at the moment. I find prose fiction the most attractive thing, despite my love of films and even though what I did most of at university was acting. At one point I thought about being an actor, but then I realized I wasn't good enough. It's always been prose fiction that's attracted me most. There are large sections of *Midnight's Children* that have very little dialogue. A lot of what I do seems to come out of nondialogue writing.

CA: *Do you have any future plans?*

Rushdie: I'd like to go back to India for a long time, because I haven't been there for a while. And I'd like to go to America again. I've been there two or three times, but the longest time I've ever spent there on any one visit is two weeks. I do think I might give myself a little holiday and do some bumming around.

Salman Rushdie

Jean-Pierre Durix / 1982

From *Kunapipi* 4.2 (1982): 17–26. Reprinted by permission.

This interview was recorded in Gothenburg, Sweden, on 5 September 1982. The questions were prepared by Jean-Pierre Durix in collaboration with Kirsten Holst Petersen, Jacqueline Bardolph, Anna Rutherford, and Carole Durix.

JPD: *What were the circumstances in which you wrote* Midnight's Children? *Did you write it in England or in India?*

I wrote it in England. I went to India and Pakistan for five months before starting it. I was going to Pakistan with my family at that time. But I also felt that if I was going to embark on something of that scale, then I could not entirely rely on my memory. So I visited a lot of the places that I had been to before and that I knew I would want to use, and also some of the places which I suspected I might want, for instance Benares, where I had never been before. I had never heard of this curious edifice there—a hostel for bereaved women. I discovered it by chance. In Benares, you can hire a fishing-boat; a fisherman will row you down the Ganges and you can look at all the palaces. At one point, we heard the sound of wailing floating towards us over the waters. It got louder and louder and then died away. I discovered that it came from an old Maharajah's palace which had been taken over by the government and made a hostel for widows who came to Benares to mourn. They literally had to do nothing to be there except mourn. I suppose that if they didn't mourn, they got thrown out . . . Because I had already by that stage had the notion of using the nickname Widow for Mrs. Gandhi, the widows' hostel suddenly seemed very useful, and so, in the book, it became a sort of prison. But then, after that trip, I just went back to England and wrote the novel.

JPD: *Were there preliminary sketches to this book on which you obviously must have worked for a long time? How did it take on that shape?*

It came in a very chaotic way. I had little bits of it, to begin with. The first chapter particularly was the first story that I had. And I had various fragments

of narrative to do with Bombay. Originally there was only one child. And
then it became two children when I decided to swap them. Then I thought
that you can't have just two children born in an hour in a country like India.
It must be more. And if it's more than two, why these two? I did mathemati-
cal calculations about the birth-rate of India, with calculators, and worked
out that, in fact, a thousand and one children an hour is roughly accurate. If
anything, it's a little on the low side. There are probably twelve or thirteen
hundred children being born every hour. So the population—allowing for the
death rate—is increasing at something like six or seven hundred an hour.
Having discovered that there was going to be a very large number of children,
I had the idea of spreading them across the hour and giving them differing
kinds of magical gifts depending on the point during the hour at which they
were born. During the first draft of the book which took, by far, the longest
part of the writing—probably two and a half out of the four and a half years
of it—I was completely uncontrolled. It was enormously long, very over-
written and loose. In a way I was just seeing what happened. I find that I've
always done this, even when the book has not been quite of that size. The
first draft is really a way of finding out what the book is about. In the end, I
had an enormous typescript, probably a thousand pages, which was completely undisciplined. But, out of that, I found myself putting the story into
the first person, as a way of controlling what was otherwise a mess of material. And the moment I put it into the first person, I really thought that it had
begun to work. Then I wrote something which was reasonably close to the
final version in about another year, and just added little layers to it for quite
a long time after that.

JPD: *How do you situate yourself in relation to other English-speaking
Indian writers, people like Mulk Raj Anand, Narayan, or Raja Rao?*

Not at all really. This idea that there is a school of Indian-British fiction is
a sort of mistake. Writers like Mulk Raj Anand and Narayan have many more
affinities to Indian writers in the Indian languages than they do to a writer
like me who just happens to be writing in English. Apart from the accident
that we all use English, I don't think there's a great deal in common. *Midnight's Children* was partly conceived as an opportunity to break away from
the manner in which India had been written about in English, not just by
Indian writers but by Western writers as well.

AR: *What about Desani's* All About H. Hatterr?

That's one book that I did very much like. I'm not sure that it's a novel, or what it is . . . But I think it's an extraordinary book. I found it by accident in a bookshop, in those grey Penguins, and it seemed so far ahead of its time I could not believe he had never written anything else since, except philosophy. The way in which the English language is used in that book is very striking; it showed me that it was possible to break up the language and put it back together in a different way. To talk about minor details, one thing it showed me was the importance of punctuating badly. In order to allow different kinds of speech rhythms or different kinds of linguistic rhythms to occur in the book, I found I had to punctuate it in a very peculiar way, to destroy the natural rhythms of the English language; I had to use dashes too much, keep exclaiming, putting in three dots, sometimes three dots followed by semi-colons followed by three dashes . . . That sort of thing just seemed to help to dislocate the English and let other things into it. Desani does that all the time in *Hatterr.* Apparently Céline does it as well, in French. At that time, I had never read Céline. But one of the American critics, because there were so many dashes in *Midnight's Children,* assumed that I had got the dash from Céline . . . His books use dashes instead of full stops, more or less all the way through.

JPD: *What are the European writers that you feel you have a lot in common with?*

I think what happens with most writers, and perhaps more with displaced writers, is that they select, partly consciously and partly not consciously, a family of writers to belong to. And it just seems to me that there is another great tradition in world literature which really hasn't been discussed in the way that the realistic tradition has been. In almost every country and in almost every literature there has been, every so often, an outburst of this large-scale fantasized, satiric, anti-epic tradition, whether it was Rabelais or Gogol or Bocaccio . . . Wherever you look, you can find examples of this kind of sensibility. That simply was the literature that I liked to read. So it seemed to me that it was also the literature that I would like to write.

JPD: *What is the importance of grotesque characters and of the Baroque in your works? How do you see characters shaping in your mind when you write a book?*

In two ways: they either come out of pieces of people that I knew, or they quite often come out of gestures or of small details of the character from which the rest of the character grows. In *Midnight's Children,* most of the characters are in some way broken. They are not fully rounded. It's to do partly with the fact that they are seen from one point of view. So you see them in the limited way that one human being would see another.

I just find myself writing grotesque characters. It's part of the fact that I think I write very badly when I write seriously. And the nature of comedy is to distort slightly.

JPD: *In* Midnight's Children, *there is a constant dialogue between some characters who attempt or pretend to be heroic and other characters who destroy that heroism. Sometimes there is a dialogue of this kind between the characters and the narrator. How important is this for you?*

The nature of heroism is one of the concerns of the book. It has a character who presents himself as a hero, although he is also aware that he isn't. And heroism is something that is very alive in Indian culture and narrative tradition. For instance, one real life incident, the Nanavati case, is very little changed in the book. The character of Commander Sabermati, and his wife, although their originals weren't neighbours of mine, remain substantially unaltered. And that did become a test-case for India, because there was this enormously good-looking, very popular and dashing young naval officer who was almost certain to become the next chief of the navy, who committed a murder, and everybody wanted him to get off, but, at the same time, they understood that he had killed somebody. There was terrible agony about this. It went on for years. And it got very political. In fact he was found not guilty by the first court that tried him. There is a curious rule in the Bombay judiciary—at least there was then—: if the jury came to a decision which the judge thought was idiotic, he could overrule and reverse it. And that's what happened in that case. The jury found him not guilty and the judge reversed the decision, and it then went to endless appeal courts. It eventually arrived at the President of India who was supposed to pardon him. Whether or not he would be pardoned became a very crucial issue. A woman is abducted by another man who then goes off and murders the abductor . . . There were newspaper articles at the time—or this may just be a false memory of mine— which compared the Nanavati story to the Ramayana story and said that, if this was Rama, would we be sending him to jail? So there was a kind of dispute between the laws of heroism and the rule of Law. In the end, he was sent to jail. And that was a major decision by India about itself. That kind of notion of the hero is still prevalent there. But it is not one that I subscribe to. And so the dispute between the two views exists in the book.

JPD: *How does a writer like yourself stand in relation to history and the problem of memory, of creating the memory?*

When I started writing the book, because, as I said, it was not then in the first person, I had a sort of Proustian idea that it must be possible simply to recreate, to bring the past back, unchanged, as if it had never been away, and found that it really was not what I could do. Instead of being a book of a Proustian kind, the novel became a novel about the past seen through memory, and about what memory did to it. It became a novel about memory, which is why the narrator is so suspect and makes all kinds of mistakes, some of which he perceives and some of which he does not. When I was thinking about the book, I had a vivid memory of what it was like living in India during the Chinese war: how frightened everybody was and how the general belief was that the Chinese would be in New Delhi within a few days and we had better all start learning Chinese, and what absolute amazement people felt when the Chinese suddenly stopped and came no further. Anyway I remembered all this with great vividness and then realized that I could not possibly have been there because I would have been in school in England at the time. I wrote to my parents and said: 'Look! Was I there or wasn't I there? Was I on holiday?' And they said: 'No, you weren't here.' But even when I knew that I had not been there, my memory refused to believe it because it informed me that I had. This showed me that memory does play very extraordinary tricks on you. So that's why I made Saleem make that kind of mistake; and even when he realizes that the assassination of Gandhi happens at the wrong point in the book, he can't rearrange his memories, because to do so would unravel too much else. I found that I did not have total recall about the past, that I was only remembering certain things very vividly, sometimes accurately and sometimes not, that, because they were fragments of the past, they became somehow much more powerful, as though they were bits of archaeological remains one had discovered and from which one was trying to reconstruct what the vanished civilization was like. They became symbolic, absolutely trivial things which had no intrinsic value, they became great totems for me, which is another reason why this book is constructed in that fragmentary way. It tries to recognize the way in which memory operates: it exalts certain things which may be unimportant in themselves and become very important because they have lodged in your mind. And then history seen through that obviously becomes a rather odd thing: it becomes distorted. What seem to be irrelevant things become very big. What seem to be very big things are treated very slightly.

JPD: *What is the importance of digressions? How do they stand in relation to the whole economy of the novel?*

I think that they are absolutely crucial. There was some attempt made when the book was with the publishers to clean it up a bit and to center it more on the main narrative. But I certainly could not have tolerated that because the digressions are almost the point of the book, in which the idea of multitude is a central notion. When I started writing, I just tried to explain one life, and it struck me more and more that, in order to explain this life, you had to explain a vast amount of material which surrounded it, both in space and time. In a country like India, you are basically never alone. The idea of solitude is a luxury which only rich people enjoy. For most Indians, the idea of privacy is very remote. When people perform their natural functions in public, you don't have the same idea of privacy. So it seemed to me that people lived intermingled with each other in a way that perhaps they don't any more in the West, and that it was therefore idiotic to try and consider any life as being discrete from all other lives. I had to find some way in which that life—Saleem's—could be constantly surrounded by all the other lives that occasionally overwhelmed it and then receded and were shown to be connected with it in all kinds of ways, whether literal or metaphorical, political, social or sociological . . . So I found the book getting bigger. The logical extension of the phrase 'to understand one life you have to swallow a world' is that the book never finishes. So you have to find some convention for limiting it. But I wanted to show a life in the context of many other lives, some of which penetrated it, some of which simply existed at its periphery. And that's why the narrator keeps telling other stories.

There's another point, which I find myself making more and more, because the part of the book that's been most criticized is the end, the way in which the central character ends in despair. The thing that happens to him is that nothing much happens to him, despite all the hopes and the optimism of the beginning. Indian critics particularly began to see the decline of the narrator as the author's message, which of course it is partially. But it is only one part of the author's message. The other part, which, I think, has not been properly appreciated, has to do with the actual form of the book itself. I tried quite deliberately to make the form of the book a kind of opposite to what the narrative was saying. What I mean is that the optimism in the book seems to me to lie in its "multitudinous" structure. It's designed to show a country or a society with an almost endless capacity for generating stories, events, new ideas, and constantly renewing, rebuilding itself. In the middle of that you have one rather tragic life. The two have to be seen together. And simply to say that the book despairs is to see it in too linear a way.

Indians are wonderful story-tellers; every Indian you talk to, if you let him, will tell you stories, for a long time. And I wanted to get some of that, the flavour of the told story, into the book, which is why I was very pleased when I introduced the device of having the book narrated to an audience. Padma is one of my favourite characters in the book, because she was completely un-planned. In the first version, she appeared as a very minor character in the last fifteen or so pages; then, when the narrator began to "tell" the book, she arrived and sat there, she simply demanded to be told the story and kept interrupting it, telling Saleem to get on with it. She became very important because she literally demanded to be important. And it's nice when a charac-ter does that and you feel that they've added something by doing it. Padma enabled the book to become an oral narrative, some kind of stylization of such a narrative, if you like. And that allowed the rhythms of the dialogue, the rhythms of the speech that I had originally invented for the dialogue sections to become the rhythm of the whole book.

JPD: *What kind of audience have you got in mind when you're writing a book like this? Have you got one? Who are you talking to?*

Well, *me* really. I had a strong belief when the book was being written that it would never be published. At that time, my track record was not good. I had published one novel which had not really distinguished itself, certainly not commercially. Actually the best reviews that it ever got were in France, where people quite strangely compared it to Voltaire. I could not understand why. But, in England, it was not compared to Voltaire. It was compared to less distinguished things . . . I thought that a writer who embarked, after that, on a novel which was a quarter of a million words long and rather weird by English standards was probably committing suicide. I found it very likely that no publisher would wish to touch it. It had the effect of making me very obstinate, and thinking that, if it was not going to be published, it might as well be the book that I wanted. So I wrote it with reference to no possible reader. I just did what I wanted to do.

AR: *How did you come to choose the map of India for the hero's face?*

It was a comic notion which struck me when I was looking at the map. I saw it as a nose hanging into the sea with a drip off the end of it, which was Ceylon. It was another way of making flesh the idea of Saleem's link with the country. But really, the nose, having come out of that, went off in another direction . . . if a nose can go off in another direction.

KHP: *It seems to me that the book resists the temptation of social satire of the Naipaul-White type. Is it deliberate?*

Well, yes! Basically this book grew out of affection and I think that Naipaul's books about India don't. So that's a simple difference.

AR: *I would like to go back to* Grimus *with the questions of time, space and reality.*

I think *Grimus* is quite a clever book. But that's not entirely a compliment. It's too clever for its own good. At the time of *Grimus,* I was very interested in science fiction. And I was taken with the liberty to discuss ideas that science fiction can give you. I suppose that's why *Grimus* plays so much with science fiction conventions. Bits of that survive in *Midnight's Children. Grimus* enabled me to use fantasy without worrying about it.

JB: *There are so many gifted children in science fiction, and in* Midnight's Children *too.*

Yes! And in a way that worried me. There's John Wyndham's novel, *The Midwich Cuckoos,* for instance. And it worried me that these children were going to turn into Midwich Cuckoos, that they were going to become demigods or monsters. And I really didn't want them to be either.

JB: *You were saying that you were compared to Voltaire. Even in* Midnight's Children *there's something of Candide.*

Well, I expect there is a bit. But Saleem is not as innocent as Candide. Candide is a kind of blank slate on whom the world writes. Saleem is also compared to Little Oskar in *The Tin Drum.* And I think he falls somewhere between Candide and Oskar. Oskar is much more demonic than Saleem. And I suppose the similarity with Candide is that he gets around a lot, too, and gets badly treated. But I don't think he is quite such a naïve person.

CD: *Do you still remain within the Indian community in Britain, as far as your writing is concerned?*

Well, I think, initially yes! It will be some time before I can think of having a non-Indian leading character or major characters. I can't really see myself doing that at the moment.

JPD: *After this book, in which direction will you move?*

In the long term, where I think the writing will go is away from India. The book I am writing now is not about India. But it's about Pakistan, a slightly fantasized version of Pakistan, which is not called anything in the book much, but is recognisably close to Pakistan. I may be wrong but I think that, at the moment, that's about it for me as far as that part of the world is concerned. At some point, the writing is going to perform the same migration that I did. Because otherwise it becomes spurious to spend your life living in the West and writing exotically about far distant lands, maharajahs . . . I am very interested in writing about the idea of migration and the effect it has on individuals and groups. And somewhere, I think, there's an enormous novel waiting to be written, unfortunately . . .

Interview with Salman Rushdie

Chandrabhanu Pattanayak / 1983

From *The Literary Criterion* (India) 18.3 (1983): 19–22. Reprinted by permission.

Salman Rushdie is a writer who possesses to a remarkable degree both the creative imagination and the capacity for objective observation and self-analysis. To hear him talk about his novel *Midnight's Children* is to be fascinated by his lucid account of his own mental processes and at the same time to acquire new and illuminating perspectives on the book, without ever feeling that the work has lost by the revelation of the author's secrets. The novel retains its autonomy.

In the course of two lectures in Mysore recently (one on "Indian Writers in England," the other on "Literature and History"), Rushdie discussed many matters relating to his own work: the autobiographical elements in *Midnight's Children,* the fragmented view of the past ("a country from which we are all exiled") that memory allows, the subversive power that the creative memory can oppose to the politicians' versions of reality. The following excerpts form an interview that may add a few more facets to the very extensive view of his writing given in his lectures.

Q: *Midnight's Children* is often compared to Gabriel García Márquez's *One Hundred Years of Solitude.* What do you feel about this comparison?

R: Well, flattered for a start. I admire all his writings very much. I think, though, there isn't a very close relationship other than that they are both books which have a political content. What I think is that the way of writing—which you find all over the world, García Márquez is not the only one—is still relatively rare in the novel, and what tends to happen is that all the people who write like that get put in the same basket. For instance, it strikes me as very odd to be compared both to García Márquez and to Gunther Grass, who seem to be enormously different kinds of writers. I wasn't conscious while writing of either of them, but that does not mean they aren't in the book.

Q: Were you conscious, while writing, of any particular writers?

R: The writers I was much more conscious of while writing are Sterne and Dickens and Swift. For instance, there is a technique that Dickens used that

17

I thought was very remarkable. He uses a kind of background or setting for his works which is completely naturalistic, down to the tiniest details. And on top of this completely naturalistic background he imposes totally surrealistic images—like the Circumlocution office, which is a civil service department designed to do nothing, or like many of the characters, who are much larger than life. Because they are so precisely rooted in a recognizable real world the fantasy works. What I tried to do—though not quite in the Dickensian way—was to make sure that the background, the bedrock of the book, was right—that Bombay was like Bombay, the cities were like the cities, the different dates were recognizably correct so that the fantasy could be rooted in that kind of reality.

Q: To return to García Márquez for a moment, what do you feel are the important differences between you?

R: Well, in Márquez it seems to me that the basic vision is the village. The reason it feels strange is that he is taking literally a village view of the world, which seems fantastic. One thing that he and I, I think, do have in common is that in India people don't really treat my story as fantasy. The fantasy elements in it are relatively minor, and are only enabling devices to talk about actuality. I gather that in South America *One Hundred Years of Solitude* is also not thought of as fantasy. I think that's quite true about "magic realism"—what is important about it is that it is realism. Whereas in the West, that is to say America and Europe, both his book and my book have been treated as fantasy. I mean I actually heard a very eminent American critic saying on television that what makes *One Hundred Years of Solitude* so wonderful is that it is not a political novel. This statement was made in complete innocence—these distortions that are made in the West seem to be the result of lack of knowledge of these societies.

Q: Where did you start from in writing your novel?

R: There are two things really. Before I even knew the idea of the story, I had the idea of wanting to write about Bombay. I wanted to restore that past to myself. That was one thing. But also it seemed to me that the period between '47 and '77—the period from Independence to the Emergency—had a kind of shape to it; it represented a sort of closed period in the history of the country. That shape becomes part of the architecture of the book. It began from lots of different places which slowly drew themselves together. For instance, there's a joke in my family about how I was born in1947 and two months later the British ran away. I suppose this joke gave me a sort of notion that you could connect a child and a historical event—and then I had the idea of making it an exact connection. And originally I thought there'd be only one child—the idea of having the exchange of children came later. That was partly because I thought of a sort of dualism between the children—they represent wealth and poverty, reason and unreason, peace and war and so forth. But also I wanted them to be not the children of their parents; I wanted them to be the children of the times. And the exchange, by divorcing them from their actual bloodlines, was a way of achieving that. And also it's a nice Bombay talkie idea; I liked it because of its melodrama and its cheapness.

Q: What happens at the end of the book?

R: I take Saleem's version of his [*sic*] and quite literally—he's cracking up and he's going to crumble to pieces.

Q: Does this imply a negative view of the future of India?

R: I am often accused of pessimism, but I don't think the end of the book suggests a negative view. Saleem's personal destiny does lead to despair, but Saleem does not represent the whole of India but only one particular historical process, a certain kind of hope that is lost and which exhausts itself with the death of Saleem. But in the way the book is written I am suggesting also reserves beyond this the multitudinous possibilities that India generates. I think I have shown that although the possibility that Saleem represents is finished, a new and tougher generation is just beginning.

Q: Will you continue to write about India?

R: I have just finished another book and it is about India. But it is not like this one. To start with it's about 250 pages long—more manageable. It is also based on India and Pakistan, but it's not connected with any particular historical event or situation. In short it's a psychological novel. I have used in it the material that interested me that was left over from *Midnight's Children*. There were still things I felt I wanted to use. After that I am going to turn my attention to my immediate surroundings. Haven't written anything yet about my life in England, a place I know perhaps better, and there are many situations worth writing about there.

The Last—and the Best—Salman Rushdie Interview in India!

Salil Tripathi / 1983

From *Celebrity* [India] May 1983. Reprinted by permission of Salil Tripathi.

Years ago, there was a Rushdie whose eyes were a clear blue, the astonishing blue of the mountain sky which has a habit of dripping into the pupils of Kashmiri men. He spoke the hushpush language, but never lived there. He was born and brought up in Sialkot and later lived in Aligarh. Our piece-of-the-moon, Salman's father was in Kashmir. Soon the family moved down south. To Bombay. Our Bombay, Salman! It was very different then. There were no night-clubs and Oberoi Sheraton Hotels and movie studios. The city grew at a break-neck speed, and one morning I found myself driving down Marine Drive with Salman. Past the great house of Malabar Hill, around Kemp's Corner (Keep Teeth Kleen And Keep Teeth Brite, Keep Teeth Ko-lynos Super White), giddily along to Scandal Point. On and on, to his very own Warden Road, right along the segregated swimming pools of Breach Candy.

The road to Westfield Estate (we are now entering Salman's kingdom, coming to the heart of his childhood, where he played French cricket) turns off between a bus stop and a little row of shops—Chimalker's, Readers' Paradise, Chimanbhoy Fathhoy jewellery stores, and, above all, Bombellis Marquis Cake and their One Yard of chocolates. There stands Windsor Villa (next to Devonshire Villa). Bougainvillaea creep across the towers, gold fish swim in pale blue pools, cacti grow in rock gardens, tiny touch-me-not plants huddle beneath tamarind trees, there are butterflies and roses and cane chairs in the lawns. A 35-year old Salman checks it all out. Things have changed. A monstrous skyscraper looms over the horizon. Sabkuch ticktock hai. A-1 Top Quality Jumbo Sized bungalow.

On June 19, 1947, Salman is born. When his time comes he goes to the Cathedral and John Connon School. And then crosses the black waters to go to Rugby.

There were Indians at Rugby, but they were sons of Maharajaha or stars at cricket and Salman was no good at games—the only thing good English schoolboys were allowed to be good at. The climax came in the second term when he went into the study he shared with two other boys (both British, whites, naturally) and found one of them crayoning WOGS GO HOME on the wall over his chair. And here is Salman picking him up by his belt, grasping him by his collar, banging him hard against the wall till the bully is knocked unconscious. Salman wants to go back home.

But Cambridge is different. He does his Tripos in history and stays on. At 20, he reads *Ulysses*—a book you have to recover from. He tells himself that there is something left to do in literature, in spite of *Ulysses*. That is Fringe Theatre. And ad jingles. But he soon gets tired of that. Allahtobah, he cries. And advertising goes funtoosh. And then comes the jolt. The realization that there are people who genuinely believe that all men are not created equal. Here he is, young and very much in love with an English girl. They are briefly engaged, but here parents manage to convince her to forget him. Marry one of our kind, they tell her. And she does. Salman is lonely, once again. He turns to eastern Sufism and writes a science fiction fantasy— *Grimus*. It is finished in 1974 and makes no money. First novels are rarely reviewed—they get tucked away in the corners. But *Grimus* gets lead positions. And most of the people give it the lead position only to be very very rude about it. Someone suggests some other way of earning a living to Salman. O ye unfaithfuls! O ye unbelievers!

In 1975 Salman comes to India, to research his coming book. In Bombay he opens the phone book—and what does he see? His father's name is still there! Eleven years after leaving the country. (It still is, on page 819— Rushdidie (sic) Anees A, Windsor Villa, BDesai Rd.-26—829761.)

It was as if nothing had happened. The city refused to disown him, and he wanted to reclaim the city. When he saw the old house, on the slopes of Warden Road, the spirit of the book was born.

He returned to England and married his sweetheart, with the most literary name, Clarissa—remember Mrs. Dalloway's first name? Or Samuel Richardson's novel?

But he was scared to begin the book. He had such rich material that an untried hand could spoil it. He found the right expression from Aragon's *Les Paysan de Paris*—of making the ordinary bizarre and the bizarre ordinary.

The book was written. He called it *Midnight's Children*. It could be an exaggerated fantasy of a lonely, neglected child. The Railway Strike and the Raj Narain case shaped up exactly to fit into the structure of his book. (Was that, too, his fault?) The book is a garrulous, talkative, oral narrative told by a suspect narrator, as colourful as the British Library Catalogue number RUSHDIE Salman/Midnight's Children / 823'.9' IFPR 9499.8R8M / ISBN 0-224-01823-X.

The India that he has reclaimed may not exist, because it is an India of memory, gossip stories, anecdotes. It is not an oracle, nor what India is like; but what his India is like. It is an India he is willing to belong to, rather than one that may have existed. Time is running out, and I must end my tale. Padma sitting at my right is getting restless.

Cut to Festival of India. With the pomp and glory befitting an Empress, The Widow—Mrs. Gandhi—arrives in London. She doesn't like Saleem's creator either—remember, she had fried Saleem's balls and fed them to the pie-dogs in Benares? Mrs. Thatcher commits the blunder of telling her how wonderful Salman is. The Widow spreads marmalade on her bread, says a polite no, thank you while reading press reports and checking whether they've noticed her new hair grooming. Salman tells Radio Australia: "She had Sanjay cloned. When his ashes were immersed, it was done simultaneously, so that even in death he was to be seen appearing everywhere at the same time."

Back-to Bom! At Warden Road, Salman ignores the ministrations of the people in the ice cream parlour to revive him. And while Sophia college girls giggle and stare at him, he goes to his old house, uses words like "pointy," which, when I used as child, teachers used to scold me. But because of him the language itself has changed, so it is all right now. In fact, it is respectable.

A fine business indeed. The booming voice of Tai, the fisherman echoes. "A wet-hended nakkoo goes away before he has learned one damn thing and he comes back a big writer sahib with a big bag full of foreign awards, foreign wife and foreign child, and still he is likable as a holy clown. I swear, janum, a too-bad thing."

Might be for Tai, who lived for aeons in his shikara, wearing those stinking clothes, ferrying Aadam Aziz to his perforated sheets and taking Ilse Lubin for her last ride.

But when Salman did return to India, third rate third world leaders sat in five star hotels, and over cognac and caviar discussed poverty. And down south four Ramas (nothing to do with Ramram Seth) searched for Rama Rajya.

The clocks tick away fasterfasterfaster and in whatsitsname Assam people die like ants and whatsitsname The Widow doesn't care a damn and the nation—itself a dream we had all agreed to dream—shatters. Was that, too, Saleem's fault?

Salil Tripathi: Are you tired of talking about *Midnight's Children?*

Salman Rushdie: Well, in England I've stopped talking about *Midnight's Children* because, for a start, everybody is tired of listening. India is a different thing and I haven't been here since it came out and it was very interesting for me to see what India's response to it was. And if everyone wants to ask the same questions again, it's not surprising. At the moment I don't mind, but probably by the end of it, I'd be extremely fed up. It's nice that I've got another book coming up in a few months' time, so I'll be talking about something else.

ST: But how does this celebrity status affect you? Was it the same in England?

SR: More or less. But India has a more affectionate relationship with the book which I'm rather pleased about. In England there are a lot of people who like it—but they don't have a sense of belonging to it, which is fair enough because it doesn't refer to them. There are lots of things in the book which English or American readers don't get and weren't supposed to get. I'm amazed how well it has done in England. I thought it'd be rather difficult in England.

ST: Do you feel guilty about not living in India? You had said somewhere that you'd like to return to India for a longer while, and then, maybe, decide, whether you'd like to stay on or not.

SR: Yes. Well, I don't feel guilty about not being here. That's for sure. But coming back here . . . well, it's a question I keep asking myself. What I think is that now I can spend time more regularly in India —whether I can come back and live is another matter. But I don't know how easy it is to uproot one's self several times in one life. There's plenty about England that I don't like, but there's quite a lot about living in England that I do like.

ST: What are those parts—the ones you don't like about England?

SR: Oh, well, those are basically political. I don't think it's a very pleasant time in that respect to be in England at the moment. But there are many aspects about the English life which I like a lot. It's just that they don't happen to be in the forefront at the moment. But it doesn't mean they're not there. Certain intellectual traditions, certain very old established dissenting radical traditions—I like those a lot. Margaret Thatcher is not England. She just happens to be in charge.

ST: Then what is England?

SR: Well, like any country there are many Englands, you know. You choose the one you like to live in. What is India? There are hundreds of them—and you choose the one that you feel the most at home in, isn't it?

ST: Do the British feel that you have mutilated their language?

SR: Oh, the British are very tolerant about things like that. They like their language mutilated. After all, compared to what Joyce did, I haven't done much! But no, it is one of the gifts of the English language that you can do it to that language. If you try to make a similar assault on, say, Urdu, the language will fall apart. English at least permits you that. In a way, it may be that the linguistic enterprise in my book is one of the things that people have enjoyed about it. After all, it is a way to enrich the language, not just to damage it.

ST: But what do you feel about the debate—linguistic energy and the robust vitality of the language as against the classic Wren and Martin's Grammar [*sic*]?

SR: Well, I was spared studying English—I mean, literature. Literature has moved on a bit. You don't have to be quite so pedantic anymore. It depends on what is appropriate. *Midnight's Children* isn't tricksy just to be tricksy. It does things in order to help me try and say, to express, to reflect, what's there. And I think, for that reason, the language hasn't attracted any kind of opprobrium—it is there for a purpose. If I'd been writing about the middle-class in London, I wouldn't use this technique—that would be absurd. For India it wasn't that hard to arrive at. All you had to do was listen.

ST: Have you ever felt that there were friends of yours who would have liked to be featured in the book? Are there people coming up and saying—"We knew you when you were *this* small"?

SR: Well, I don't think anybody is featured directly. I've stolen pieces out of people—you know, somebody's hair-style, somebody's fatness . . . it hasn't to do with portraying people. I know there are people who believe themselves to be portrayed and I suspect there are slightly more people who believe themselves to be portrayed than there are characters in the book! And as far as I can see, in Bombay there are no direct portraits. There are one or two, in the whole book, though—like Indira Gandhi.

ST: Is this The Great Indian Novel?

SR: I don't know why people make league tables out of books. It seems to me of no interest whether the book is THE Great Indian Novel or the Second Great Indian Novel or the 97th Great Indian Novel. It is a book which people should read. I don't compete. Literature isn't about scoring points. What I do think is that the Comic Epic is the natural form for India. I was surprised how little it had been used. It was somewhat surprising to me that the book was still there for me to write.

ST: And you have said that there are peculiar Indian themes which throw open a lot of possibilities which haven't been adequately used. Like the partition.

SR: Yes. Khushwant Singh's *Train To Pakistan* is about the only good book on that theme. *Midnight's Children* uses the partition somewhat at a distance because the action is in Bombay.

ST: And what do you feel about Nissim Ezekiel's criticism? That you are peddling exotica to the west?

SR: I can't argue with the reader's reading of the book. If that's what he thinks, that's what he thinks. But I'm sure there are one or two people who don't think that way.

ST: Do you like being called an Indian writer?

SR: Yes. If you have to choose a nationality as a writer, I'd call myself an Indian writer. There is a tendency to assume that if one were to call himself an Indian writer, he can only write about India. And that's not my intention. In that sense, in ten years' time people may find the term problematic about me, because I'd have written a couple of books which are not about India. I don't know what they'd call me then.

ST: Now will you be writing an autobiography?

SR: An autobiography? I'm 35 years old, you know! I know some writers write 5 autobiographies by the age of 35. But I have no plans for an autobiography.

ST: Tell us about the racial scene over there. From the reports we hear, it seems a pretty bad situation.

SR: It is.

ST: Your sister has had a terrible experience.

SR: Yes.

ST: And you have used the word "scandalous" to describe the treatment meted out to the blacks and the Asians. Sometimes.
SR: Yes. Sometimes.

ST: And at the same time you've said that a fair skin and an English accent distances you.
SR: It doesn't distance me. It protects me.

ST: Why? Why should Salman Rushdie need protection?
SR: Well, I'm very closely involved in it. I've been doing voluntary work in Race Relations for 6–7 years now. So I know what's going on. And what's going on is not nice. And what's more, it's getting worse. The tensions are worse now than they were five years ago. And the kind of nervousness inside the blacks and the Asians is more. Unemployment is much higher among the immigrants than among the whites. So, at the time of recession, we are getting hit quite badly. The interesting thing about England is that the racial problem is of a special kind. The National Front is a small organisation and it is an alarming organisation. But it is small. It is not even slightly representative of even working class attitudes. National Front's danger is that it is an army on the streets. It never gets votes, it has no kind of national support. In the classical meaning of the race riot the blacks and the whites fight each other. In that case there has never been a race riot in England. The troubles in England happen because the Indian community has come to it with the feeling that certain parts of the organs of the state are hostile to them—so the troubles are between the blacks and the police. And in that sense the term race riot is somewhat misleading. The more dangerous problem is that there is a feeling among Indians, and to me, quite justified, that certain parts of the organs of state are not free from racial prejudice.

ST: Are you talking about Lord Denning's judgement?
SR: Partly. I'm talking about the police force, the immigration service, the judges, some of the practices of the Home Office, the housing authorities. One of the minimum requirements of the state should be that whether or not individuals are prejudiced—because India itself is not free from that—the state does not enshrine the principles of prejudice. And in England, in some places, it does. That's alarming. Things are changing. Forty per cent of what are called immigrants are born in England. They are all young, they've grown up in England, and they all have exactly the same expectations from that society as the white kids. Then they discover that they don't get it. So they

are angrier. It is not uncommon for the first generation of the immigrants to come for a quiet life. They want to give a better standard of living to their children and they often don't want to rock the boat. So they are willing to swallow a few difficult things. The second generation doesn't do that. It's always been known in England that the troubles will come from the second generation if things are not sorted out. And nothing is done to sort out the problem. So the second generation is a much bitterer generation. I'm talking about kids of 16 and 20—they are much tougher. Most of them have never been to India.

ST: For them, I guess, it's just the land of their forefathers.

SR: Yes. And they've no connection to it. Many of them, when they come here—occasionally their family brings them here to their old villages—they go away feeling how revolting and dirty it all is—they're not Indian in any sense as you and me. But of course, they are all Indians. And one of the things which interests me is that how the concept of "Indianness" changes when it is exported—like now, there is an Indianness in England, America, Africa. And they are all different kinds of Indianness. Those shades of Indianness are what I want to write about at some point in the future. Not from the point of racism, but from the point of inside the community—because one of the problems about racism is that it dominates one's thoughts and so much of one's thoughts are spent talking about how the whites treat the blacks, that very little is being said about what's happening inside those communities. What are the stresses and shifts there. I think it is just as important that we should talk about ourselves and not just about us and them all the time.

ST: Are you doing a book about Pakistan?

SR: Yes, I mean, one thinks about all sorts of things. It's a very difficult time when you are between projects. And at that time you are asked about your future work and you have half-a-dozen ideas in your head and they may change. This book that I've written. . . .

ST: *Shame.*

SR: Yes, it is not specifically about Pakistan. It is about a Muslim country. And it is not named because I don't want to repeat *Midnight's Children.* I know I can recycle that every two years and get away with it. But I don't want to write another book which has the same relationship with history. This book is not so precise about dates and places. Maybe it could be about Pakistan.

ST: You had told someone that Mrs. Gandhi subsists on a diet of Mills and Boon.

SR: I was misquoted. I don't believe that. What I said was that Benazir Bhutto survives on that. They were asking me about the Bhuttos and the Gandhis and I know that Benazir does read a lot of romantic fiction. And I said that, and Benazir and Mrs. Gandhi got united by the journalist. Not my fault. No, I know Mrs. Gandhi reads things.

ST: Like what?
SR: I don't know. Maybe *Midnight's Children?* I don't know. I don't think so.
ST: She isn't very happy about the book is she?
SR: Well, these are just noises. I haven't heard anything directly.

ST: But you didn't meet her in London at the time of the Festival.
SR: No, I never met her. I don't get put in those places. But I've heard little noises dribbling out of the High Commission—I don't know whether she has read it, or she's had it read for her. But if you were Mrs. Gandhi, would you be pleased with the book?

ST: How do you feel when she is treated so well in England—you know, wined and dined like a democrat?
SR: It is very embarrassing. And it is also very ambiguous. There is a thing about being an Indian abroad—you want to support Indian things when they manifest themselves abroad. But her . . . well! The thing is that for Mrs. Gandhi the west has always been very important. And she's always been very anxious to be well-thought in the west. And they seem to help her now-a-days! The fact is that Mrs. Gandhi is just about the only politician that most people in the west could name, and because that's so, there's an assumption that she is the only leader. And so they give her a lot of good press—rather uncritical—which they wouldn't do for their own leaders. And that's rather depressing and sickening.

ST: Have you seen *Gandhi?*
SR: Yes.

ST: Did you like it?
SR: Well. I liked certain things, and I disliked other things about it.

ST: What did you *not* like about it?
SR: It's falsification of history. I was rather puzzled by the simplifications. For instance, it would have made a better film if the genuine historical rela-tionship between Gandhi and Nehru was allowed to be portrayed. Their rela-

tionship was first of all a relationship between equals. Secondly, it was an explosive relationship. They argued about the future of India. And, in fact, that argument is central to independence—homespun vs steel mills. And by and large India chose Nehru. It may have emotionally chosen Gandhi, but practically it chose Nehru. That dispute would have added a great deal of drama to the film. Instead, Nehru is being made into a disciple of Gandhi— sits at Gandhi's feet and says *"Haan bapuji, nahi bapuji,"* cries when Gandhi goes on a hunger strike. I think that made the film rather silly. And I did find it very odd that Subhash Chandra Bose was left out. I know they couldn't put in everybody, which is their defence; but Bose seems like a huge omission. All right, they didn't put in Tagore or Sarojini Naidu.

ST: They did have her.

SR: Really? Of course, the Dandi March. But not having Bose is a great distortion of the reality of those times. There are also peculiar things—like the killings in Calcutta have been shown after the partition—whereas a schoolboy could have told you that it happened in 1946. Deification of public figures is an Indian disease. We've done it to all sorts of people all the time. Why should Attenborough do it? Gandhi was a sharp, crafty, streetfighting Gujarati lawyer who was a brilliant politician. He didn't win because he was a saint. In that generation they weren't saints. They were brilliant politicians. Tough men. And to present them as these kinds of reborn Christs may conform to a desire in the west for re-makes or new versions of Bible epics, but it seems to me an insufficient film about Gandhi. And the sad thing is that it makes sure that there won't be a good film now about Gandhi.

ST: You aren't very happy about the Raj nostalgia.

SR: In itself, it's just rather boring, you know. But it is once more a manifestation of many other things—and there is evidence. For instance, during that little war in the South Atlantic last year, the thing that you heard most often was "Let's put the great back into Britain." And it seems that the British are desperately anxious as the recession appears and as they shrink, to try and cling on to that image of themselves—world-beaters and world rulers. Falklands was all 18-year old kids and I think that at the end of the empire, the imperialistic ideas got very quickly suppressed—the experience, the pain of losing the empire and working through that, I don't think they ever did. They just squashed it. And pretended that they had gone away and that they were modern people. But it means, it is still there just under the surface and every time something like a war scratches that surface, it all comes bubbling out again.

Salman Rushdie

John Haffenden / 1983

From *Novelists in Interview*. Ed. John Haffenden. London: Methuen, 1985. 231–61. Reprinted by permission.

Salman Rushdie's *Midnight's Children* (1981) won the Booker McConnell Prize for 1981, the James Tait Black Memorial Prize and the English-Speaking Union Literary Award. A fecund, dynamic, baroque, transformative fable of memory and politics—"a commingling of the improbable and the mundane"—the book has been equally acclaimed on both sides of the Atlantic, and in the subcontinent. 250,000 words long, it has sold more than a quarter of a million copies in this country alone, and has been translated into twelve languages. After the critical unsuccess of his first novel, *Grimus* (1975), Rushdie "went for broke" in reclaiming India for himself in this "great, encapsulating" comic epic: "There were times," he has admitted, "when I was convinced that I was mad."

His most recent novel, *Shame* (1983), shows us Pakistan in the looking-glass: "however I choose to write about over-there," he writes, "I am forced to reflect that world in fragments of broken mirrors." Its subject is truly shame—"*Sharam,* that's the word . . . shame . . . embarrassment, discomfiture, decency, modesty, shyness, the sense of having an ordained place in the world, and other dialects of emotion for which English has no counterparts"—and shamelessness. Malcolm Bradbury has written of the book, "Like Márquez and Kundera, with whom he is so naturally contemporary, Rushdie shows us with what fantasy our sort of history must now be written—if, that is, we are to penetrate it, and perhaps even save it" (*The Guardian,* 8 September 1983).

Born in Bombay in 1947 into a Muslim family who emigrated to Pakistan in 1964, Rushdie was brought up bilingually in English and Urdu; he was educated at Rugby School and at King's College, Cambridge, where he read History. "I am an emigrant from one country (India) and a newcomer to two (England, where I live, and Pakistan, to which my family moved against my will)," he writes. "And I have a theory that the resentments we *mohajirs* engender have something to do with our conquest of the force of gravity." After Cambridge he became a professional actor, working with a multi-media theatre group, and then supported his creative writing by working for a time as an advertising copywriter. He is married to an Englishwoman, Clarissa, and has a young son, Zafar.

Occasionally interrupted by telephone calls, builders calling at the door to talk about roofing and pointing, and Rushdie's own eagerness to check the Test match scores on teletext, I talked to him in 1983 at his comfortable terrace house in Tufnell Park, London. (In 1984 Rushdie and his family moved to another address, though still in London.)

Many readers of Midnight's Children *have felt that the childhood of Saleem Sinai must approximate to that of Salman Rushdie. Speaking now* in propria persona, *can you say something about your early life and upbringing in Bombay and Karachi?*

I don't like Karachi, whereas I did like Bombay very much. But even Bombay has been more or less ruined as a city; it's now an urban nightmare whereas it used to be a courtly, open, hilly, seaside city. It has become a kind of Hong Kong, only more incompetent than Hong Kong. In Bombay nothing works. When I was there in February there had been a fire in the telephone exchange on Malabar Hill, which is the ritziest residential area, and they had still not got around to providing a telephone service four months afterwards. If I were to go back to India now, I would not live in Bombay, which is something I would never have said before. It still has the feeling of being my home town, but it is no longer a place in which I feel comfortable.

My family moved to Pakistan in 1964, when I was 17. I had come to school in England in 1961, but I went back for most of the holidays; and until I was 14 I had never left the subcontinent. I was a complete Bombayite until I was 17. Karachi I gradually got used to over many years; I have come to know it better and to feel more connected to it as a place, but it's not a big city the way Bombay is. Karachi is a city that has almost no urban life, because of the repressions in the culture. Very little happens on the street, and there is a problem with sexual segregation, which makes life odd. You see men holding hands—and that is not because they are homosexual, it has to do with the need for physical contact. I find society in Pakistan very closed, and that closed world is expressed in *Shame*.

Was your father a businessman?

Yes, he was: business covers more or less everything in India. He's now retired, 73 years old. He and I have a good but sometimes explosive relationship: we have the same kind of bad temper. My mother and I also get on very well . . . and I have three sisters, not one like Saleem.

Is your father at all like Ahmed Sinai in Midnight's Children?

No. But he was the one member of my family who was a little worried by the book, not because it gave a portrait of him but because people might think so. Obviously there has been a certain assumption about the book being autobiographical, but that has faded away. My mother could never see what the fuss was about: she could see that they were not the characters in the novel. In actual fact my childhood was relatively uninteresting, though it has certain superficial similarities to Saleem's in so far as the school is the same, and the house is the house I grew up in. But my childhood was uneventfully happy. Saleem's childhood is tempestuous and disturbed, and in that respect we're not the same at all.

You went to school at Rugby, where I think you had a bad time?

The first half of my time there was very bad, the second half less bad, but the whole of it was bad enough to make me not want to go on to Cambridge, and I had to be more or less bullied by my parents. I had my place at Cambridge, but there was a six months' interim during which I went to Karachi and told my parents that I did not want to go back to England. My father was appalled because he had gone to King's, and in the end I think I went to Cambridge because they wanted me to do so.

Did your schoolmasters persecute you as much as the boys?

No, to be fair to them, it wasn't the masters. I had a pretty hideous time from my own age group: minor persecutions and racist attacks which felt major at the time, the odd bit of beating up. But I grew to my adult height very young—which meant that I was for a long time taller than my contemporaries—so there were not many physical attacks. People would go into my room and tear up my essays or write slogans on the wall. I found it odd because I had never thought of myself as foreign before—largely because I had never left my own country before, but also because I had been educated in an English mission school in Bombay. For a long time I had been taught by English and Scottish teachers, and I knew quite a lot about England, so I did not feel strange in coming here. I went home for the holidays, but I didn't tell my parents what a bad time I was having, I only told them when I left school. I remember very bad moments when I felt very depressed, but it did get better as I got older. I never had any friends at school, and I don't know a single person I was at school with: when I left school I consciously determined never to see any of those people ever again, and I never have, I just wiped them out. I did decide to be cleverer than them—which wasn't difficult—and Rugby did have brilliant teachers. Obviously, it helped to be in classes of six or seven, and I certainly had the impression of being better taught at Rugby than I ever was at Cambridge. Although Cambridge had the great historians—I was studying history—not many of them were great teachers. I think my real problem at school was that I wasn't good at games; other Indians and Pakistanis at Rugby had no trouble if they were good at games: everything was forgiven them.

Did you lack interest or facility?

Both, really. I liked the games that weren't glamorous—table tennis and chess—and I was reasonably good at both of them, but they didn't count. I hated rugby football, although I was made to play quite a lot of it because of my early size.

I had somehow assumed that you must have read English at Cambridge, since you are well read.

Well, with huge gaps. I made the mistake of going on a TV quiz show and admitting that I'd never read *Middlemarch* . . . and I don't think I'll ever live it down. When I saw I was in trouble I went out and bought it, and I'm planning to read it. I hear it's good.

Did you have any mentor in your life, someone who inspired you to write?

No. My father never wanted me to be a writer, and I never had any encouragement to write. My grandfather—my father's father—was a writer, but then I never knew him: he died before I was born. He was a good poet and published a couple of volumes of Urdu poetry, and he is the only literary ancestor I have. Apart from that, there was no reason for me to become a writer, but it was the only thing I ever wanted to do; I never had any other ambition, except—briefly—to act.

And going to Cambridge did revitalize you?

Yes, it was a great pleasure to know that the persecution was over, and to be surrounded by intelligent people, so that intelligence ceased to be a factor in one's encounters. It was nice to know that you didn't always have to be in the company of idiots whose idea of literature was the *Daily Mail*. Public schools are basically composed of philistines. It was an exciting time to be at Cambridge, from 1965 to 1968: it was a very politicized period. There was the Vietnam war to protest about, student power to insist upon, drugs to smoke, flowers to put in your hair, good music to listen to. It was a good time to be young, and I'm very pleased to have had those years: there was an energy about student life then.

How did you catch the acting bug?

I had done a little acting at school in Bombay, then some at Rugby, and quite a lot at university. I enjoyed it without ever being outstanding at it. After Cambridge I worked for a while as an actor, mostly at an extraordinary place called the Oval House in Kennington which had an enlightened administrator. It began as a youth club, with a huge room he turned into a theatre, and a great many groups flocked there. A lot of the people who are now mainstays of the British theatre were beginning there, stretching their wings in different groups, and you knew that this was the most interesting theatre being done in London: the people involved had great originality. Most of the people were unemployed, living off the pittances we earned, and I had no other source of money. The standard was very high—professional productions on no money.

I remember a Brecht production . . . and a rock play called *Viet Rock,* a musical written by Megan Terry: we did that, with certain parts being improvised. I also remember what was probably the worst thing that ever happened to me in a theatre, one night in 1969, at a time when it was an interesting thing to insult the audience every so often. During one sequence each member of the cast had to take a section of the audience, which was arranged in a horseshoe, and abuse them for their complacency about Vietnam. But this night we saw that the first two rows of the audience was composed of a coach party of paraplegics, and we were panic-stricken. I was in a cold sweat, but the producer said we had to do the show, so we had to abuse those cripples while being mortified at what we could hear ourselves saying. At the end they came rushing around in their wheelchairs to say that they'd never had such a good evening in the theatre. They felt wonderful to have been sworn at as human beings, because normally everyone treated them with excessive respect or assumed that they're deaf because they're crippled.

And after the acting?

I was starving, and I got a job in advertising for a year. Then I gave it up to write a book that nobody published; then advertising for another year. I worked for Ogilvy and Mather, and more recently for a firm called Charles Barker, which is the oldest advertising agency in England. At both firms I eventually got a deal where I had to work between two and three days a week, and that effectively gave me between four and five days a week to write for myself. I thought it a kind of luxury I wouldn't find anywhere else. I thought of it as industrial sponsorship. That was how I wrote *Midnight's Children*. It is possible to write commercials which are not dishonest, without telling lies, and I don't remember writing anything which I don't think was true or at least arguable. But the people you have to deal with are mostly appalling, and they make you feel suspicious of what you're doing. I never really enjoyed it, and in fact it got worse and worse. When I finished *Midnight's Children* I simply ceased to be able to write advertisements; it was as though—quite without my volition—something in me had pulled the plug out. I was disillusioned with the process of advertising, but it was odd that it happened that way. When I realized that I couldn't do it any more—this was before *Midnight's Children* was published—I told my wife to prepare for poverty. So I left in the spring of 1981, and I was fortunate when the book came out. There were some press reports that said that I had won the Booker Prize and then left my job, when actually I had done something much more risky.

Fay Weldon believes that working as a copywriter did influence her style of creative writing.

I can see that it does in Fay's case, but I don't think it taught me anything other than self-discipline and regularity. It also taught me self-criticism, the ability to edit myself. With so few words at your disposal in advertising, you have to condense. It seems odd to say this, after I've written three long books, but one of the things about *Midnight's Children* is that it is actually condensed. I felt that a book of such length had to feel almost too short for its length, not prolix, and *Shame* is also an attempt at density.

In writing Midnight's Children *did you feel any element of compensating to yourself for the lack of tempest in your own early childhood?*

No. When I began the book it was more autobiographical, and it only began to work when I started making it fictional. The characters came alive when they stopped being like people in my own family. You see, my grandfather was a doctor but he never lived in Kashmir, he never met my grandmother in that odd way, nor was he particularly involved in politics. One of the discoveries of the book was the importance of escaping from autobiography.

Your first draft was 900 pages long, and written in the third person.

It was messier, much more direct. It was a very uneven draft, because I was discovering things as I went along. The character of Saleem in the draft was not the same at the end as it was at the beginning; I was learning about him as I was writing the draft. At the beginning of that draft he was probably quite like me, or quite like what I thought I wanted to say about me.

Did the pattern of incidents change much as you revised?

No, although a certain amount didn't happen until Saleem took over the narrative. One couldn't have those discursive passages until the first-person voice took over. I thought that by putting the book in the first person Saleem's voice would organize and hold together the material. But basically the sequence of events and the structure of the story didn't change, except that a lot of it got left out, and some things that were very long in the original draft either vanished completely or became very small pieces. All the sentences changed, because in the first draft I wasn't too worried about the actual words, I was trying to get the story down. I use first drafts in a very rough way, almost to find out what's happening. Some passages do survive, but almost all the sentences change, and in the case of *Midnight's Children* it was almost inevitable that they would change because of the switch from the third person into the first. *Shame* had three complete drafts. I tinker between the second and third drafts, but there's not much change of substance then, mostly technical things.

Do you now feel at all dissatisfied with anything in Midnight's Children?

I do feel that it's no longer my property. The reaction to it in India has been so enormous that it belongs to hundreds of thousands of people, and in a way my view of it is now no more or less valuable than anyone else's. I also feel quite detached from it, since I finished it more than three years ago, and I started it in 1976—seven years ago—and one simply forgets. I can remember feeling alarmed at the size it was turning out to be—frequent feelings of panic that I was losing control of the material and that what was happening was no good—and also being nervous that nobody might wish to publish it . . . and having to proceed in spite of that. What I can't remember is the day-to-day process of discovering the story.

Was there a time-lag between writing the first two Books and the third, which seems to be written with a different sort of moral energy?

It wasn't written at a different time, it was deliberately written to be quite different. I think the book would not work without Book Three, it would be much less unusual—a kind of *Bildungsroman*—and that part puts the rest of it into perspective. Book Three grows so naturally out of the earlier stages, it was essential to have it. I personally think Book Three contains some of the best things in the novel—the jungle chapter, for instance, which is the passage that divides the book's readers most dramatically: readers dislike it intensely or they like it enormously.

Because it is a phantasmagoria?

It seemed to me that if you are going to write an epic, even a comic epic, you need a descent into hell. That chapter is the inferno chapter, so it was written to be different in texture from what was around it. Those were among my favourite ten or twelve pages to write, and I was amazed at how they divided people so extremely.

Yes, it is quite a short section in the context of the book as a whole, yet it seems to be an eternity of disintegration and mania.

I like that: a lot is imagined to be happening by the characters. I also very much like the magician's ghetto. The jungle section and the magician's ghetto are two parts I still feel very affectionate about in the book. There are things in Book Two which I don't like so much any more, although, by and large, that section has been most praised.

Do you feel there were more gimmicks, as it were, in Book Two, more opportunistic details and excursions?

It's not that, though I put in some things just because they were stories I remembered. But one of the deliberate efforts in the book was to leave loose ends; I was very interested in the idea of implying a multitude of stories in one's structure, through which one picked one narrative path. There are stories you just happen to bump into and that you never see again, or stories that are just fragments of themselves and not completed. It was structured to contain that kind of waste material in it, because that was part of what I was trying to say.

One of the things that slightly puzzles me about the book is the question of tone. The book is fundamentally about the destruction of potential in a new, independent India, and one might have expected more overt anger to have emerged from that context. Did you feel you needed to establish a consistency of tone geared to that impetus?

The tone is basically comic and remains so even when it darkens: I thought that was a kind of constancy.

A black comedy, do you mean, almost like Candide?

There is a comedy that doesn't always make you laugh, and in that sense it is a comedy . . . even at its worst moments, and that is one of the elements *Midnight's Children* has in common with *Shame.* The moment when Sufiya is discovered surrounded by decapitated turkeys is a comic moment, but black comedy of that sort doesn't make you laugh. I think of *Shame* as a comedy, although in a way it is even nastier than *Midnight's Children,* or at least the nastiness goes on in a more sustained way. Kafka can unite comedy and tragedy, and I was interested in doing that.

Did you none the less have to make deliberate efforts to countervail the anger you must have felt at the real events which lay behind the action of Midnight's Children, *consciously to translate it into the genre of comic epic?*

The book was conceived and begun during the Emergency, and I was very angry about that. The stain of it is on the book. The Emergency and the Bangladesh war were the two most terrible events since Independence, and they had to be treated as the outrageous crimes that they were. I was in India near the beginning of the Emergency, but not throughout it; I felt the shock of having it imposed. Fortunately I wasn't in Bangladesh, but I know a lot of people who were there—on all three sides. It is a complete fallacy to believe you must always experience what you put into a book, what matters is whether you can imagine it or not; there is no automatic connection between experience and imaginative writing.

It must have taken some nerve to write such a spirited novel, full of anecdotes and divagations, while taking as your context a series of horrific and devastating public events. The perilous paradox seems to me that one of your impulses in writing both Midnight's Children *and* Shame *was an urgent political one, and yet you compose the subjects with such inventive bizarrerie . . . as entertainment, in fact.*

It didn't strike me as being too difficult to achieve, since it is a matter of ear: you just have to listen to whether or not you're overdoing it. There is a danger that things which are fun to write about will take over from what you're trying to say, but it is a matter of craft: you can hear the strained applause if you take too many encores. I find it much more of an effort of nerve to write without jokes. The first draft of *Shame* was much darker, oppressively and unremittingly gloomy, and I thought nobody would ever get through it if it was that sad. But I also felt that the characters involved didn't deserve high tragedy. Although the relationship between Raza and Iskander is basically tragic, the actual figures are clowns—gangsters, hoodlums—and not people who deserve Shakespearian tragedy. So you have to bring comedy into it—you have to write black comedy, because they are black-comedy figures—and I rewrote the entire book, changing the tone, making it lighter. I find, in a book where the plot is dark and the characters unsympathetic, that if you can make it comic it doesn't lose the tragic content—the story is still the story—but it gains an extra dimension which makes the characters more human. Even when the characters are not sympathetic, you find a way of seeing what they're thinking.

In Shame *I found that the characters of Iskander and Raza, because they are in some sense buffoon characters, become palatable, almost sympathetic, and yet one knows that they are based on Bhutto and General Zia of Pakistan. I felt uneasy as to whether that mode of burlesque was right, the one you felt it appropriate to hit.*

I was trying to say that there are moments when both of them are sympathetic characters. When Raza stakes himself to the ground, for example, one does feel on his side. When Iskander gives up his mistress, he tells his daughter that men are bastards and that she should never have anything to do with them; he's talking about himself but she takes him literally, and I felt quite warmly towards him at that moment. If one is not going to make cardboard characters it is important to say that even people who do terrible things are not unrelievedly terrible people, or at least that they are not always terrible: there can be moments when they behave well.

Which is not to say that their stupidity redeems them, but it humanizes them?

Yes, nothing redeems them. I didn't want just to make hate-figures, I wanted to make people. Although there is clearly something of Bhutto in the one, and something of Zia in the other, I have no way of knowing whether the personalities of Iskander and Raza are actually like those actual personalities. It really wasn't my purpose to invent portraits of them, but what I took from them was that kind of tragic connection—of the one being the protégé of the other and ending up as his executioner—that was what interested me, that was the given from history.

There were two or three starting points which glued together. Another was the title, *Shame:* I kept finding instances of that emotion or concept at work

in societies, at all different levels from the private to the public, and I began
to think that it was one of the most central means of orchestrating our experience. The more I looked for it in human affairs, the more central I discovered
it was, and I wanted to explore that area. When the book starts, the shame is
private and sexual—to do with being pregnant when you don't know who
the father is—and the book develops by building variations on that theme,
showing how shame is part of the architecture of the society the novel describes, and perhaps not only that society. I have a feeling that it is not
peculiar to the east, but I didn't explore that; I thought that if it were universal
the only way of showing that was to be concrete and particular. People who
read the book can decide whether or not it has applications outside the society
under discussion. It seems to me that it does exist elsewhere.

In Midnight's Children *you acted, as it were, as the recording angel of the
experiences of India since Independence, whilst in* Shame *you seem to be
more sternly controlling a story about an alienated place, Pakistan . . .*
      . . . as the exterminating angel, if you like. That felt partly good: I felt in
charge of the material, probably more so than I had ever felt before—except
at the end of *Midnight's Children,* where I felt great relief that I had somehow
managed not to fuck it up. I felt with *Shame* that I knew what I was doing
from a much earlier point. It is a harder book, and it's not written so affec-
tionately, although—as I say somewhere in the book—Pakistan is a place
I've grown to have affection for, so that it's not written entirely without
affection. The episode of the wedding scandal may be satirical, but it is affec-
tionately written. But by and large it is a harder and darker book. And that's
because of its subject matter: Pakistan is very unlike India.

To my mind there was more satire in Midnight's Children. Shame *seems to
be composed in parts with a fierce sarcasm.*
      There were parts of *Shame* that disturbed me to write, because they were
so savage and I wasn't quite sure where that savagery was coming from. The
later sections of the book were very disturbing: they disturb me to have written them. It's a book which comes from a very different place from *Midnight's Children.*

Did you think of Midnight's Children *as proposing a continuous allegory—
the allegory of Saleem's body as being the mirror of a disintegrating state,
for example, or the allegory of the Midnight's Children's Conference?*
      There are those allegorical elements, but I always resisted them in the

writing. Allegory comes very naturally in India, it's almost the only basis of literary criticism—as though every text is not what it seems but only a veil behind which is the real text. I quite dislike the notion that what you are reading is really something else. The children in *Midnight's Children* become more a metaphor than an allegory, a representation of hope and potential betrayed. They are not developed along any formal allegorical lines, and when they operate in the plot—like Parvati the witch—they don't operate allegorically but just as characters. Similarly, although Saleem claims to be connected to history, the connections in the book between his life and history are not allegorical ones, they're circumstantial. Although the book contains those large allegorical notions, it tries to defuse them.

You've said elsewhere that the book is written from the point of view of a child who feels responsible for everything that happens in the larger sphere, and yet it seems to me that the form you gave the novel suggests something different, that things that happen in the public domain just happen to answer to states of collapse in his own being.

What I meant was that Saleem's whole persona is a childlike one, because children believe themselves to be the centre of the universe, and they stop as they grow up; but he never stops, he believes—at the point where he begins the novel—that he is the prime mover of these great events. It seemed to me that it was quite possible to read the entire book as his distortion of history, written to prove that he was at the middle of it. But the moment at which reality starts to face him it destroys him: he can't cope with it, and he retreats into a kind of catatonic state or he becomes acquiescent and complacent.

A number of critics have found it a rather despairing book, but perhaps nihilism is the better word. Nihilism supposes that there was no possible rectification of the events that have taken place—they're something appalling and absolute—whereas despair would imply that things could have gone better, with a programme or strategy which has failed in a desolating way.

I wouldn't really accept either word. The book wasn't written as a social tract, it was written as a fiction which forces you to obey the rules you've laid down. It seemed to me that the Emergency represented the dark side of Independence, and that there was a progression from one to the other—from light to dark—and that was going to be the progression both of the book and of Saleem's personality. It never occurred to me that people would read the book as showing the end of all hope. It's the end of a particular hope, but the book implies that there is another, tougher generation on the way. The book exists to be a reaction to events as the author has reacted to them. It was written in the light of a very dark time.

Saleem offers us a hope for the next generation, as you say, and yet we have learned to look ironically at his narration, his self-illusions and delusions, and we might therefore judge that his hopes are frail and ill-founded. Authorial irony has made us sceptical.

Yes, you are supposed to be sceptical, but what I'm saying is that the book does not present the end of possibility . . .

. . . which would be a cynical view to take.

Yes, and actually stupid, objectively disprovable, untrue. It has somehow been taken that way, but I think it's a misreading. People in India actually say much worse things than anything *Midnight's Children* says; it's an optimistic book by comparison with present Indian attitudes about the future, which are much bleaker. The book contains nothing that people in India don't say every day, and my point was to put it down. People chicken out of saying things; they become optimistic and talk about rays of hope, but at the time of writing there didn't seem to be much hope. First of all there was the Emergency, and when that ended the world got taken over by 80-year-old urine drinkers, and that didn't seem to be much improvement: they proved to be just as corrupt and more incompetent.

Is it true that Morarji Desai drinks his own urine?

Yes, every day. He lives on urine and pistachio. He calls it "taking his own water", and he thinks it's very good for him. Maybe he's right: look how old he is—he's endless, immortal.

Your first book, Grimus, *is a sustained work of fantasy, with a plethora of characters and incidents. The story concerns a group of people who perpetuate their mortal lives and discover that the intrigues and jealousies of life go on, so that the final endeavour of the hero—Flapping Eagle—is literally to explode the arrangement. Did you find it difficult to control a fantasy of such length and complexity?*

It was easy in the sense that it was the only book I've written which had its source in another book, a twelfth-century Sufi narrative poem called *The Conference of the Birds,* which is the closest thing in Persian literature to *Pilgrim's Progress.* The characters are all birds, which is why the central character of *Grimus* is a bird, Flapping Eagle. In the poem twenty-nine birds are persuaded by a hoopoe, a messenger of a bird god, to make a pilgrimage to the god. They set off and go through allegorical valleys and eventually climb the mountain to meet the god at the top, but at the top they find that there is no god there. The god is called Simurg, and they accuse the hoopoe of bringing them on—oh dear—a wild goose chase. The whole poem rests on a Persian pun: if you break Simurg into parts—"Si" and "murg"—it can be translated to mean "thirty birds", so that, having gone through the proc esses of purification and reached the top of the mountain, the birds have become the god. Although the plot of *Grimus* is not that of the poem, it has it at its centre, and that gave me something to cling on to. I was trying to take a theme out of eastern philosophy or mythology and transpose it into a western convention, and I think it didn't really work. I find the book difficult to read now: the language in it embarrasses me.

Yet you obviously wanted to say something about a hell on earth in it.
     Yes, I think the interesting part of the book is the town where nobody dies, and the horror is that life goes on. I thought that if one was going to transpose something as rarefied as Sufi metaphysics into a western context, one needed consciously to use a genre in a way that now makes me cringe.

Since you use fantastic and fabulous elements in both Midnight's Children *and* Shame, *I wonder if you draw any distinction in your own mind between fantasy and fable?*
     What I didn't like about *Grimus* was that it seemed too easy to use a fantasy that didn't grow out of the real world, a kind of whimsy. I don't even really like the word fantasy as a description of that kind of non-naturalistic material in my books, because fantasy seems to contain that idea of whimsy and randomness, whereas I now think of it as a method of producing intensified images of reality—images which have their roots in observable, verifiable fact. Except for the character of the girl, Sufiya Zinobia, *Shame* is somewhat less fabulated than *Midnight's Children*. When Bilquis's father is blown up in a cinema there is a kind of hallucinated sequence; but then she is in a state of shock, so that there is a naturalistic basis for why it is hallucinated. I do think that one thing that is valuable in fiction is to find techniques for making actuality more intense, so that you experience it more intensely in the writing than you do outside the writing.

You mean that any intensification should not become sheerly fantastic, it must have some political or social context to which it is the response?
     Yes, I think so. It has to come out of something real, and in that sense I

had to reject certain things about the way *Grimus* was written. I had to re-examine everything I had thought about writing and put it back together another way.

At one point in Shame *you actually call yourself a fantasist, and you write, "I build imaginary countries and try to impose them on the ones that exist." I would have thought that the usual definition of fantasist would be to abstract or extrapolate things from the real world and to pursue their imaginative logic.*

I think the writer has a kind of vision which he tries to project on to other people, and the fit between that vision and other people's is the tension between the writer and the reader. As a writer I am trying to say, "This is the shape of how it is," and the more I can persuade you that that *is* how it is, the greater my success. In *Shame* the author sometimes knows less than a character, and he's obliged to say that there are things he doesn't know. Normally an author is omniscient or not, and to try to make an authorial voice which would shift between the two positions was technically one of the things I enjoyed in the book—sometimes the author is the writer of the story, sometimes he's the reader of the story, and I thought that was quite valuable in providing shading.

William Golding has written—specifically with reference to Lord of the Flies—*that the fabulist is a moralist: "the fabulist is didactic, desires to inculcate a moral lesson."*

He's right about the fable—*Aesop's Fables* or the *Panchatantra*—where the machinery of the tale is designed inexorably to reach that moral statement which the story is seen to have proved. It carries with it the dreadful warning against not behaving in the moral way the fable recommends. In that sense I think the term "fabulism" as it applies to contemporary literature is false, though in the case of Golding it may well be true. What's happened recently is that writers are using the machinery of the fable but without wishing to point a simple moral. I don't think of either *Midnight's Children* or *Shame* as containing a moral. *Shame* is about ethics, about good and evil, but it doesn't tell you how to behave, whereas fable does. *Shame* is not morally didactic; it shows you something. Italo Calvino is described as a fabulist, but his stories don't have morals: they're shaped like fables, they have the characteristics of fables, but without the purpose.

I'm also very fond of myth, but it isn't possible to sit down and say that I will now write a myth. Myth is a cultural accumulation—a collective experience, not an individual achievement—and you can learn from and use its shapes, since they provide a strength in the work. The greatest compliment I received for *Midnight's Children* was when students in Bombay, and not only in Bombay, said that they knew everything in the book and that I had just written it down. I thought that was wonderful, because they really were saying that I had expressed a shared experience. Naturally, I had not made a conscious attempt to articulate the shared experience of my generation, but the students were saying that the book had some mythic content.

Do you feel that there's no place for didacticism in your work?

In terms of politics *Shame* contains certain political criticisms, which makes it didactic in that sense. If you're going to write about politics it is almost impossible to escape having a view about it. I have a simple view: I believe military dictatorships to be bad and that it's desirable to end them. But I was also trying to show in *Shame* that the last time there was an elected civilian government in Pakistan it actually did worse things than the Army is now doing, that the civilian government was a different kind of dictatorship. Just to have the ballot box doesn't automatically destroy totalitarianism, if the people elected are sufficiently unscrupulous, which—both in the case of the characters in the book and in the case of history—they were.

In his essay on fable, Golding also says that "the writer has to have a coherent picture of the subject; but if he takes the whole human condition as his subject, his picture is likely to get a little dim at the edges . . . literary parallels between the fable and the underlying life do not extend to infinity." That strikes me as an interesting comment on what you tried to do in Midnight's Children, *where Saleem speaks of swallowing a world. Golding regards fable as dealing with a much more contained and demarcated area of experience.*

I think that's a difference between Golding and me. Golding's books do take small metaphors, an island or a ship. But what I was trying to do in *Midnight's Children* was to make a plural form, since it seemed to me that I was writing about a world that was about as manifold as it's possible for a world to be. If you were to reflect that plurality, you would have to use as many different kinds of form as were available to you—fable, political novel, surrealism, kitchen sink, everything—and try to find an architecture which would allow all those different kinds of writing to co-exist.

So that what you produce is a kind of kaleidoscope without insistent purposiveness, whereas Golding would insist on a moralistic purpose in his novels?

If *Midnight's Children* had any purpose in that sense, it was an attempt to say that the thirty-two years between Independence and the end of the book didn't add up to very much, that a kind of betrayal had taken place, and that the book was dealing with the nature of that betrayal. To that extent there was a kind of public purpose.

I also had an idea about personality. I was trying to write about one person, and finding—as he says—that in order to do so you have to swallow a world. In order to create one character, you would theoretically have to create the universe. I was interested in what it meant to be an individual in the middle of that many hundreds of millions. The normal response would be to say that it means less to be an individual in the midst of the billions, but I thought it could mean the opposite. The book therefore made a kind of comic inversion: instead of being one speck on the beach, Saleem became the speck which contained the beach. Now that's not really a purpose in the sense of having a message, it was a way of examining personality. Once upon a time you could have written novels in which the public world and the private world were discrete from one another—Jane Austen didn't have to mention the Battle of Waterloo, and that was all right—but it seemed to me that one of the things we've learned about ourselves as a species is that we are very closely inter-connected. Originally the first line of the book, which is now buried some-where, was "Most of what matters in your life takes place in your absence," and that was a central idea. An important idea for me was that people leak into each other—"like flavours when you cook," as Saleem says at one point—and I was trying to write about how people are pieces of each other. It's not just that public life affects private life, but separately lived private lives can affect each other quite fundamentally: things which become a cen-tral part of you can actually have happened three stages away from you, and have been passed on to you through successive leakages.

Some critics regard the form of a novel as being the pattern of an author's personality. Do you feel any discrepancy in yourself between the free-wheel-ing and exuberant personality we feel in Midnight's Children *and your social self, which seems on first acquaintance to be urbane and intellectual?*

I think, like most writers, that I am most completely myself when I write, and not the rest of the time. I have a social self, and my full self can't be released except in the writing. *Shame* is a different sort of book from *Mid-night's Children,* and that's me too. Books are interim reports from the con-sciousness of the writer, and that changes. I don't think I could write *Midnight's Children* now.

Midnight's Children *has been compared to novels like* The World According to Garp *and other large-scale, potentially absurdist books, and of course it has strong affinities with a tradition stemming from Sterne.* Shame *also fits the modern form of the reflexive novel—you take pains to draw attention to yourself-as-author and to the fictiveness of the book. To what extent did you decide your literary pedigree when you began writing* Midnight's Children, *or to what extent did you take any models—Márquez, Gogol, Kundera . . . ?*

I don't like *The World According to Garp,* I don't think it's a good novel. I didn't consciously think of a single writer as a model. Even the correspondences with Sterne were for a time unconscious, and I only realised that *Tristram Shandy* had gone before me when I was some way into the drafts. When I remembered it, I did little bits of stylistic underlining, to make sure that people knew that I knew.

Gogol saw Dead Souls *as being a book which might reform Russian society.*

Actually Gogol got that into his head at the end of volume one, and fortunately not much of volume two got written. I was under no illusions that *Midnight's Children* could change the world. But I did think that there were certain kinds of conversation which were not taking place in India and Pakistan, because certain things had been swept under the carpet. I had not read Kundera when I wrote *Midnight's Children,* but the point he makes about the connection between memory and politics is, I think, relevant to what I was doing. I thought that because I write about these things people who read the book will be obliged to think about them. So I did want to say how it was, so far as I could remember; and when your version differs from the official version, then remembering becomes a political act.

Would you subscribe to Kundera's concept of the novel as "investigation into human existence"? That definition comes from an article he wrote in the New York Times *(24 October 1982) about his novel* The Joke—*I suppose the emphasis should be put upon the word "investigation"—and he also says that the novel proclaims no truth, no morality.*

Yes, I think so, though that formulation actually says very little. *Midnight's Children* is very orchestrated, full of architecture—it's as though the skeleton is on the outside and the flesh on the inside—but I felt that *Shame* was much more of a voyage of discovery. When I had the Iskander-Raza plot, for instance, I thought it was a very *macho* kind of book—all about careerism, coups, politics, revenge, assassinations, executions, blood and guts—but then I kept discovering more and more in all the peripheral characters, particularly the female characters. It became very interesting to me to find that I was writing a book in which the central characters almost never took the front of stage, and that in a way there were no central characters: there were a dozen or so major characters, and they would sometimes step into the centre of the plot and sometimes move to the edges of it. That struck me as an enjoyable thing to do after writing a novel in which the central character had been so dominant. Omar Khayyam in *Shame* is constantly described as the hero, but he's clearly *not* the hero. That was a piece of deliberate fun. Omar Khayyam is not important, except as the person who brings Raza Hyder to the killing ground.

He's described as Iskander's confederate in debauchery, and he marries Sufiya.

Yes, he has peripheral roles all the way through the plot, and I wanted to have a peripheral man as someone I called the hero. He's central to none of it, and he's not important enough to arouse real rage. After Saleem in *Midnight's Children* I wanted to have a kind of nonentity at the centre of *Shame,* a zero who happens to be rather a good doctor. During his nightmare towards the end of the book he confesses that "Other persons have been the principal actors in my life-story." What he is saying, and what I was saying, is that the sum total of the events of the book adds up to his life. There can be people who are peripheral to their own lives: that's what his character is about, that there can be people whose lives are led entirely as spectators, and everything that's interesting in their lives is done to them or by others in their presence.

Do you feel any emotional identification with that position? I ask because of what you said earlier about your uninteresting childhood.

No, I'm not very passive, really. Saleem has been accused of being excessively passive, and I don't think that criticism is fair in his case: he finds it difficult to act as an adult, but he's not passive in the way Omar Khayyam is passive . . . and even Omar Khayyam is not entirely passive—he saves a girl's life, for instance, and later marries her, without which there would be no plot. But he is an irritating character, and irritating to write about—because there's nothing there.

Your mention of passivity reminds me of Saleem's remark about making oneself grotesque in order to preserve individuality. And yet his grotesqueness happens to him, either by inheritance or circumstances. He purports to be taking control of his life, when in fact he can't and doesn't.

Yes, he tells the story retrospectively, and I'm not sure I believe him. One of the problems with *Midnight's Children* is the almost complete impossibility of pointing out that there are moments when Saleem and I don't think alike. I accepted that as the price I had to pay for his narrative voice, which was very useful to me.

Do you identify with Saleem's remark about establishing a "philosophy of coolness and dignity-despite-everything"?

I probably did then. I think I was a less relaxed individual when I wrote that book than I am now; I've been gradually calming down. At the time I had many more uncertainties about my writing and therefore about myself. There's nothing like the fear of doing the work and not having it see the light of day; I don't think it's a constructive fear, it's something you have to banish in order to have the energy to do the work. Not having that problem calms you down, makes you feel a little less frenzied. *Shame* is the first book I've written with the expectation of an audience.

Do you find that you can now write with less self-consciousness . . . or perhaps more?

Less rather than more. There's less performance in *Shame* than there is in *Midnight's Children.* But then performance is usually regarded as showing off, at least in western criticism. I don't see it like that. One of the things about the Indian tradition is that the performer and the creator are almost always the same person. The idea of performance as being central to creation is present in all Indian art. The dancer is the artist, for example, and not simply the exponent. But *Shame* seemed to be a book which forbade the kind of display in *Midnight's Children.*

Perhaps one of the keys to your transition from Midnight's Children *to the more harsh treatment of* Shame *rests in Saleem's observation that whereas India embodies alternative realities, Pakistan consists of falsenesses and unrealities.*

I hadn't remembered that particular opposition. The first part of the statement—that India has multiple possibilities—seemed to me to be true, whereas contemporary Pakistan seems to represent a closure of possibilities, a loss of possibilities. That affected not just the tone of voice in the book but also the plotting, because I thought that this time I couldn't write an open-structured book. The plot became like a clamp in which everybody is held: they can't escape from it. Instead of saying, as in *Midnight's Children,* that here is superabundance, one was saying that here is constraint. But it's also wrong to see *Midnight's Children* as the India book and *Shame* as the Pakistan book, and actually the Partition section of *Shame*—in Delhi—is one of the sections I'm most proud of, because it is still very difficult to write about the Hindu-Muslim troubles in 1947. It seemed to me important to write about it because that sort of communal tension is starting up again in India—quite apart from the difficulty of writing about something that happened when you were unborn or just born. I showed the typescript to Anita Desai—she was about 10 years old and living in Delhi at the time of Partition, and she has memories of it—and I was pleased that she liked that chapter very much. So the book is not just an attempt to slam Pakistan, because the book is not just about Pakistan. I discovered that I seemed to be writing about the nature of evil, and that isn't exclusive to any part of the world, but it acquires more external resonances when you remain concrete about the place you're writing about.

Did you feel more nervous in writing Shame *than in writing* Midnight's Children?

No, in a way I felt more relaxed, partly for this feeling of having got into control of it at an earlier stage. The moment of control happens, if I'm lucky, at the end of the first draft. I have abandoned two novels at that stage because they didn't seem to be going anywhere.

And at that stage in writing Shame *you found out how important it would be to refract the story through peripheral characters, and that you had come to be writing a story of malign familial crises rather than a political allegory?*

I discovered bits of it in writing the first draft, and then I saw that the most interesting things were in that area. I didn't want to write a political allegory, though it is a political story: it's a book about the private life of the master race. In Pakistan the numbers of people who settle the fate of the nation are very small, so that it is a kind of domestic story about kitchen tyranny.

Sufiya Zinobia, the demon child, is perhaps the most discomforting character in the book. She personifies nemesis, incarnating all the shame and vengefulness of the family. She's both alarmingly real and a metaphorical agent which explodes the tyranny of her father, Raza Hyder. The last image of the book, which encapsulates that phantasmagorical dimension of Sufiya's character, suggests the explosion of a nuclear bomb. I wonder why you felt compelled to bring the novel to a conclusion by toppling the military-bureaucratic dictatorship through a metaphorical-fantastic mechanism?

I wanted Raza to fall, and it was also—having set up the idea of the nemesis—in the logic of the plot. One of the interesting things is that Sufiya does
not get Raza, although she is the instrument of his fall. I find she is the most
disturbing thing in the book, and she was very disturbing to write because
she more or less made herself up. For instance, I hadn't originally thought of
her as being mentally retarded, but it suddenly became clear that that was the
only way in which she would operate. I hadn't fully understood in the first
draft the way in which she would develop into this completely monstrous
being. I thought that the reason why she and Omar Khayyam arrive as opposite figures in the final moment is that in their different ways they are both
the repositories of the society, and that's why they are married.

Originally I wanted her father, the military dictator Raza, to end up in exile
in Gloucester Road, as many fallen figures might—not to die in that appalling
way but to be living in a Kensington flat, with no pictures on the walls, stick
furniture from Pontings, curtains that are never opened, lots of lights and
heaters on all the time. I felt quite anxious to get him out of the country and
into England—the first draft didn't have that final carve-up—but it then became clear to me that the characters were refusing to leave the country; it
was as though they were saying to me that they had an imaginative life but
only within the frontiers of that world, and that if I brought them to Gloucester Road they would cease to exist: they would crumble like characters coming out of Shangri-la. I tried several ways of getting them out of the country,
but they wouldn't go.

*So you had to take your chance with melodrama, with this incredibly alarm-
ing and literal image of the feral girl?*
Yes, it is a bloodthirsty ending. I find it very affecting; she did frighten me.
I think it's unusual to be frightened by one's own creations, but she did make
me worried about her. I worried about what she meant. Why is it that the
character who is the most innocent in the book is also the most terrible? In
the end I thought it would be dangerous to go on asking that sort of question—since that unresolved ambiguity was obviously at the centre of her, and
it is what makes her moving.

*One incentive to your creation of her was clearly the anger you felt about
the white boys who set upon an Asian girl in the London underground, as
you mention in the non-fiction part of chapter 7, entitled "Blushing."*
Yes, I know where she comes from and the process of making her, but she

seems to transcend her source material. There is a dark area at the centre of her, and the book is about that dark area.

Is Sameen, to whom you dedicate the book, your sister?
    Yes, the one of my sisters who lives here.

And she was the girl who was beaten up?
    That was actually much exaggerated by the press. She had some trouble on the tube during the time of the Brixton riots. Three kids began to be abusive—I think one of them slapped her once—and a black man in the next carriage came to her rescue. It was upsetting and it made me angry, but it was a very small thing. It was exaggerated when it came out in the papers, and she was furious with me. I mention it in the book in the context of saying that the girl is not one girl but many, so that the instance in the book is not just my sister.

Can you say something about the enjoyable but ultimately sinister complex of the three mothers of Omar Khayyam?
    They came about more or less by chance. The book is partly about the way in which women are socially repressed. I think that what does happen in that state of affairs is that women become very close to each other, and there is a female network of support which is very powerful. There are various expressions of that in the book—the telephone link between Bilquis and Rani, for instance, a connection in which the power relations shift, and eventually that umbilical cord is cut by the intercession of the men. Omar Khayyam's mothers are another instance of female solidarity, which is really brought about by the way they are obliged to live in the male-dominated society. The group-baby was an intensification of the idea that if they wanted to share everything they would even want to share a child. I like them very much, but for a long time—even before I wrote the first draft—I wasn't sure whose mothers they were. I even tried to write it so that they were Raza's mothers (Omar Khayyam was already present, as an adult), but they clearly didn't belong there. I didn't want to lose them, because they seemed a very strong image. Eventually they discovered their son, and I structured things so that the book began with that curiously fabulated chapter.

To a western reader Omar Khayyam's betrayal of his mothers might seem perfectly understandable, and even right in the circumstances. After living for so long in their perniciously claustrophobic environment, we can see how he would want to get away and never come back, disavowing his family.

Yes, and even to eastern readers it would seem like that, but they would never completely forgive him.

Since Shame *says a great deal about the position of women, do you anticipate that the book might be used as a women's text or tract?*
Books have authors and readers, and it seems to me that the sex of either is of minor interest. I don't think anybody could use *Shame* as a tract, because it contains too many ambiguities.

Do you have any sense of having used the fiction to enunciate your own view of political change in Pakistan?
It has to change, but I try very hard in the fiction to avoid saying what I personally would like or dislike. I think that if the society does not change it will explode. If Zia is to fall, he will fall by a palace revolution. But at some point—since the stresses inside the society are so great—unless something is done to defuse the bomb, it will blow up. Whether that is a good thing or a bad thing is not my point. It will be a bad thing in the sense that a lot of people will die. Whether or not it is desirable or undesirable that Pakistan should exist is really a question that the book doesn't discuss. If you ask me, I don't think Pakistan has a long-term chance of surviving.

It's difficult to see the military regime being displaced all the while Pakistan is a client nation of the USA, neglecting democratic rights and the federal aspirations of its peoples.
Yes, the military will be kept there as long as the west chooses. But there is a tendency in Pakistan—and I do it myself—to blame the west for all the problems, and I thought it would be worth writing a book to say that there's no point in blaming other countries, because actually we're doing it to ourselves. The point I'm making is that these plants—tyranny and so forth—are not grafted on, they grow naturally in this soil.

Do you mean, for example, the way General Zia uses Islamic fundamentalism as a political weapon, a device that seems particularly alien to a western audience?
It's actually very alien to the Pakistani audience as well. One of the things I say in the non-fiction parts of the book is that Zia cloaks what he does in the language of the faith, and because people respect the faith they don't want to question what he does: that's the way religion legitimizes tyranny, the way Islam is *linguistically* protecting Zia. I don't think Zia will destroy Islam, but he may well destroy the basis of the state.

Are you religious yourself?

No, I'm not formally religious. But it's like being a lapsed Catholic: you don't lose it—you have that intellectual tradition, and it's an important part of what you are. In that sense I'm a Muslim, but not in any practising sense.

I found that reading Shame *had a useful educational purpose for me, in so far as it prompted me to go away and read some books about Pakistan, to refresh my memory—including Tariq Ali's book* Can Pakistan Survive?, *which struck me as setting out the issues clearly and conclusively.*

That's interesting, because he sent that book to me quite recently, long after I'd submitted *Shame.* I found there were really quite a lot of meeting-points between the ideas in the two books. Although we had never discussed it, we had both—in a position of exile—reached the same conclusions.

Would your wishes for Pakistan be the same as Tariq Ali's—a secular-democratic, socialist state?

Yes, certainly, and at one point in *Shame* I talk about the possibilities of the country disintegrating—once the Islamic myth has been devalued as a basis for the state—and the book then says that we could replace it with different myths, such as liberty, equality, fraternity. I do think that if the state has a chance of surviving it has to remove religion from itself, and when it does that it has a chance of removing the generals.

I do think that in a way the question about Pakistan doesn't matter to *Shame,* because the book has to make its own world. Whether or not you know anything about Pakistan shouldn't be a factor in reading a fiction, because the book has to tell you what you need to know, and if it doesn't it fails. You make a world, and you try to make it cohere and mean something about the world that you don't make, the actual world.

Midnight's Children *is a rich and elaborate concoction obviously rooted in your early love for Bombay and for India in general,* Shame *more of a dark decoction. Since you have never lived full-time in Pakistan, did you feel at all parasitic in writing a novel based there?*

Certainly my relationship to the material is different. I feel more detached, but not in the sense of feeling like an outsider—because in fact, in the last two decades, I've known Pakistan rather better than India. Still, you couldn't write that kind of exuberant, affectionate book about Pakistan, it would be a false book; and there will be plenty of people who won't like *Shame* because it is harder and sometimes cruel. But I don't think *Shame* is just unrelieved darkness: I went to some trouble to provide that light and shade we've talked about. In a way, I can write the book from the outside because I can stay alive; nobody in Pakistan could write the book, because they'd die.

Is there any danger to your family from the fact that you've written it?

Not as far as I can see. It's only a novel, after all, written in the English language—which most people can't read—and it will be stopped from entering the country. I now have a British passport, so in that sense they can refuse me entry to the country or they can deport me if I get through, but that's about it—given that I haven't broken any law in Pakistan.

But that's a risk you felt morally obliged to take?

Yes. When I started writing *Midnight's Children* the Emergency hadn't ended, and at the time the idea of writing a book which might prevent me from going to India ever again was very sad. But it hasn't happened.

Has Mrs. Gandhi read Midnight's Children?

Of course she's read it, she's a very literate woman. She doesn't like it very much; she hasn't commented in public, but she's let her displeasure be known. It would have been amazing to me if she had not been displeased, because it is very rude about her.

When you return home to visit your family, do you feel any tension in yourself about re-accommodating yourself to their way of life . . . or just to Pakistan?

The first few days require a certain shift, but after that there's no strain—except that I do find Pakistan a strain. My parents speak very good English, but we don't speak that much English at home because they prefer not to.

Does your wife speak Urdu?

She understands a lot, but she hasn't acquired the courage to speak the language, and I don't blame her. Her vocabulary is not small, but I don't think she's mastered the syntax.

How did you meet your wife?

I met her in 1969, in London, through a mutual friend. She used to organize publicity work for a charity, and then she went into the publicity department of a publisher, but she stopped working a year or so ago.

Did you have any difficulty from your family when you chose to marry a white English girl?

I think there's no doubt that my parents would have rather I had not, but fortunately they both got on with her very well—very quickly—so there's never been a difficulty. And, to be fair, there's never been any difficulty from her family about her marrying me.

Are you active in working for race relations? You've written a strong article—"The New Empire within Britain" (New Society, *9 December 1982)— about racism here.*

The background knowledge for that article came out of about five or six years of doing voluntary work in race relations—I was involved with the local community relations council, here in Camden—but now I simply don't have the time: it's sad but true. I've resigned from the executive council simply because I could never get to the meetings any more.

Your conclusion to that article is that "Racism, of course, is not our problem. It is yours. We simply suffer the effects of your problem." I think many people would consider it a joint problem, to be mutually overcome . . .

The victims of racism are the people who suffer from the effects of a problem which exists in the minds of the racists and in many of the institutions of this society. The argument began when the second generation grew up: it makes them bad-tempered when they are treated as foreigners. It would make me bad-tempered.

At least I know that I really am a foreigner, and I don't feel very English. I don't define myself by nationality—my passport doesn't tell me who I am. I define myself by friends, political affinity, groupings I feel at home in . . . and of course writing. I enjoy having access to three different countries, and I don't see that I need to choose.

Salman Rushdie

David Brooks / 1984

From *Helix* 19/20 (1984): 55–69. Reprinted by permission.

An interview conducted by David Brooks in Adelaide on 6 March 1984. Also present was Mary-Anne Paton.

Brooks: I wanted to talk to you about the "new fiction." Fairly clearly, your work, that of Chatwin, Thomas and Hoban, and in other areas Calvino, Kundera, Márquez, amounts to some sort of departure, and I wonder whether you think this has some social explanation, whether fantasy has become so much more important over recent years for reasons of political exigency.

Rushdie: I resist being put into schools myself, and that makes me nervous about the question. But apart from that, well, I do think that it looks as though Queen Victoria's finally dead. The fiction of the Victorian age, which was realist, has to my way of thinking been inadequate as a description of the world for some time now, and nobody has noticed the fact until quite recently. The fiction and most of the drama of the 1950s for instance—in England at any rate—was entirely realist, and at the time it was praised as a new departure, whereas it seemed to me to be anything but that. As they have developed and time has passed it has become very clear that the writers of the 1950s were not revolutionaries, were not out to change things. They were in fact fairly conservative, and the idea of the "angry young men" is almost a laughable misnomer. After that, I suppose, the 1960s represented a kind of a shift in people's perceptions. The simplest of these was the perception that reality was no longer something on which everyone could agree, which it *had* been at the time of the great age of the realist novel. For realism to convince, there must be a fairly broad agreement between the author and the reader about the nature of the world that is being described. I think that for Dickens, George Eliot and others, that would by and large be true. But now we don't have that kind of consensus about the world.

Brooks: A lot of writers I have spoken to about such things resist "intellectualization," as some of them have called it, of changes in the nature of fiction over the last fifteen years or so. But you seem to be much more . . .

Rushdie: Prone to it?

Brooks: Prone to it. And more interested in reading what others are writing, and so, I imagine, also much less inclined to shy away from the notion that this might be a sort of post-structuralist phenomenon, part of a far wider change in the way of viewing the nature of human perception in the first place, and of human agreements about reality.

Rushdie: Well that might be so; I have almost no knowledge of the Structuralists, except from what you read in the papers. I've read some Barthes, because he writes quite well, but I've never read Lacan, Derrida, Foucault. That doesn't mean that their thought doesn't filter through, and I do think that there is a good and a bad part of structuralism. The part of structuralism that does not interest me is the idea that the book is self-referential, that the book is a kind of closed system.

Brooks: You're very concerned with the inter-relationship of the book and the world.

Rushdie: Books are about things which are outside books. If books are not about the world then they are not interesting to people, not even interesting to write, to me. One has to withdraw immediately from everything that sounds like a prescription because, for instance, *Alice in Wonderland* is a book about which the idea of a closed system could almost apply. But actually the reason why *Alice in Wonderland* lives is because it seem to tell us something about the way in which we live. The part of structuralism which talks about the text as the kind of entity which is first of all separate from the world and secondly almost separate from its author is something which I'm not very . . . well, I don't find that very plausible.

Brooks: Are you conscious—this is taking that answer in a different direction—of adjusting the strategies of your narrative to your purpose in any significant ways?

Rushdie: Yes. I think I'm fairly conscious about form and technique, and sometimes that consciousness shows in the writing. I suppose that is the bit the people talk about as post-modernist—moments when the books occasionally discuss themselves. You see, one reason they do that has nothing much to do with fashions in criticism. One of the feelings I do have about both India and Pakistan is that the literary problem in those countries is not to do with good writers arriving, but to do with the absence of a critical method which is flexible enough to cope with the rapid changes that are taking place there. What you find in both countries is that the critical method tends to be rather atrophied into either a very traditional, classical Arabic and Persian, or Hindu and Sanskritist approach, or else something handed down from the English—the Great Tradition view of literature—and there seems to be nothing else; so it's seemed to me almost necessary to provide critical tools *in* the writing, because nobody else out there has had any.

Brooks: So in a sense you see yourself as some sort of import agent, providing the literature of India and Pakistan with some important exotic equipment.

Rushdie: No! Heavens! Good God, no! I *hate* the word exotic. No, it's not that you have to import a criticism in order to provide appropriate tools; you just have to develop them. Not everything has to be brought in from outside, because what's happening in Indian literature and Pakistani literature now is, in many cases, that the people who run the media, the people who have access to review space, and the people in the universities, can frequently simply not understand what's done, and so fall back on rejection, and rejection in very old fashioned language, so I had to try and say—you know—this book works like this for these reasons. It was an attempt to increase comprehension, rather than to pay lip service to structuralism. One of the strange things about the oral narrative—which I did look at closely before writing *Midnight's Children*—is that you find there a form which is thousands of years old, and yet which has all the methods of the post-modernist novel, because when you have somebody who tells you a story at that length, a story which is told from the morning to the night, it probably contains roughly as many words as a novel, and during the course of that story it is absolutely acceptable that the narrator will every so often enter his own story and chat about it—that he'll comment on the tale, digress because the tale reminds him of something, and then come back to the point. All these things, which are absolutely second nature in an oral tale, become bizarre modern inventions when you write them down. It seems to be that when you look at the old narrative and use it, as I tried to do, as the basis of a novel, you become a post-modernist writer by being a very traditional one. By going back to ancient traditions you have done something which is bizarre. For instance, in *Shame,* I knew that the interjections by the "I" figure would be the things that created most problems about the book—that, when people didn't like the book, those would be the bits they wouldn't like—and that I was taking a risk to do it, but it struck me that if I'd been sitting down *telling* the same people the story they would never even have noticed if I occasionally digressed to a story only loosely connected to the main story—though that's how people tell stories.

Brooks: Another association made very strongly in *Midnight's Children* and *Shame* is that between personal history and national history.

Rushdie: Well, in the case of *Midnight's Children,* there is that obvious connection. In the case of *Shame,* I felt that the material I was taking from history—the thing about the story of Zia and Bhutto—was very explosive. The execution of Bhutto, in particular, is an event which left deep wounds on everybody in Pakistan, of whatever political coloration. It's one of the strange things about his execution that it united his enemies in his support. So I thought, if you are taking this recent wound, very easy to open again, you need to handle it with particular delicacy, and it seemed one of the ways of doing it would be to present the author in the work at the same level as the fictional material, instead of saying *here I am above the story telling you what to think about this thing that you already think strong things about.* To put yourself into the story, or *my*self into the story, was a way of saying that I was only a part of the thing that I was discussing, and to explain where it was that I was coming from, where it was that my point of view emerged from, and to make myself part of the dispute, part of the debate. Because then, it seemed to me, it was legitimate to use that material in the way that everybody else would in a discussion.

Brooks: There have been times, reading *Shame* and *Midnight's Children,* when I've actually winced, thinking of what the things you were saying must have been doing to your own life, because you're proscribing whole areas of possible existence for yourself by attacking in the way that you do certain of the people that you do. I was wondering what effect in fact these things have had on your own life, your own freedom or options?

Rushdie: Well, there are plenty of people who don't like me nowadays. The difference between India and Pakistan is that in India the fact that there are people who don't like me doesn't prevent my going or staying there. In Pakistan things are more complicated. Before coming to Australia I went to India and was advised not to go to Pakistan. So . . . But you know, all things change.

Brooks: Do you think they are going to be swifter or slower to change in Pakistan?

Rushdie: Well last year I thought that there was a possibility that something was about to happen. But I think one must be honest and say that the General won that round, because Bhutto's daughter Benazir made a bad mistake in agreeing to go abroad for medical treatment. But you never know, it's hard to say. On the one hand, I've blamed her for being guilty of a kind of colonial reaction—going abroad to get her illness fixed, because the local doctors aren't good enough—yet it may not be as simple as that because she might also have been worried about what would happen under the anaesthetic if she stayed in Pakistan. So one can't blame her so readily. But I do think that the episode, if not an error on her part, was a triumph for Zia. He won't let her back now if she tries to re-enter.

Brooks: Well this brings up another question which is to do with something that Kundera says in an interview with Philip Roth, published in the back of the Penguin edition of *The Book of Laughter and Forgetting*. There he says that, in a place where a great deal is going on (he's talking about Czechoslovakia and 1968 and its aftermath) very little writing is being done; whereas a great deal of writing is being done, and the writers per thousand of population are far more plentiful, in a place like France where not so much is happening. I wonder whether you felt you had to be away from Pakistan and India to write the kind of novels you have, whether in fact exile is a precondition of being your kind of novelist in the first place.

Rushdie: That sounds a bit as though I could have worked it out as a programme. It wasn't quite like that. Put it this way. In the case of *Shame,* as we've just been saying, if I'd been in Pakistan and writing it I would have been making plans to leave before it came out. There are certain books that could only be written from outside, and which in a way if you are outside you are obliged to write. I find myself a political novelist. It was never particularly my intention, but there I am. I didn't do it in order to argue with governments, I did it in order to tell stories, and make things up. It seemed to me that the thing that was attractive about fiction was that it is a kind of formalised lying.

Brooks: Are you now conscious, though, of writing fantasies, writing fictions in order to do something else?

Rushdie: Well I don't think that I do write fantasies. I think I write understatements, pale shadows of the world. But no, I don't know what novels do. I'm not saying they don't *do* things. The idea that art has no effects is a complete mistake. The only reason that people make the mistake is that it is

very difficult to know exactly what the effect is, and the effect is very wide—
different for everybody who experiences the world.

Brooks: So you wouldn't like to hazard a guess on the probable effects of
the kind of fiction that leaps from improbable event to improbable event.

Rushdie: Maybe it just shows you that the word improbable is not appropriate here.

Brooks: So these not-so-improbable improbables make the kind of fiction
you're writing a more realistic fiction?

Rushdie: Absolutely, of course, that's the point about it, that it wouldn't
be interesting if it were not true. There's a famous exchange of letters between Brecht and Walter Benjamin. At some point during this exchange
Brecht talks about how, when people talk about realism, they normally talk
about it as if it were an aesthetic: if, say, you were to observe certain unities,
and if people did not fly, and nobody had miraculous gifts and you talked
about observable phenomena, and you were psychological in your approach
and so forth, then you would be writing what is called realism, and that would
in some way describe the objective world. And Brecht said of course realism
is not an aesthetic, realism—to paraphrase him—is whatever you have to do
in order to describe what you see. If that involves golden angels coming from
underneath mountains, then *that's* realism. Realism is whatever it takes. To
be metaphorical does not mean that you cease to be realistic. Take as a concrete example the beginning of *Shame,* the three women who share the child.
Now, I'd had that idea before I had the book, really, and in a way I thought
maybe there would be a book for it at some point. Then it turned out to be a
part of this book. What I'd been thinking about for a long time was the
position of women in a closed society. What observably happens in such
societies is that the women form their own kind of networks of support, of
solidarity, of sustenance and so forth, and they become close and intimate in
a way which is impossible for people until their lives are circumscribed,
because actually they would reject that closeness if the doors were open. But
because the doors are not open they live in this hothouse way. All I wanted
to do was to say here are women who share everything, and to find the most
extraordinary thing they would wish to share, and that ended up being the
child. So the fact that you have a child who has three mothers, which sounds
like a fantasy, is actually only about half a step further from what actually
happens.

Brooks: This raises interesting questions about metaphor in your work and whether in fact you are very happy with people's attempts to treat parts of your work as allegory or to try and interpret them symbolically. I mean, I found myself at one point this morning, as I was wandering over here, thinking the three mothers of Omar Khayyam Shakil were perhaps the three countries of Salman Rushdie . . .

Rushdie: Oh yes, yes I know, it's funny how people keep doing that.

Brooks: I don't necessarily like doing that, but it is one of the functions of the human mind.

Rushdie: All I can say is that I don't construct like that. I mean, I think that it's wrong, really, for writers to prescribe readings of their work, so the fact that I don't construct like that doesn't mean that you're not right—who knows? I've also heard that the three mothers stand for Baluchistan, Punjab and Sind. As far as I can tell, they don't, but who am I? I'm just one of the book's readers! In India allegory is a kind of disease. Indian philosophy has this idea of Maya, of reality as a veil, in which what we in fact can think of as being real is an illusion born out of our limited perceptions, and if you can move this veil aside then somewhere behind it there is reality. And you move the veil aside through a process called religion. Because there is this idea of the veil, almost all great classical Indian literature has been allegorical in its form, and so—we're talking about the limitations of Indian criticism—one of the problems is that there's an expectation of allegory which is so great that almost everything you do is always translated allegorically. I don't think that anything I've done can be translated in that simple way.

Brooks: So you find yourself actually fighting that possibility?

Rushdie: Yes, except that, if it's an Indian disease, it also affects me, so it does get into the books every so often. But I keep trying to sidetrack it.

Brooks: What about the choice of the language in which you write the books?

Rushdie: It wasn't a choice. By the time I started writing there was only one language I could write in. I still speak Urdu but one of the problems with Urdu is that . . . well, there are several problems. Although it is a very beautiful language, it's also a language best suited to certain methods which are not mine. For instance, metaphysical or lyrical or romantic writing. Its grammar, its syntax, are very rigid, unlike those of English. It's not a very flexible language in that sense. So you couldn't attempt a Joycean enterprise in Urdu, the language would just disintegrate and you'd be writing things that meant nothing, nobody would know what the sentences meant. It's a language which says keep the rules, and which of course reveals something about the people who use it. It is a language which is very beautiful as long as you keep the rules, but there's no elbow room in it. The way in which Urdu is being adapted in Pakistan today is by adulteration, by the incorporation of Punjabi and Sindhi, which are much more colloquial down-to-earth languages. The Urdu now spoken in Pakistan is not Urdu really, it's really Punjabi and Sindhi with some other elements, Urdu is bad at colloquialism, bad at the everyday. It's very good at the moon.

Brooks: I was interested in what you were saying yesterday about metaphor and the English language and your need to find ways to make that language more metaphoric.

Rushdie: Somebody who interviewed me recently was rather upset because I called English a language which resisted metaphor. They said many would think that English is a language very rich in metaphor, which of course it is, but what I was saying is that at the level of everyday speech, at the level of *good morning,* and *what would you like for breakfast,* English is not metaphorical, but Urdu and Hindi are. When you say in English *the sun rose,* you might say in Urdu *the sun woke up,* which sounds peculiar in English.

Brooks: So the languages that you are familiar with increase your demands on English, and give you—what do you call it—an angle of dislocation?

Rushdie: Well, yes, you have to find angles to enter a language, I suppose, and that's mine. On the other hand, nothing is true forever. In my case the subject precedes the decisions about the forms, and the subject in a way tells me it must be written in such and such a way. I felt after *Shame*—a book of great violence, somewhat disturbing to me—that I wanted to write a different sort of book, and about different kinds of things. It was time to remember that there were other things than dictatorships and corrupt classes. Love, for instance. I thought I'd like to make that kind of a shift, and what I've found— and I'm not particularly going to talk about the unwritten book—is that it has required a shift towards a simpler, purer language, which in a way might seem like a contradiction of everything I've been saying, except that I don't think that I could have found that language without having done the other book.

Brooks: How do you feel about your first book, *Grimus?*

Rushdie: I don't know really. I haven't read it for ten years. I don't mind him, and I don't feel quite able to reject it, but I know it has more mistakes than the other books. The thing I feel most uneasy about in it is to do with the language, because—what should I say?—I don't recognize my voice in it, whereas in the other books I do. But this may have to do with the fact that I was a different person then. Maybe at the time I *did* talk like that; now it seems somewhat distant to me. There is a small character in it, if I remember rightly, who is standing on the edge of a cliff trying to discover a voice in which to speak, and I find, I think, that is the best bit in the book, or the most truthful.

Paton: I was interested—if you don't mind back-tracking a little—in that point you made about the violence in *Shame,* and how it was disturbing to you. Could you expand a bit on that? Before you started writing the book, were you aware that you would be writing about violence?

Rushdie: Yes, I knew. I do plan quite a lot, but then you also get taken by surprise. I always thought that it would be a book about the connection between shame and violence, and that it would inevitably contain certain acts of violence. I tried at first to convince myself that I could make these largely comic. I mean beheading turkeys, for instance, may be disturbing, but it is also funny, or at least is supposed to be. I thought maybe I could keep the thing in control by the use of farcical imagery like that. But then, you know, if you create a figure of nemesis, there is a point at which you have to accept that nemesis is not funny. That was the difficult bit.

Paton: When Sufiya Zinobia becomes a beast?

Rushdie: Yes, when she starts killing people, and, yes, the further the book went on it really became . . . I mean, it came out of the dark. There was a dark thing that she came out of and I'm not quite sure where. Somewhere inside me. I was rather surprised to find it was there.

Brooks: Are your books a *finding* as you write them, or do you plan very carefully beforehand?

Rushdie: I do both really. What I do, it's . . . it's a sort of insanity. Imagine yourself to be an explorer going to a country for which there are no maps, and which you've never seen. What you do is you draw a map. You console yourself with this map. You say *I know all about this place I'm going to, it looks like this, these are the towns and these are the people, these are the* *principal exports,* and then you go there, and of course the map really bears no relationship to the place and then you have to redraw it, but if you don't have the map to begin with you can't begin the trip. I do find the first draft of everything I've written has really been just a way of finding out what I was doing. Yet it takes up by far the greatest part of the process of writing, because something out of nothing is the hard bit. I do quite a lot of planning, and some of the things I plan don't change, but a lot does. For instance, I didn't know that Sufiya Zinobia would turn out to be an idiot until a long way into the writing. I didn't know that the dictator would die until quite a long way in. I thought he would just go into exile at one point, you see, and then he refused to, or the logic of the book demanded a different sort of ending. I think in *Midnight's Children* there was an even bigger problem, which was that at the point I began writing it the events that come at the end had not yet happened in history. I started writing the book in 1975 and the Emergency ended in 1977. That obviously was a very peculiar and dangerous gamble, to write so close to events and yet claim to be writing not journalism but something else, and it required some fast moving, and some rewriting. You see, one of the things was that I knew, in my picture of the book, that I didn't want to end with the Emergency; I thought that if you put that at the end it would give disproportionate weight to that strand in the book. On the other hand I thought, you know, what do I do? I can't end it in the book if it's not ended in actuality. So I was very grateful to Mrs. Ghandi. I remember cheering.

Brooks: Because she came in on cue?

Rushdie: Yes. For calling the election then having the grace to lose, just as I was getting near the end of the book. It's the one moment in which I understood how the character in the book feels, believing that he effects history at a distance.

Paton: I've been thinking about the end of *Midnight's Children* as compared to *Shame.* They seem to be a long way apart.

Rushdie: The moods of the books? Well that's really to do with India and Pakistan, with the difference between the two. Maybe there was a shift in my own mood also. I don't know. But I had the feeling, with Pakistan, of claustrophobia, and in India of wide open landscapes, and in simple terms the two books reflect those two views. The compass of *Shame* is more confined. *Shame* is not a portrait of a nation, it's a portrait of a ruling class, and *Midnight's Children* tries to be a bit broader than that. But what happens at the end of *Shame* . . . well, I'm not entirely sure about that explosion. I don't know what it is, or signifies. I don't think it necessarily means anything as simple as the end of the world. It's a kind of question mark. I suppose it implies a kind of cleansing of the stables.

Paton: So you wouldn't really see it as pessimistic?

Rushdie: Well, it is sometimes necessary to wipe things out in order that you can write other things. That's true of writers, and it's also true of history.

Brooks: I was very interested to hear you saying yesterday that among other things the different structures of *Midnight's Children* and *Shame* reflect different perceptions of their respective countries—the idea of multitude in *Midnight's Children,* and of a fabric that could accommodate a multitude of stories, one story in a way fighting its way through the crowd. I like that very much and it does seem to come from the book in the first place, but I was wondering whether you thought there was also a number of things you learnt through the writing of *Midnight's Children* that were then applied to *Shame.*

Rushdie: I was conscious of doing things the opposite way in *Shame.* For instance, India is a society about which not only multitude, but plurality is basic—there are all these different religions and different kinds of people, so you have to accept a kind of plural concept. The word Indian doesn't really mean anything—Bengali means more than Indian; India, if it means any thing, means plurality. Although it also has different races, Pakistan feels much more like a singularity, because there is just the one religion and there's a much greater homogeneity both of language and faith, especially since the loss of the east, so it required a different treatment. Also, as far as *Midnight's Children* is concerned, the problem of the narrator was something. Saleem was very useful, but when you have such an overwhelming narrator there are always moments when the author and narrator don't agree and it becomes impossible to tell the readers, so there's an assumption on the part of the readers that the narrator speaks for the author. Also, when the narrator is placed so close to the author in age and place and so forth, there's an assumption towards biography which increases that sense of unity of view. And so I felt that what I would do in *Shame,* after having had a book with such a dominant centre, was to have a book in which the centre was a hole. I mean, to call Omar Khayyam the hero is actually a way of not having a hero. Instead you have a dozen characters or so who are of roughly equal importance and who at different moments in the book become the point-of-view character or become the person about whom the story *is,* and then they step out of the centre and somebody else steps in.

Brooks: I wanted to ask a question concerning Omar Khayyam and Nishapur and that strand in the book—why you placed it there, whether you were conscious of various dominant reasons for it, or whether it was more of a metafictional game.

Rushdie: Well, it was a joke to begin with, you know, but it was one of those odd jokes that, once you have made it, you start discovering is relevant. I suppose it began as a joke about a poet who is only interesting in translation, but also there is this thing about Omar Khayyam as an astrologer—the *real* Omar Khayyam was an astrologer—and astrologers, astronomy, telescopes, things seen through the eye, are quite present in the book. There were all kinds of little reverberations that I found between the actual figure and the fictional figure, by chance really, but principally it was just a joke. Jokes in Pakistan are just about the last kind of political protest possible.

Brooks: Everything else having been tried.

Rushdie: I mean everything else having been murdered . . . But I also made up one or two of the jokes, and I found they were by far the hardest bit of the writing. It is very hard to invent jokes from scratch—there's a one page story in the book about God coming down to Pakistan and asking successive leaders why the place is a mess—well I made that up you see, that's not a real joke, and I feel very pleased because nobody seems to have picked that up.

Brooks: You find writing a great deal of fun?

Rushdie: Yes some days, some days. You know, I have all the standard views about writing, which is that it's lonely and you sit in a room and it's hell and sweat and it takes a long time and you despair and so forth, but also it's better than having a job.

Paton: As a writer, where would you see yourself—in an Indian tradition or a European?

Rushdie: One thing that I do think is that there seems to be a spot of imperialism left over in the idea of what material a writer can legitimately use: an American can write about anywhere in the world, but an Indian writer is supposed to write only about India, African writers are supposed to write only about Africa. I do want to write at some point books which are not set in the East.

Paton: I think in *Shame* you say that.

Rushdie: Yes, yes, but one can't prophesy quite that accurately. The next book in fact is set in India or Pakistan. It is difficult; it is very hard.

Brooks: Yeats wrote very progressive critical essays about where poetry was going and what poetry should be doing, and what was worst about current poetry, and at the same time, sometimes, he was writing poetry that fitted his description of the worst. It's very hard to break the mould.

Rushdie: It's not just that. It's that you are the victim of your imagination. I don't think it's because I'm falling into a habit, I think it's because, for a start, this material is so rich; there is so much to write about that it seems stupid not to do it. It's such a luxury for a writer to have all that stuff about. You just pick the stories up. You don't have to make them up—you just pluck them off the trees. On the other hand, I was talking yesterday about migration and so forth, and I do think that is an important subject; I'm working on a fairly large long term project in that area. You see, one of the things that I have discovered is that migration has a kind of suppressed history, somewhat like the way in which women have been erased from history. Take England, for instance; the history of what migrant communities have contributed to that society has been suppressed in the interest of creating the idea of a homogeneous society. It's been suppressed for a kind of politically dominant race and reason, and if you want to excavate that history, it's very difficult because you have to read 200 books instead of 20, because there are only fragments everywhere. I'm happy and relieved to say that there are some historians who are beginning that process of excavation. I want to have some knowledge at least of that suppressed history before beginning to write fictions and I've somewhat delayed my start because I've got a couple of years' reading to do. Meanwhile, to my great relief, I've got this book to write.

Paton: In *Shame,* you keep coming back to ideas of history and time.

Rushdie: Yes, well, history was my academic discipline. I suppose I have always used a kind of historical method, in the completely unmethodical way which is the luxury of fiction. I do think this connection of history and story important to remember. The Italian word *storia* means both things; the Urdu word *qissa* means a tale and it means history. This connects with a view I have that what is happening now is a return towards narrative in fiction—not a naive return, not an attempt to pretend that Joyce didn't happen, but a return to narrative in the light of everything that has happened. It's the end of the century, and time for synthesis, and that seems to be what's happening.

Paton: You seem concerned, especially in *Shame,* about the corruption of history.

Rushdie: Yes, because it's going on everywhere. I don't think there has ever been a time when the truth has been so manipulated, because the weapons of manipulation are now so sophisticated.

Brooks: I just realized something, listening to you now, about my own reaction to *Midnight's Children.* I enjoyed it a great deal, but I also found that it was oppressive. And I felt that this had something to do with aesthetic rhythm. Ezra Pound, in a thing called *The Treatise of Harmony,* suggests that any two sounds, no matter how disharmonious they may be in a normal structure, can be harmonious if there is a sufficient space left between them, if a sufficient silence is allowed to intervene. Harmony becomes a matter of appropriate interval. I was a bit disturbed half way through *Midnight's Children* by the close succession of enchanting pages, the rapidity with which remarkable events followed one another, and then I remembered someone, an American, telling me about her own experience of India, and that one of the things that struck her most forcibly was the different idea of intimate distance, and that in fact in India people . . .

Rushdie: They don't leave space.

Brooks: Yes, and it seems to me that that's actually entered the book, that it's evident from the structure of *Midnight's Children.*

Rushdie: Yes. You don't leave volumes of empty air around people, because there are too many people.

Brooks: Well this is a fundamental difference, say, between your work and work that is remotely comparable, like Márquez's, and a lot of modern European fiction, too.

Rushdie: I've noticed that, except in certain defined spaces like a football stadium or a rock arena, people with a western sensibility feel oppressed by crowds.

Brooks: And even there of course, the crowd has an immediate emotional effect; people go to a place where they want to be excited and the crowd makes it happen.

Rushdie: Yes. So being in a crowd is a special event which creates special feeling. In India this is not true. Nobody is afraid of crowds, because the crowd is the norm, so a crowd does not create special behaviour, nor does it create any special fears.

Paton: It was interesting, in *Shame,* when you put the women out into those remote houses, and you created that sense of space. There really was a sort of a horror . . .

Rushdie: Yes. Emptiness *is* frightening. You get to the frontier and there is a cloud there—people faint when they get to the frontier, because there is nothingness.

Paton: It seems to be your image of hell: one person miles away from another person.

Rushdie: Hell is not other people.

Fictions Are Lies That Tell the Truth: Salman Rushdie and Günter Grass: In Conversation

Günter Grass / 1985

From *The Listener* 27 June 1985: 14–15. Reprinted by permission.

Rushdie: I was thinking about the Second World War and what it was like for the losers as opposed to the winners. And I wondered if you felt that coming from the losing side, so to speak, has advantages or has had advantages for you in writing.

Grass: If you accept that you are a loser, and for German people it was very hard to accept—I did, and, looking back, I think I did win something by this acceptance of being a loser, of losing a war. I was 17 years old. By losing the war I lost my home town, Danzig, that's now Gdansk, which is Polish. And I tried to bring something back to write about, to win it again by writing. I think also it is a chance, if you lose a war, to go on thinking about the reasons how it could happen in Germany, this terrible crime with a short name: Auschwitz. When I'm visiting other countries who still believe they belong to the winner's side, I am very often astonished how much less they are able to think about things they have lost.

Rushdie: I am interested in what you said about losing a city, because I had exactly the same sense, though for different reasons. It was a simpler reason: my family migrated from my city when I was 14. I left to go to school in England and then the city itself was transformed. The city that I remember, that I grew up in, was knocked down and replaced by high-rise buildings, like concrete tombstones. So even the people who still lived in the city lost that city, because it disappeared. And I had very much the desire of wanting to reclaim it. It was very useful for me that the city itself was built on land-reclamation. The whole city, where it now stands, is mostly built on land that was reclaimed from the sea—by the British, in fact. Bombay is, in a way, a British invention as a city. I felt I had to go through a similar process of land-reclamation to get the city back for myself.

Grass: Reading your book, I had the feeling that it was somebody who

tries to reconstruct something for himself writing this book, what he has lost
and to keep it.

Rushdie: The question of a loss is also connected to memory, I find it
interesting that a number of leading writers in contemporary European literature approach this subject of reclamation, of regaining the past, of remaking
the past, reinventing it for their own purposes. That's to say, there is all over
Europe a kind of historical project among many writers.

Grass: In the middle of the Fifties I discovered for myself that I needed a
confrontation with history, with Germany history. I couldn't look away any
more to other parts, nice parts. It had to be confronted. It was also the reason
I changed from West Germany to Berlin, because here, in West Berlin, every
day you are confronted with the result of the last war. Also seeing the wall
every day you have this feeling. And another reason was that just after the
war the Germans in both parts tried to belong to the winner's side. We were
the best democrats afterwards, and we did everything the United States
wanted. And you can say the same of East Germany; they were the best
socialists and belonging to the winner's side, they did exactly what Moscow
wanted at the time. And the official, political language about the end of the
war was not that of capitulation, it was "disaster," it was a "catastrophe," it
was "hour zero." Nice lies, covering the truth. They said of the Nazi period
that it was a time when it "became dark in Germany." This kind of demoni-
sation of the SS, of the Nazi party, didn't tell the truth.

This was one reason to look back and to show in telling my story that all
these things happened in clear daylight. Very slowly, there were special
groups who were interested: the arrangement between capital and Hitler in
the beginning, but also the petit bourgeois people, who were lost after the
First World War. It was very easy for Hitler to win those people. He really
did speak out the dreams of the petit bourgeois, and he realised in a terrible
way what he promised them. And I tried, both in my first novel *The Tin Drum*
and also in *Dog Years,* not to explain, to tell the story of this slow, very petit
bourgeois way to go, slowly, with all knowledge, into crime. Political crime.

Rushdie: What you're saying is that the purpose of the fiction was, in a
way, paradoxical: that the fiction is telling the truth at a time in which the
people who claimed to be telling the truth were making things up. You have
politicians or the media or whoever, the people who form opinion, who are,
in fact, making the fictions. And it becomes the duty of the writer of fiction

to start telling the truth. This is a kind of paradox which, perhaps, is true of many countries now.

Grass: I think that our dreams, the unspoken things and the fantastic ideas people have, they all belong to reality, and in one sentence I jump from the flat reality that you see, you can touch, to inside things.

Rushdie: There are two bodies of thought at the moment which would hold that politics is none of our business as writers. There is, certainly inside English literature, but I suspect in all literatures, an attitude towards writing which says that it is somehow separate from these public issues, and ought to be separated from them. And, on the other hand, you have the whole apparatus of the post-modernist critique, which also, for very different reasons, seeks to separate the text from the world. So you have both a radical and a conservative discourse suggesting that writers should not meddle in public affairs. My own inability to believe that that's the case is very strong. Now in your own work you've taken the public road, both inside the novels and in your statements and writings outside the novels. Was that why you become a writer, do you think, or did it come as a secondary impulse? That desire to take issue with the affairs of the time?

Grass: No. For me, every problem I see I see as an artist—also in writing. But the reality with which I'm crowded around is touched by politics. If sometimes I wish to write or to do something that has nothing to do with politics, in the second sentence the history of my country, my own history, is taking me back to this ugly reality we are living in. I think it's a stupid question. In Germany they always try to say, "Writer, go write, please, nice things or sad things and poetical things." As long as we have literature, it is confronted by political questions. And what is moving me in recent years more and more, is that the situation of writing has changed: because the situation of life has changed. Human beings, for the first time, are able to destroy themselves. After Hiroshima the situation from year to year changes more in that we are able from one day to the next to finish human beings. To finish the history.

If you live here in the middle of Europe, in Germany, you know that here the nuclear weapons are crowded from East and West more than in any other place of the world. You must be a lucky man and a bit of a stupid man if you don't realise this. Lucky and stupid in the same moment not to realise this every day. Sure, it's very difficult to go on and live like this, but in Germany we have a lot of young people who are afraid and they are brave enough to show that they are afraid. I'm afraid of people who still go on and say, "Well, there is no reason to be afraid and life will go on and we have to trust," and they don't believe any more. And I think that one of the mistakes the Germans made, in this century and also in the time before, was that they were not brave enough to be afraid. I think we have, with all this knowledge, to go on to tell stories. But in this knowledge we have now.

Rushdie: Is it a question of telling stories, then? Because it seems to me that the reason, the thing that made me become a writer was that desire: a desire simply to tell stories. I grew up in a literary tradition. That's to say that the kind of stories I was told as a child, by and large, were *Arabian Nights* kind of stories. It was those sort of fairytales. But beyond that, the kind of context in which I began to think was one in which it was accepted that stories should be untrue. You know, the idea that fiction should be a lie, that it should be a wonderful story. That horses and also carpets should fly was expected. And the belief was that by telling stories in that way, in that marvellous way, you could actually tell a kind of truth which you couldn't tell in other ways. And so I grew up assuming, again, that that was the normal way of telling stories, and found myself struggling when I began to write seriously in the context of a literature which had for a long time formed a sort of opposite view about what a novel was. That's to say, a novel should be mimetic, it should imitate the world, obey the rules of naturalism or of social realism. So I find myself constantly struggling with the fact that my assumptions are opposite to the assumptions of many people in the West, for whom fantasy or the use of the imagination is exceptional. For me it seems to be normative. I wondered what was the kind of literary context that you came from, whether you had a similar experience or not.

Grass: Just after the war I really started to read again and to read other things and was interested in all this forbidden literature, the early expressionism in Germany, the surrealistic authors. I couldn't work with this short-minded kind of realism, just to imitate reality. I was also, from my childhood, very much touched by the German Romantic tradition also: the fairytales. They are telling truth. The flying horse is really flying.

Rushdie: The fish talks.

Grass: Yes, he talks and I used in many books those archetypal figures of German fairytales. Like in *The Flounder* perhaps, and also in *The Tin Drum*.

I think using these fairytales is bringing us to another kind of truth: to a much, much richer truth than you can get by collecting facts of this flat realism.

We have many realities. Our problem is that we don't accept that there are many realities. This side wants only this reality, and the other only their own reality. This is one of the reasons we still have this struggle.

Rushdie: In India the thing that I've taken most from, I think, apart from the fairytale tradition that we were talking about, is oral narration. Because it is a country of still largely illiterate people the power and the vitality still remain in the oral storytelling tradition. And what's interesting about these stories is that they command huge audiences, the best storytellers with literally hundreds of thousands of people. They'll come to sit in a field while a man tells stories. It's a very eclectic form; and, of course, not at all linear. I mean, the story does not go from the beginning to the end but it goes in great loops and circles back on itself, repeats earlier things, digresses, uses sometimes a kind of Chinese-box system, where you have the story inside the story inside the story and then they all come back. It seems formless. When you look at it, it appears chaos—that you are at the whim of the storyteller and that he can do whatever he wants. Now, it occurred to me to ask the opposite question. Let us assume, for the sake of argument, that this is not formlessness but a form which, after all, is many thousands of years old and has adopted this shape for good reasons. And it struck me that the storyteller, much more so than the novelist, has the problem of holding of the audience. The novelist doesn't see the moment at which people shut the book and get bored; the storyteller always sees the moment because people get up and walk away or they throw eggs, or whatever. And so everything he does is done to hold the audience. This suggested to me that what we were being told was that this very gymnastic, convoluted, complicated form was, in fact, the very reason why people were listening.

Then I found in novels like *Tristram Shandy,* for example, a very similar spirit. So it seemed to me that what I was finding out was the kind of writing that stood, so to speak, at the frontier between both the cultures. That I could, as a migrant from that culture into this culture, bring with me that luggage and already find that there was a similar thing going on. So I had something to connect myself to.

Grass: I have this feeling of arriving when I go back to Gdansk and I see the city as it is rebuilt by Polish people now, but after some minutes I know it is no more Danzig and I know that it's lost. And I accept it is. To be now without a place, to be with many places, I don't complain about it. I think it's a very good feeling to be without one place. To be nervous, to be disturbed, to be out. To belong to the loser, to know what you have lost and to carry it in language. Language can be something like home for a writer, but I think I would also have this feeling and this relation to language if I did have a place, and I think the same would happen to you. But we have this special problem, that this is a reason for our neighbours to be nervous again. For other people it's very simple, for young people to explain themselves as English or Dutch or French or Spanish. But it's much more difficult for young people in Germany; they have to explain that they're from West Germany or from East Germany.

We are afraid to use a word like nation. If somebody speaks about the French nation, *la grande nation,* there can be chauvinism behind, but if somebody in Germany speaks quite normally about the German nation, everybody is afraid that a new nationalism is emerging. It's a kind of taboo.

Rushdie: I was very struck by a curious fact I discovered which showed me something about the reason why my writing, or perhaps one reason why my writing had fallen towards this metaphorical, imaginative kind of writing, which is that if you look etymologically at the meaning of the word "metaphor" and the word "translation" it turns out they mean the same thing. Translation, from the Latin, means "to carry across." Metaphor, from the Greek, means "to carry across." So again this comes back to my preoccupation with the idea of migration. People are also carried across, you see; they're carried physically from one place to another and I formed the idea that the act of migration was to turn people somehow into things, into people who had been translated, who had, so to speak, entered the condition of metaphor, and that their instinctive way of looking at the world was in that more metaphorical, imagistic manner.

If you consider where your sense of self has always been located—in the idea of roots, the idea of coming from a place, the idea of inhabiting a kind of language which you have in common and the kind of social convention within which you live—what happens to the migrants is that they lose all three. They lose the place. They lose the language and they lose the social conventions and they find themselves in a new place with a new language—

and so they have to reinvent the sense of the self. This is, after all, the century of the migrant as well as the century of the Bomb; there have never been so many people who ended up elsewhere than where they began, whether by choice or by necessity. And so perhaps that's the source from which this kind of reconstruction can begin. People who are no longer caught in the old definition of the self, but capable of making new ones.

Angels and Devils Are Becoming Confused Ideas

Salil Tripathi and Dina Vakil / 1987

From *Indian Post* 13 September 1987. Reprinted by permission.

He sits on a plush red sofa in his Bombay hotel suite, surrounded by type-writer, breakfast tray, a stack of newspapers, and a carefully arranged bowl of roses. An incomplete draft of his script, *In Search Of Midnight's Children,* which he is currently filming for British television's Channel Four, lies unat-tended on the coffee table in front of him. But what really engages author Salman Rushdie's attention is a batch of current clips of the comic strip *Mandrake.* Predictably so, "I rather like the idea of people turning into aspar-aguses and all that," says the magician of words.

In life, as in his art, the celebrated Booker Prize-winning writer revels in the ordinary turning into the bizarre, the bizarre masquerading as the ordi-nary. Villains with unexpected vulnerabilities and heroes with disastrous vices crowd his novels. The outrageous and the banal, fact and fantasy, his-tory and fable dominate his work: In *Midnight's Children* (which inspired the documentary he is filming), he discovered an India he would have liked to belong to, not the one which existed; in *Shame,* he created a Pakistan that hurt not only the generals, but also some of his family; in *The Jaguar Smile,* he discovered Nicaragua's revolutionary culture of masks with bullet-holes in their foreheads and Sandino recognizable only by his hat.

Salman Rushdie may have left his native Bombay when he was just 17, but he admits to "withdrawal symptoms" if he stays away from the city for too long. Not surprisingly, therefore, he returns to Bombay in his new novel, with a film star hero who fancies himself to be the Archangel Gabriel.

Clad in a checked green *lungi* and a yellow handloom *kurta,* Rushdie does not look his 40 years. His clipped British accent has quickened, as if irritated by the limitations of speech which cannot keep pace with his myriad thoughts. In a wide-ranging interview, he talks to Dina Vakil and Salil Tri-pathi about why he chooses to live in England but continues to return to India, his new novel, and why he never meant *Midnight's Children* to mean Rajiv Gandhi's Dosco chums.

79

Q: After *Midnight's Children* was published, Satyajit Ray said the book was unfilmable, in the sense that it would have to be simplified so much that it would not be itself. How far do you think that is true?

A: I think he might well be right about *Midnight's Children* as a film. But the film we're making has very little to do with the novel, apart from the title, because, after all, it's a documentary.

I thought what might be interesting would be to do something more personally interesting—to revisit the ideas out of which the book came, but to do it in the context of real people. The book is, as you know, all about people born at midnight, 15 August 1947. In the film, we are going to be talking about people who are going to be 40 this year, like the country. And I thought there was something quite intriguing about going to meet people that you had, in a way, invented *(laughs)*. Except that what I didn't want to do was to go and find exact parallels of characters in the book, in the sense that that would be very forced.

That began to intrigue me as an approach, because it seemed to be a way of making a kind of snapshot of the country, which was not mediated through the normal channels of public figures or expert analysts. It would just be a group of ordinary people describing the conditions of their lives and how they saw things in the country to be developing and what they thought, at 40 years, the idea of Independence had come to mean. And, in a way, the attraction of doing it was that I didn't know what the answers would be.

Q: How do you feel about 40 years of Indian Independence?

A: To tell you the truth, it seemed to me as no more than an excuse to make the film. Anniversaries are just anniversaries, really, they're not in any sense really significant events. It's a way of getting films made; it was as useful a point as any other to make a film about the present, because the one thing I wanted to make clear was that the film was not going to be about 1947, it wasn't going to be about Partition. It could only be about the intervening period [between 1947 and today] in so far as it covered the background of people's lives—you know, where they'd been and how they'd grown up.

I wanted it to be a picture of the country now, as far as possible, rather than of the country then. Already in England, they've got onto the bandwagon of the 40th anniversary; there have been a lot of articles and television programmes about the period of Partition and the end of the empire, as you can imagine. And I didn't at all want to be a part of that thing. Originally, people were stressing that we should have the film ready to show on 15 August, and I said that that really wasn't it, that I'd much rather be here on 15 August, filming it.

Q: Were you?

A: Yes, we were, in Delhi. We've already been in India three and a half weeks, so we've only got another ten or twelve days of the total shoot. I went to the Red Fort celebrations [on Independence Day] and we filmed that. We were up on the ramparts, and we also had a second camera [trained] on one of our characters who happened to be an ordinary tailor from Paharganj. We thought it would be more interesting, really, to see the whole thing from the point of view of just one person in the crowd.

So this is how the film came about. The question about whether the actual novel can ever be filmed is quite separate. My feeling is that it's very hard to get it into a feature film and that, if it is at all possible, it would have to be something longer, like a television series.

Q: Do you think that works by writers such as you, or Milan Kundera, or Gabriel García Márquez, for instance, can ever be filmed?

A: I have no theoretical position or reason to believe not. The film that I have seen is of Márquez's *Chronicle of a Death Foretold* and it was appalling. It's very sentimentalised and, in a way, misses the point of the novel. I believe they are filming [Kundera's] *The Unbearable Lightness of Being*—so, obviously, they think they can do it.

I would think that there always is a solution with film. I think there would be all kinds of problems with [filming] *Midnight's Children,* of which the most obvious one is the problem of language. You can write a novel in English and the reader will accept the convention that most of the characters are not really speaking English, or speaking in English only part of the time.

In *Midnight's Children,* it is clear that, at least in the Kashmiri section, and in the sections involving the grandparents in Agra or even Delhi, it's very likely that the language used is not English. In a film, you can't duck that issue and you have to decide what language the characters are speaking in. And if they're not speaking English all the way, it might look rather peculiar. It also has an implication for the budget. You're not going to get a massive international budget to make a film if the characters are all speaking in Hindi.

Q: Why don't 40 years of Pakistan interest you as much as 40 years of India after Independence?

A: Well, they do, but not as much. I suppose it's because I grew up here. Until I was 17, I was based in Bombay and either living here or coming here on holiday when I was at school in England. That's a very important part of one's life. I know Pakistan very well and, in many ways, in my adult life I've been to Pakistan more than to India because of family being there and so forth.

But, in answer to your question, there are two reasons. One is that [Pakistan] doesn't seem to me as diverse a subject as India. The other is that it's more difficult to make a film there because one is talking about a much more controlled environment. I suppose, if I went to Pakistan, I'd want to make a film about the political situation whereas, in India, there's a whole range of things to make a film about, of which the political situation is only one.

There's also, I suppose, a clue that I found in the novel, which is that when Saleem Sinai [the protagonist] goes to Pakistan, he loses his powers. He is not able to communicate telepathically, or to build a comparable group in Pakistan as he does in India. It suggested to me that one should perhaps respect that *(laughs)*—that when one wished to make a contemporary reassessment of *Midnight's Children,* if you like, the children should also be confined to India, because they were in the book.

Q: At the PEN (Poets, Essayists and Novelists) Conference in New York in 1986, you had an argument with Saul Bellow on the role of the writer—to you, commitment mattered more; to him, inspiration. How do you see your role?

A: It's two things, really. I think there's a role inside the writing and a role outside the writing and those aren't always the same thing. It seems to me that any writer would wish to reserve the right not to write about public issues—there are other things to write about as well. I don't feel it's absolutely obligatory every time I write any fiction to make it a public fiction.

It so happens that both *Midnight's Children* and *Shame* are of that type. But it's not necessary to do that. I mean, if I wanted to write a love story, I'd write a love story. In short stories, for example, quite often I've not written about big public issues. So, it seems to me that the public role is not necessarily what one has to do inside the writing, although I have obviously been temperamentally drawn in that direction. But I wouldn't have any objection to a writer who chose not to do that.

The question about a public role outside the writing is again a temperamental thing. There are plenty of writers who don't want to do it. So far, I have wanted to use the writing, or the voice one establishes as a result of the writing, to talk about other things, or to talk directly—say, not in fiction—about things that capture one's attention, or the hot issues.

I think it has to be done very sparingly, because one of the things that I have always not wanted to be is some kind of backdoor political commentator. For instance, I've always resisted offers to write regular columns and to have any kind of regular base in journalism. I think it's more the question of finding it important to have the ability to make the interventions at moments when it matters to me.

Q: Is that why you decided to do the recent book on Nicaragua, *The Jaguar Smile?*

A: Well, in a way, yes, although it came about by a series of accidents. I went to Nicaragua because I had been involved in the campaign against the American aggression, and I went out of interest. I really didn't go to write a book. It became clear when I was there that the place was having a strong effect on me and, therefore, it was probable that I would write something, but even then I thought it couldn't be a book, because I was then in the middle of another book.

I thought that I'd come back and write some articles and that would be it. But it just got longer and longer and, in the end, I had to accept that it wasn't an article. It became a book because it existed in the form of a book rather than because I set out to make a book. That was in a way very irritating because it interrupted my novel for six months.

Q: Can you talk about your new novel?

A: Well, it's very difficult to talk about it. I have been working on it for years now and I hope to finish it by the end of this year. It'll be five years since I finished *Shame.* It's a novel about the Archangel Gabriel. I think *(laughs)*—that's the simplest way of putting it. The main character, who is not an Archangel, is kind of going insane. He is an Indian movie star who decides to step out of his life and step away from it, and actually leaves Bombay and goes to England; but, at the same time, he is losing his mind and is becoming convinced that he is, in some way, the Archangel. That's a one-sentence answer on what it's about.

It's about angels and devils and about how it's very difficult to establish ideas of morality in a world which has become so uncertain that it is difficult to even agree on what is happening. When one can't agree on a description of reality, it is very hard to agree on whether that reality is good or evil, right or wrong. When one can't say what is actually the case, it is difficult to proceed from that to an ethical position.

Angels and devils are becoming confused ideas. One of the things that happens in the process is that what is supposed to be angelic quite often has disastrous results, and what is supposed to be demonic is quite often something with which one must have sympathy.

It is supposed to be a portrait of, in part, an attempt to come to grips with that sense of a crumbling moral fabric or, at least, a need for the reconstruction of old simplicities.

What I think the novel is also conceptually about is the act of migration, and of hybridisation, of the way in which people become combinations. One of the things that is observable about Bombay, perhaps above all Indian cities, is that kind of cultural hybridisation. All cultures are, to an extent, adulterated anyway. This process of intermingling is what I referred to in *Midnight's Children* as leaking, in which people 'leak' into each other; so do cultures—that's very central to what the novel is all about.

I suppose it is also about the attempt of somebody like myself, who is basically a person without formal religion, to make some kind of accommodation with the renewed force of religion in the world; what it means; what the religious experience is. It is clear that there is such a thing as transcendence, that mystical events are not entirely spurious, that people see visions and they are not always lying.

The question is, what is the nature of that experience, assuming that one does not immediately look to the miraculous for an explanation, but, at the same time does not dismiss it as a fraud. That middle ground about what the nature of transcendence is, or might be, is also what the novel is about.

Q: You just mentioned the renewed force of religion. How do you look at the growth of fundamentalism and communalism in India?

A: It seems to me inescapably at the centre of things right now. It is very hard to look at the country without having to look at that. In a way, I've wanted to find out what people were saying about it. It seems to be the most dangerous thing happening in the country and it appears to be on the increase. Obviously, that's something I feel extremely alarmed about.

The good news, if you like, is that even though, basically, all the people we've been talking to (during filming) have expressed concern about these issues, there is still, underneath, a kind of acceptance of the idea of hope. Even when you go into areas where there has been a lot of communal trou-

ble—old Delhi, Ahmedabad and Kashmir—it's not that the trouble is mini-
mised, but there is still something underneath it which is worth recognising.

Q: Do you at all identify with the Muslim world?

A: Yes and no. I am not a religious person. I don't say prayers. I don't
think of myself in any religious sense. However, I've been very affected by
Islamic culture and very interested in it. So, although I don't identify with
the Muslim world, obviously one of the major formative elements in my
intellectual make-up has been Muslim culture in the broadest sense.

I think Indian Muslim culture is rather unlike other Muslim cultures—for
example, in Kashmir there was a Sufistic form of Islam, actually rather similar to the kind of Islam that originally took root in Pakistan, until the present
dictatorship attempted to stamp it out. I do find it attractive and sympathetic.
But no, I would not place myself in another sense inside a Muslim world.

Q: You had once said that one of the things you liked about Britain was its
old, established tradition of dissent. In this context, how do you see the recent
ban on Peter Wright's book, *Spycatcher*?

A: It's clear to me that that particular dissenting tradition is out of power
(laughs). It seems that it has been for quite a long time. England is becoming
a rather dislikable society in many ways. There are levels of repression and
the State can now make intrusions into private lives. There is also the increasing power of the police—which one notices, incidentally, in New Delhi, too.
All these things mean that ten years of Thatcherism have done a great deal
of damage to the country. It's a structurally damaged society.

To take the example of the *Spycatcher* case, an attack has been made on
the freedom of the press—a very significant attack—and outside the community of the kind of people who are interested in the media, nobody is really
bothered. Nobody really thinks that something fundamental has been done to
the country; so, all these things are going on without any real objection or
real rage.

Q: How do you see the raid on the *Indian Express*?

A: The simple answer is that India is in a terrible mess. I have views very
similar to what is being (editorially) said in the Indian papers. The country
often seems like a rudderless ship. The fact that the raid was conducted on
the *Express* at the present time suggests to me that it was not coincidental. I
am, therefore, worried for the same reasons that I am worried about the
Spycatcher issue.

Q: Would you still rather continue to live in England?

A: The answer has to be yes, because I do. I stay there for all kinds of reasons which have to do not with the political structure of the country, but with reasons of friendship and habit. I do regularly think about not staying there. I don't particularly wish to grow old in England—it's not a very pleasant country to be old in. I don't like being cold.

I have always seen it as a kind of impermanent settlement, but it is an impermanent settlement that has lasted 25 years. All that I can say is that it is a question that I ask myself and that I have not stopped asking. Going back to India, for example, would be the easiest thing to do, [but] there is a sense in which you can't go home again. Your life takes you in a certain direction. What I would like to do, and I do try and do, is to maintain a regular connection with India. I get withdrawal symptoms if I don't come back fairly regularly, so I'd like to make sure that that connection doesn't get broken. But as to where one lives permanently, I don't know the answer.

Q: Since most of the ethnic Indian programming in Britain is concentrated in Channel Four [the BBC2 equivalent of the commercial network], do you think it leads to a ghettoisation of the Third World on British television?

A: No, that's not true. Channel Four is the least conventional of the four channels in its approach. It is actually structured differently in that [unlike the other programme stations], it does not make its own programmes. It acts as a publisher; it commissions programmes from independent companies. What it does is to open up television to a whole range of independent film-makers who have not previously had access to it.

So, for instance, the documentary on *Midnight's Children* is being made by a company called Antelope Films, which I have been working with for Channel Four. So, I don't think it ghettoises [Third World material]. It's a much freer way of working than the other television channels make possible.

Q: When Rajiv Gandhi came to power with all his Doon School chums, some people said Midnight's Children were ruling the country. Do you at all feel apologetic about coining the phrase?

A: *(Laughs).* I saw a lot of those articles [saying just that], and I had wanted to say that that was not what I meant. One of the problems of phrases getting into the language is that they get unstuck from their original purposes. Well, I suppose the use of the phrase in that context is correct in the sense that it was a generation that didn't remember the independence struggle which came to power. But it wasn't what I meant. I never meant Rajiv Gandhi.

Salman Rushdie: *Satanic Verses*

W. L. Webb / 1988

From The Roland Collection, ICA Video, Writers talk—ideas of our time #89, 1989. Reprinted by permission. The Roland Collection of Films and Videos on Art includes an extensive collection of interviews with contemporary writers and artists. They can be contacted via email at sales@roland-collection.co.uk, or via phone in the USA at 1-800-597-6526 or in the UK at 01797 230 421. Their catalog is available on the web at www.roland-collection.com.

Webb: Well, welcome to another ICA/Guardian conversation. I'm Bill Webb, representing *The Guardian.* I don't have to tell you this is Salman Rushdie, amply representing contemporary art. Salman's fourth novel, *The Satanic Verses,* was published yesterday, just in time to go on the Booker short list once more.

Salman has done a remarkable thing. When he arrived in England, India was primarily in the general British consciousness a literary property belonging to English novelists . . . Kipling, Forster, Paul Scott, J. G. Farrell, and even lesser writers. Now, a very few years later, less than a decade, probably the best known contemporary English writer—the one whose name comes to the lips of foreign publishers and critics as naturally as Grass does when they think of contemporary German literature or Margaret Atwood when they think of new writing in Canada or Peter Carey when they think about new Australian writing—is an Indian born in Bombay only weeks short of that which brought forth "midnight's children," the babies born at the continent's turning point, on the eve of independence, which gave him the idea for the novel that made his reputation. Well, though Salman's besetting sin is not a false modesty, I don't think he's actually made that claim for himself. But he has made "the empire strikes back" something of a slogan or rallying cry in his polemical writing, and has indicated clearly enough what it is about his experience and his work that has, with a great deal of talent, made this triumphant irony of literary history possible. He probably said it as well as anywhere in a review he wrote for *The Guardian* about Jeff Dyers's book on John Berger, talking about Berger's meditation on the *Gastarbeiter* ["guest laborers"] in *A Seventh Man,* he wrote, "To migrate is certainly to lose language and home; to be defined by a list or become invisible, or even worse, a target. It is to experience deep changes and wrenches in the soul. But the migrant is not simply transformed by his act; he also transforms the New World. Migrants may well become mutants. But it is out of such hybridization that newness can emerge." Now that perhaps does as well as anything to introduce his new novel, *The Satanic Verses,* which is partly about that experience—the death the migrant dies in the agony of mutation or rebirth—and which continues to demonstrate the transforming and emblematic newness that makes readers around the world think of him as currently the best of British.

Like *Midnight's Children* with its one thousand and one babies, *The Satanic Verses* is another exhilarating, hair-raising attempt on the great encompassing novel he tells us he aspires to. It's told in great swirls and loops of story, like the epics of the traditional Indian storytellers, with their pointed ambivalences, a world in which "it was and it was not so." I find myself often thinking of it, as I read it, as a kind of Whitmanesque *Song of Myself*: "Do I contradict myself? Very well, I contradict myself. I am large, I contain multitudes." At any rate, I seem to think that Salman said somewhere the other day that this was a novel into which he had put more of himself than any of the others—perhaps all of himself, including the little Indian boy who's confronted with a bristly great alien kipper on his first morning at Rugby, where no one showed him helpfully how to deal with it—and through this ordeal, he discovered that he was a bloody-minded person and swears "I'll show them all. You see if I don't." Which is not of course to say that this innocent, with already something of a diabolical urge, is the author himself. Naturally, it's not a naturalistic novel. On the one hand, it sort of comes from a culture whose narrative tradition is not a realistic tradition. And then, his experience leads him to agree with Norman Mailer that the trouble with reality is that it isn't realistic anymore. We live in fantastic times and it is about as good a measure of the fantasy of the times as any that just when Salman had finished writing a novel that begins with the blowing up of a plane remarkably like that Air Canada flight full of Indian passengers, that wires immediately began to hum with news of that exploding plane that finished off General Zia, whose bad end had been foreshadowed in his previous novel, *Shame.* Salman is aware of this; he has something of a track record in that respect. And one notes with a kind of awe in this novel some pungent tropes on Maggie Torture herself. So it begins, out of thin air, a big bang, followed by falling stars, a universal beginning, a miniature of the birth of time. And then a remarkable headlong representation of the surrealism of such a reality: the explosion, the bodies, the seats, the drinks trolleys—all tumbling through the air. And in the middle of them, two Indians, both actors: the flamboyantly vulgar Gibreel, movie star of a thousand, well, perhaps a hundred Bombay reincarnation epics, and the stiffly Anglophile Saladin, clutching each alter ego, free-falling to Earth to be reborn miraculously. The one is parody archangel, the other is rather more than a pantomime devil, who will incarnate a long and desperate debate throughout the novel about the nature of good and evil. From this dream-like fall, a sequence of tales or dreams or deliriums unfolds, some of them taking place in Bombay, some in proper London and improper London, Babylondon, some in the desert city of Jahilia, a territory not to be found in atlases or my history books. The novel ends finally with many corpses, like the last act of a Renaissance tragedy, and a beautiful account of the death of a father, extraordinarily lucid and unsentimental and very moving. So, an encompassing novel, full of Salman Rushdie's powerful narrative traction and fizzing with scenes and ideas. But, to put it mildly, not a simple novel, not easy. So let's discover what we can from the horse's mouth about it.

The unifying idea of *Midnight's Children,* one of the greatest ideas since Joyce's "day in the life of," was of this historic moment in the century. And in *Shame* it was the polarity of shame and shamelessness put to work in the unhappy politics of this invented country of Pakistan. Can you tell us something about the ruling idea of *The Satanic Verses,* and if you will, something about the events in reality which seeded it?

Rushdie: Yeah, I . . . Thanks for that, by the way. You can come again. . . . I suppose the novel began in a number of places, one of which is the incident from which the title of the book comes, which I suppose I've known about for twenty years. When I was studying Islamic History as one of my papers of my final year at college, I came across this amazing incident in which the Prophet Mohammed, it is said, flirted with—or at least God had said—flirted with the idea of tolerating the three most famous and lucrative pagan goddesses of Mecca as acceptable at the level of archangels, as kind of intermediary beings. And there were verses of the Koran which accepted them, which said that they were exalted birds and their intercession was greatly to be desired. And then, at some later moment, Mohammed repudiated these verses and said that the devil had appeared to him disguised as the archangel. And these had been Satanic verses, which had to be expelled from the Koran and were to be replaced by new verses which said that these creatures were completely unimportant, that God wanted nothing to do with them.

A number of things were interesting about that. One was that the fact that they had been goddesses, being female, was in fact an explicit part of the repudiation. There's a verse which is in the Koran to this day that says "Shall He (that's to say, God) have daughters while you have sons, that would be unjust division." So that was striking as something that happened at the very beginning of Islam which seems to me that has implications for what happened afterwards.

Also, of course, the problem of distinguishing angels from devils it seems to me is one of the things the novel is about. After all, even the Prophet Mohammed seems to have had some trouble doing that. It doesn't offer much hope for us. And so, in the novel, the ideal of angels and devils is somewhat confused or interpenetrated. That was one place it began from. And I think the place from which it began in the sense of when I knew how to write it. But it went from that to my wanting to write a series of variations on the life of the archangel Gabriel. And I found myself writing down connected stories about various historical and imaginary manifestations of the archangel down the ages and connected all together by the idea of this Indian movie star called Gibreel, who comes to think of himself as a reincarnation of the archangel. And as the reader, I suppose, you're asked to accept at least the possibility that he might be telling the truth.

Then I suppose what I finally understood, which actually let me start writing, was that the novel is about, unsurprisingly I suppose for me, about divided selves. That the character of Gibreel loses his faith is what happens to him is that he gets very ill and calls upon God and nobody arrives and he finds it impossible to believe in God. And then that part of himself which has a great connection with religious faith, and need for it, splits apart from that part of himself which can no longer accept the idea of God. And that division of himself is really his story, it seems to me, in the book. And I then found myself counterpointing him with another character, Saladin, in whom there is also a split, but which is a secular split; where the split in him is not between God and disbelief, but is a cultural split between East and West. So I have this, if you like, a sacred and a profane character, who are both in different ways divided—and at the same time, you know, begin the novel falling out of the sky holding on to each other, so in a sense are a composite being as well, a kind of many-headed monster. And I discovered, only now, really, only in the last few weeks when I've been obliged to start talking about the book, that I keep doing this, it seems. That, it seems to me I've done it, if you look at every novel . . .

Webb: Doubles, duality . . .

Rushdie: Doubles, yes, and people . . . I mean in . . . Even in *Grimus*—which nobody reads, thank God—there's the character of the American Indian, Flapping Eagle, going up the mountain to discover this mysterious figure, Grimus. When he gets up there they become kind of alter egos—one is the other's other. And I suppose, when, obviously Saleem in *Midnight's Children,* and Shiva, the baby for whom he's exchanged, becomes his kind of dark opposite. And even in *Shame* the two male characters of the general and the civilian politician, Raza Hyder and Iskander Harappa, in a way define each other, in a way they're kind of stuck together. And here I am doing it again. I feel ashamed at this. It seems to me that that kind of . . . it's time I stopped perhaps. Maybe becoming conscious of it is a way of stopping.

Webb: Well, a question I thought we might end with, but it comes sort of apt exactly now, is, at the end of this very beautiful section about the death of a father, there is a strong sense for the character, for Saladin, of sort of reconciliation, acceptance of a more stable version of the reality which is reality. And the sense of it being a point of departure too. And obviously one wonders whether this is something in your own head, whether this seems a point of departure for you?

Rushdie: I think that's right. I think I do think that. I do think that what happens in the novel, one way of saying what happens in the novel, is that the fantasticated character, the kind of grotesque mythological character, comes to a bad end. And the one who is more rooted, or becomes to be more rooted, in some kind of more real version of the world, if you like, survives.

Webb: So it would be a thing of large implications for a writer of phantasmagoric . . .

Rushdie: Yeah, I think . . . I don't know whether it means I don't want to do it anymore. I don't really. Certainly at the end of the novel that's what I thought. But, you know, in a way, you can't tell yourself those things; you have to wait and see what happens. What I do think is that there is in me always this kind of pull on the one hand to make things up and to, to have invisible cities and all that; and, on the other hand, towards making sure that I don't just completely fly off to outer space, to keep some kind of feet on the ground.

Webb: And there is a sort of problem whose tip sort of emerged for me once or twice in this novel, which I found more kind of wild and headlong than the others. And it is this: that since realism, since reality is not real, and since we no longer have a notion that the consciousness operates in a linear way, we have a much more kind of . . . we accept and hold [that] modernism is about the exploration of the complexity of consciousness. Don't you feel if you go, you're going a long way along this road? You tread a tightrope when you get into a position of producing a sort of mimesis of chaos, in fact.

Rushdie: mmhmm.

Webb: Especially when the consciousness that's involved is, as the case with both these characters from time-to-time, rather schizoid and paranoid. And I mean, there is a simple answer: it's a matter of control. But might it be that after a decade or a couple of decades in which this kind of fantastic novel and the energies which it has put back into the sort of form, that one might begin to feel that either the steam is running out or that one has pressed the form as far as it can go in the balance between energy and order?

Rushdie: Well, I think that's the point really. Because I think I can't think about it theoretically, really. I can't settle down and say what kind of novel does one need to write in the 1990s, in what sense has a form been exhausted? I mean I think in the end you have to follow your own kind of sense of where the energy in your work is. And I do feel at the end of this novel that I've come to if not an end, then certainly the end of a paragraph. And I felt that somehow *Midnight's Children, Shame,* and this book together—and in a way, even *Grimus,* which has certain metaphysical concerns to which this book returns—I just feel that I finished a bit of what I set out to do. And it was the sense of great liberation. It means I can do anything next. I don't have to go on laboring in this particular garden, which is partly to do with trying to write about the things that made me, really. And I suppose that *Midnight's Children, Shame,* and this book are, if you want to define the thing that they have in common, I would say that they're an attempt to deal with the things out of which I feel that I came and which shaped whatever it is that is my consciousness.

Webb: And now you are here wherever it is.

Rushdie: And now I am here wherever it is. Yes. I remember feeling about Naipaul's novel *The Enigma of Arrival*—which I had a rather rocky relationship with—but the thing that I very much recognized in it, and responded to, was this sense of his having to invent the ground on which he stood. That there he was, as a migrant, arriving in Wiltshire, or whatever, that in order for Naipaul to be in Wiltshire as opposed to for an English writer, he has to describe each hedge into existence. He has to describe every garden and country lane and tree and farmer and so forth. And only when this colossal act of description takes place does he feel he has something to stand on. And I think I feel exactly like that. I don't have a territory, you know, in the way that William Faulkner has Yoknapatawpha County, in the way that Eudora Welty has her bit of the Mississippi, in the way that Hardy has Wessex, in the way that a rooted writer has his ground and his writing just comes out of it and goes on and on in exploring it and is inexhaustible. I don't have it. I mean, literally, every time I settle down to write a sentence I fell I have to invent that ground, the ground to stand on. And I think maybe I've done it. That's the point. I think maybe now, you know, maybe I could stand on these books and then take off somewhere . . . I don't know.

Webb: How shall I put this? I suppose I want to say one of the reasons why you are spotted and recognized—setting this small matter of talent aside for one moment— as this representative British figure, in this splendidly ironic way as a writer, now, is that you are recognizably a writer of a kind that one could put roughly together with Grass and Peter Carey and García Márquez, who are all writing in this kind of high-energy sort of form. I wondered whether that doesn't suggest, and then as against that, you are recognizably not writing the sort of shy English novel—not all English novelists write shy English novels, not [Angela] Carter, or [J. G.] Ballard, or Martin Amis, or [Ian] McEwan—but there's nevertheless each week, almost every month, quite a lot of these novels. What I am groping towards is whether you think there is now a kind of, a real international literature, world literature, which happens at the moment to be defined by this kind of high energy writing, if we can call it that, and then regional literatures, which are bigger than they used to be and which now encompass the culture of a small country off the north coast of Europe, for example.
Rushdie: What I think about that.

Webb: It's a long question.
Rushdie: Yeah. I'm certainly going to somewhat find myself resisting the idea of being called a representative British figure. I think I'm flattered, but . . .

Webb: Well, it was always ironic.
Rushdie: No, but I think there are certain British figures who would contest quite seriously the idea that I represented anything British. And that's

alright, too. It's . . . I think there is . . . The reason I'm stumbling is because I think the idea of an international literature contains certain kinds of danger.

Webb: That's what I hoped you would say and then I would address it.

Rushdie: I mean at its worst it produces the airport novel, doesn't it? At its worst, it produces Jackie Collins. I mean that's a kind of international . . .

Webb: Yes, I wasn't even thinking of the economic dimension. Of course that's a very urgent sort of dynamic . . .

Rushdie: I mean, that's an international novel, if you like. It takes place, it's consumed, on airplanes. And after all, this novel begins with a plane crash, so perhaps it's an attempt to sabotage the airport novel. But I discovered that people enjoy reading this on airplanes, which I find very paradoxical. A lot of people have read this novel on airplanes. I would make . . .

Webb: When they get over the first bit, it's not so bad . . .

Rushdie: It's alright, yes. Exactly. You get the worst over to begin with. The reason I worry about it is for the same reason that you know I would worry about speaking Esperanto. And I think what happens is you can lose any real sense of a relationship with a language or a relationship with a place or a relationship with a particular community if you find yourself appealing to this international body. And, actually, although I can see that there is kind of a commonality of project between this kind of writing and Peter Carey's writing and Grass and all these things, it actually seems to me that the way in which we are unlike is more interesting than the way in which we are like each other. If I read Peter Carey's novels, which I admire enormously, the things that, of course, I mean I see echoes in the way in which his cast of mind is and mine, but actually, what I like about his writing is the way in which it tells me new things. And I think that that's . . .

Webb: It's a crude category and the initial notion I had, the notion about the irony that you spotted as this representative figure of modern British writing, and it's sort of a practical one, because it's what publishers, when you meet them in Frankfurt, they identify you as being of this company, and they identify these other writers as being in this company.

Rushdie: Well, mercifully, I don't have to be at Frankfurt. I think that the reason that my writing has had this international, this sort of multinational dimension, is just that my life has. It's for no other reason than that I've been very closely connected with at least three countries—and so you know, I write out of that. But I wouldn't wish to make some kind of larger claim that

that kind of writing is better because I admire enormously kinds of writing that I've somehow never yet been able to do. When I say Japanese novels, these very very short, enormously controlled, obsessive explorations of tiny strands of human experience, which makes them mean everything, which makes the tiny strand mean everything. I would like to be able to do that just as much as I would like to be able to do this. So I don't think there is any sort of justification just by the reason of being that one can write big fat books which invent the planet, to say that that's somehow the best way to go. It's just the way that I do it, because I can't do it any other way.

Webb: Well, let's go back to this particular one. One notion that I was taken with, one of the sort of other ruling notions of the book, or recurring preoccupations, is with something which one comes across very often in life and in relationships. But I can't think particularly of it being presented this way in a novel. And it's the idea of worrying about what is the unforgivable, the quantifying of it, the defining of it, the uncertainty of it—would you like to say something about that?

Rushdie: Sure, it was something . . . I do think it's very central to the way in which the characters in the novel connect with each other. One of the questions that the book asks is "Is there such a thing as a thing that cannot be forgiven—an unforgivable act?" What is there? Is there an unforgivable thing? And just to take an extract, there's a story that one of the characters in the novel says that they read, a story which they then tell another of the characters, which in fact they haven't read, because I made it up. But the story was an attempt by me to try and crystallize this notion of what might be an unforgivable thing. And it's about two people, a man and woman, who have been very very close friends most of their lives, and without ever having had a kind of sexual relationship, it's been friends. And when they're starting out in the world, poor and all that, the woman gives the man a present of a deliberately very cheap, nasty vase: a kind of joke present that is extremely ugly and totally valueless, and which he values enormously and keeps on the mantel piece and all that and invests a great deal of affection and meaning in. And then life goes on and they become successful and rich and all that. And then they have a fight about something, and in the course of this fight, she picks up this little cheap thing which he's still got on the mantelpiece and smashes it. And he never speaks to her again. And it becomes something he absolutely can't forgive. Forty years later, they haven't spoken to each other again and she's dying and emissaries come from her deathbed to him and say that this is crazy, the two of you loved each other so much. You've completely lost your life together, you've lost forty years of your friendship. At least now at the very end, all she wants to do is see you, why don't you come? And he says "no," that she should have thought of that when she broke the vase. Now the question about that as a parable is "which side are you on"? In a way the book to an extent explores the nature of that parable. To an extent you think the man's crazy. But on the other hand, I think any of us could see that there might be a thing that would be impossible to forgive. And what I wanted to do was in that parable to choose in the novel something which was quite in itself of no value, a thing which has no value or meaning except that it's given, and also a thing that when broken can't be put back together. And, I don't know, I'm interested to hear what you think about that. But one of the things I think happens in the novel is that. For example, in the relationship between the son and the father, which has been coarsely bad in the beginning of the novel and between the two of whom things have happened which they would both call unforgivable things. They discover that in that curious moment immediately preceding death that all these things become unimportant—that, in fact, it is possible to forgive the unforgivable. And it was, to me, very important that that did happen in the writing of the book. It was rather odd, because it didn't happen in the first draft of the book. Because in the first draft of the book, the returning son misses the death of the father—he comes too late, arrives after the death. And then he has to deal with all that unresolved material. And I think that worked too, actually. But I just thought in the end there was more in it, in that final moment, than could be explored if they didn't meet. So I rewrote it so that they did meet, and I think for me it made a colossal difference in the novel, that I did it that way.

Webb: One reviewer I read suggested I think that perhaps there were, that it was not altogether a forgiving novel and that some characters got their— well, it wasn't quite clear whether their desserts were just, but they were abrupt and sudden and grim.

Rushdie: Yes, it was a rather strange review, that. The characters she complained about were both women.

Webb: Yes.

Rushdie: And a kind of feminist point was being implied, that this was, she said it was not a novel for strong women or something. A thing which does disturb me a little bit because I think in almost all my writing there have been very strong female characters which in many ways are the characters who carry the weight of the books. It's not an exception, this book. It's true that two of the strong female characters come to bad ends in this novel— violent ends. That's to say, in different ways, murdered. One by the police, the other by her former lover. It seems to me quite extraordinary to suggest that if in a novel written by a man a female character comes to a bad end, this suggests that the author hates women. It seems to me a very difficult position to sustain and I don't feel in that review that she managed to convince me that that's what I've done or that's what I do. Because the implication of that is that a woman character in a novel by a man can never experience tragedy.

Webb: I guess she was thinking that the women of these tragic pairs fared worse than the men.

Rushdie: Well, I don't.

Webb: For the pattern, you started out with men . . .

Rushdie: I think everybody, everybody has a bad time in this book. I don't think there's any injustice there. But no, and I think what's true, for example in the writing of *Shame,* as I've said often, the experience that I had writing it was that the female characters somehow came in from the wings of the novel and took the novel over, and that although there was this sort of central pair of opposed male figures, increasingly the kind of action, the moral weight, the dynamic of the novel was through this galaxy of female characters around them—sort of wives and daughters and lovers and mothers and so forth. And this time it is true to say that something different happens. Which is I think that there are very strong female characters in the novel whose stories are struggling for space against the stories of the men in the novel, and quite often explicitly struggling. The female characters say "when is it my turn?"

Webb: They had esteem, but desperation that the males . . .

Rushdie: . . . with the competing characters, yes.

Webb: They had a desperation, they're up against both of sort of the dual male characters . . .

Rushdie: And it's true to say that in this novel what happens is that the female characters' stories are in fact crushed, do in fact not get space, the kind of space that in many ways they merit. That's true and that happens. That doesn't mean I'm writing a misogynist novel. It means I'm trying to write something about the relationship between the men and women in this book in which the men do crush the women. That doesn't mean I'm on the side of the men.

Webb: Well, it's possible that people want to take up that later on. In fact, why not, not necessarily now, but would anybody like to put questions to Salman?

Audience Member: One of the things that strikes me now as I remember the book, rather than in the act of reading it, is that although there were a great many tableaus, and indeed, film sets, in this crumbling and changing city, through it all, I have a very vivid sense of the voices. And it almost struck me that the main characters lived through their speech. And that's what I can hear, I can hear them now, rather than see them. And I was wondering whether you actually concentrated on that speaking, the dialogue, and that as a point of identification?

Rushdie: Yes. I've always found dialogue the hardest bit in books and as a result I suppose it did get disproportionate amounts of attention from me because I find it easier to get it wrong than I find the prose stuff. So, yes, I do in a way. I remember when I was studying history, the history master at college gave me a piece of advice which I have now used for ahistorical reasons. He said that you should never write history until you can hear the people speak. And I don't know what he meant. I've never written history, but I do find it difficult to start writing until I can hear the people speak. And I think it's important to make a trivial point: if you're writing dialogue, the reader should be able to tell who's speaking without "he said, she said." It should be possible without naming the speaker for the speaker to be clear. And that's hard to do, I guess. And easier for some people to do than others. You get the feeling that Noel Coward did it in his sleep. I have to be awake.

Audience Member: . . . this kind of polyglot feeling of metropolis . . .

Rushdie: Well, what I wanted, one of the things I did try a lot in this novel to do is a progression from the kind of language of *Midnight's Children,* which was an attempt to allow more voices into English, if you like, an attempt to allow more ribbons, and therefore more thoughts, more kinds of things into English then I'd noticed there. I suppose that goes on, I guess, that process, because I've still got those voices in my head. But I also wanted to try and make in this a language or way of speaking or combination of ways of speaking, which I characterized to myself as having a great degree of fluidity so that you could move between different sorts of language at great speed without it seeming to be a problem. And parallel to that, that you could move with equal speed between different sorts of writing or different kinds of emotional meaning, that a sentence could begin hilariously and end in tragedy. Or the other way around. And those kind of very fast transitions I've been trying to affect really since I've started writing. And I think that I've spent a lot of time in this novel trying to do that not only in terms of story but also in terms of language. So that was linguistically the thing I had tried to do here more than I had tried to do before.

Webb: One of the most resonant, sort of political sentences in the novel is the, is that extraordinary sequence where the immigration police keep a kind of clinic which is full of Max Ernst-like figures who are half-beast and half-human, and one of them says to . . .
Rushdie: . . . Saladin . . .

Webb: Saladin, who's there, "They have the power of description, and we succumb to the pictures they construct." Would you say there was kind of a positive as well as negative implication in that sentence?
Rushdie: Well, not there, there isn't. What I . . .

Webb: The power of description is a liberating power—it can be a liberating power as well.
Rushdie: The point is that if you come from the black communities in this country, the power of other people to describe you is much greater than your power to describe back. And so, one can't see it as a fair struggle at the moment, because we are described, and we are described into corners, and then we have to describe our way out of corners, if we can. And it seems to me that that's one of the things I was trying to do: I was trying to contest descriptions.

Webb: As a political act, it would be a description back.
Rushdie: Yeah, exactly. Because I think there's a moment in which Gibreel, who is after all somewhat more aggressive towards the idea of England than Saladin is—I mean Gibreel is of the view that the English are cold fish who take baths in each others' dirty bath water. A thing that is obviously untrue (*laughs*). He says that, and other people in the novel say, the activist called Uhuru Simba, who is arrested by the police and ends up being killed in police custody, says in court, "Not only are we not going away, but it's

our turn." This is where we get to tell you who you are. And I think there is a sense in which that's true. That's part of the project, yes. Because I think it's time that we got to tell them who they are.

Webb: A project for novels?
Rushdie: Yeah, sure. And other things.

An Interview with Salman Rushdie

John Clement Ball / 1988

From *The Toronto South Asian Review* 10.1 (Summer 1991): 30–37.
Reprinted by permission.

This interview was conducted for broadcast on CKLN-FM's Title-Waves, a half-hour interview programme about new books. It took place in a room at the Harbour Castle Hotel during Salman Rushdie's visit to the International Festival of Authors in Toronto in October, 1988.

JB: In your last two novels you wrote something akin to a fictionalized history of two countries, India in *Midnight's Children* and Pakistan in *Shame.* Is *The Satanic Verses* a different kind of project for you?

SR: For me it seemed like the natural next thing to do, which was to write a novel out of the experience of migration, really. In a way I wrote *Midnight's Children* and *Shame* as if I had never left: as if I was an Indian who had never left India or a Pakistani who was still living in Pakistan. And it would have been very disappointing to me if those books had been received in those countries as outsider books because, in a way, I dislike the outsider books myself, and I would have hated the idea that I was adding to them. So it was very reassuring for me that the books were received as insider books in India and Pakistan.

JB: Even though you hadn't lived there for quite some time.

SR: Even though—yeah, although I'd been going back and forth. It wasn't as if I'd been cut off completely: my family were there, friends were there. But then I thought that really, having finished *Shame* I thought to myself, well I really ought to admit to myself that I did leave, and that my experience is that of a migrant into the West, with all the ambiguities and hybridizations that that involves. And so I decided I would try to write a kind of hybrid novel, a novel which was about that conjunction of East and West which happens inside me.

JB: In that sense I get the feeling that this book is perhaps even more ambitious than *Midnight's Children,* if that's possible. You're setting a large part of it in England, but a number of other stories from other cultures find their way into the novel as well, including the dream sequence that's got the Indian politicians in such an uproar. With so much going on, is it possible that you've given yourself an even bigger canvas to paint on in this book?

SR: It certainly feels like that to me, yes. It certainly feels to me as if this is the biggest chunk I've ever bitten off, and certainly was hardest to wrestle into shape. Because of course the point is if you're going to do something very complicated, to make it read as if it's very simple. And what took five years, really, was to make it seem simply to flow in a natural way, so that the reader can simply say, "Oh yes, this comes next, and that's right," as opposed to getting bothered by the many different sides of it. And I suppose I used in my mind an idea of construction which was mosaic rather than linear, so that I would take a number of stories which were fitted together in a mosaic pattern rather than a straightforward linear pattern. Although each story in itself has obviously—at least I hope so—a strong linear narrative drive. But they fit together at tangents to each other, and that job of making them fit was what was difficult.

JB: Yes. There's no obvious structural scheme, as in *Midnight's Children,* where the personal and national histories complement each other. In this novel the structure seems a lot more complex, at least on first reading.

SR: Well it's a novel about metamorphosis, isn't it? It's a novel about all sorts of transformation, whether it be the transformation that comes from moving from one part of the world to another, the changes in the self that involves, or rather more dramatic and surrealist kinds of transformation. And I thought that, well, if you're going to write a novel about transformation, then the novel itself should also be metamorphic in form, so it should constantly change. It can be naturalistic for a passage, then it can become very surrealist, then it can become naturalistic again—that, you know, a love story can be followed by a tragic section which can be followed by a farcical section—and that the novel should in that sense be kaleidoscopic and should constantly change form, and that would be an equivalent—a formal equivalent—to the story of the book, which is about people changing.

JB: One of the remarkable things that struck me about *Midnight's Children* is the way that the I-narrator, Saleem, managed in the course of telling his story to also provide so much commentary and explanation on it that he ended up having written not only a novel but also the essay that kind of explains his story, all at once. You seem to be steering away from that writing, though, in *Shame* and especially in *The Satanic Verses*.

SR: It's true, that this—well, it doesn't have a first-person narrator. However, it seems to me that what I've tried to do is offer the explanations, offer the material you're talking about, through the characters, through the action of the novel, perhaps more than as in *Midnight's Children* where there were kinds of glosses on the action offered by the first-person narrator. So I guess that is a progression, and I think that one of the things I've tried to do in this novel is to create a language which can make very fast transitions very smoothly, so that a scene, or even a sentence, can begin in comedy and end in tragedy. And that kind of doubleness in everything, it seems to me, is really what the novel is about: that tragedy has a comic side, that comedy has a tragic aspect; that good has an evil dimension, that evil has a good side.

JB: So you're playing around with the ambiguities of everyday life.

SR: I think it's a progression for me. I mean, it seems to me that if the novel is about anything other than these sort of large ideas about good and evil and metamorphosis, it seems to me it's about how one becomes a human being. I have this notion we're not just born as human beings, but that we actually have to learn how to become human beings, and many of the characters in the novel are for a long time not really unitary selves, they're just collections of selves. They're kind of masks, they put on this or that role, and they can change very dramatically. And I think that's also true about people, that we are not unitary selves, we are a kind of bag of selves, which we draw out from; we become this or that self in different circumstances. But in the end one has to learn how to be a person, you know, and it seems to me that the way in which the main character in the novel, this Saladin Chamcha character, does that is by confronting the great things about human beings, which are the great issues of birth and love and death. And it's through confronting those things and learning how to deal with them that by the end of the novel he does qualify, I think, to be called a human being.

JB: There's a kind of a wild energy to the writing of the two "subcontinent novels," if I can call them that, that seems to grow right out of the colour and the vitality and the apparent chaos of the countries themselves. When you turned to England as a primary setting in *The Satanic Verses* did that require a change of approach for you?

SR: It required a change, yes. I mean, you couldn't write about England quite in the way you write about India because it's a different place. But on the other hand the England or more precisely the London that's in the novel is very much a kind of bizarre place. And it seems to me that a lot of the spirit of the novel grows out of my sense of what it is to be a metropolitan creature, what it is to be a city person, which after all I am. I've spent my life very largely in two collosal cities, Bombay and London, both of which are in the novel. And in a way, as somebody says in the novel, the act of migrating from Bombay to London is perhaps not as far as to go from an English village to London, because these two cities have great things in common. And I think the things that cities have in common are precisely their fantastic nature—that cities are, after all, invented spaces, artificial spaces. They're spaces which look very permanent, solid, but which in fact are extremely ephemeral and transitory, and huge buildings can fall overnight. The shape of a city constantly changes, but at any given moment it looks absolutely solid and permanent, so it's a kind of fiction. In a city you have endless varieties of lives which in many ways contradict each other, which one would find very hard to reconcile with each other, yet coexisting. I mean, you can live literally next door to a life which in many ways negates your own. That aspect of the city as being an irreconcilable space, as well as an endlessly shifting and illusory space, I think obviously is "magical." And I think that people often write about cities in a way which assumes that what they look like is what they are—write about cities as if they were permanent sociological spaces.

JB: And as if one person's version of the city could be the same as another person's. . . .

SR: Exactly. Whereas instead, in my view, you have all these conflicting versions of the city, and one of the things I wanted to do in the book—for example in the love affair between Gibreel, the actor who comes to London, and the English woman he loves, the mountain climber, is that in fact they quite literally belong in different kinds of story: you know, that actually the kind of person she is, the kind of life that she's had, the kind of story she needs told about her, is in fact a very different sort of story to the story that Gibreel needs told about him. And, I thought, that's actually something that happens to us in cities: we're constantly bumping into people and falling in love with people and finding ourselves with people who are actually people from a different sort of story. And then sometimes we manage to make the two stories the same, and sometimes we don't and they split apart again. And so I wanted these two people to be—she keeps saying or thinking that this is not the kind of story she ever thought she'd find herself in. And she's right, really, she doesn't belong in it. And the fact that she doesn't belong in the story, in a way, is also a way of saying that she doesn't really belong in his life or in the relationship, which is very damaging to her and actually in the end destroys her.

JB: So for you as a writer, you've got to take the two very different kinds of stories and let them kind of bump against each other.

SR: Let them smash into each other and see what happens.

JB: Do you see this as being a political novel to the extent that the other books were?

SR: Yes, I think it's a political novel in a different way. I think it's not a novel which, like *Shame* and *Midnight's Children,* deals centrally with actual political events. There aren't any independence riots in it, there aren't any dictators in it, but I think it deals with, for example in its Indian sections, it deals a lot with actual central issues of Indian politics at the moment, which have to do with sectarian tension, and rather ironically the book itself has become a victim of those tensions in its banning. In the British section I've tried to deal with, or to write from, the experience of not being white in Britain, and obviously that's political in its nature. The reason why the long central section of the novel, the longest section of the novel, is called "A City Visible But Unseen," is—and that city is of course London. . . . one of the points that I've tried to make in that section is that that's not an imaginary city. It is not an invisible city in the sense that Calvino's cities were invisible cities, fantasy cities; that this is a real city whose streets I know; you know, it would be possible to guide anybody down those streets and to show them the locations out of which, and the kind of life experience out of which, the experiences in the book come. But that city is certainly in English literature, and even in English society, ignored, not looked at—in fact is unseen. So there you have the experience of a lot of people, millions of people now in Britain, invisible to the rest, and I wanted to try and make it visible. So that of course is also a political ambition.

JB: Is that a major job of the writer, to find things that people perhaps don't know exist, and show that they do exist? In your books it often comes across as being something you've dreamed up because of the fantastic nature of many of the things that happen. Do you feel that people take your books as being real enough? Do you want to make sure that *that* London is seen as a real London?

SR: Yes, I think that people ought to see it as a real city. Obviously the characters in it, against this realistic background, are often very phantasmagorical, which is after all an old and honourable tradition. I mean Dickens did much the same, setting very much larger-than-life characters against a meticulously observed social context. And not only that, he would insert into the social context very surreal images, such as, you know, the Circumlocution Office, a government department which exists to do nothing—

JB: In *Little Dorrit . . .*

SR: Yes, or the trial of Jarndyce versus Jarndyce, a trial which literally never ends. These are images of pure surrealism, which work because they're embedded in beautifully observed naturalistic detail. And I suppose that is something I've tried to learn from the great man, that fantasy, surrealism, those elements work as intensifications of the real; they work as metaphors of the real world when you can embed them in a believable setting. So I have tried always to make the places—place is very important in my work—to make the places very believable, very real, and then I feel that these strange flowers of the imagination can grow out of that ground and mean something to people.

JB: Critics are constantly reeling off lists of writers that they suspect must have influenced you: Márquez and Günter Grass and various others. I'd like to hear from you who you think are the writers that have influenced you.

SR: Well, in this book I wouldn't say—I could say it, yes, that Grass in particular was important for me at the time or before I wrote *Midnight's Children,* but I don't think that either Grass or García Márquez really are people who have anything to do with this particular book. I think that if I had to name people who helped me write this book, so to speak . . . that I could name . . . oh, Blake for example. I think "The Marriage of Heaven and Hell," for example, is a text which is centrally important in this book.

JB: It's quoted quite often . . .

SR: It's quoted quite often, and in its union of heaven and hell, in the marriage of heaven and hell that takes place there, of course, it provides a kind of key to what happens in my novel as well. Another book that I think is very important for me in the shaping of this book was the Russian novel *The Master and Marguerita* by Mikhail Bulgakov, which did give me some clues about to how to shape this book. That's a novel about the Devil coming to Moscow; my novel is about both an angel and a devil, who may or may not be angelic or demonic, ending up in contemporary London. Like *The Master and Marguerita,* my novel contains interpolated narratives; actually, I've got many more than the Bulgakov novel. But it's also true that the interpolated narrative in the Bulgakov novel is also religious: it's a religious retelling of the life of Christ from the point of view of Pontius Pilate. So there's an obvious parentage there, and it would be foolish not to recognize it. Beyond that, I'm not really sure that there were any specific writers or books that helped me. There are a lot of writers from whom I have learned: Saul Bellow, for example. It seems to me one of the things about Bellow that he is quite rightly revered for is the ability of his sentences to kind of swoop from high philosophy to street language. And that kind of very rapid transition is also something that I'm interested in doing, so that a text can include, you know, high literature, could include classical references, in my case both to Oriental and Western culture, and at the same time be kind of streetwise, you know, and have the language that people actually speak to each other in it.

JB: One impression I get from your work is that the actual act of writing and of creating these various kinds of languages that you're working with is great fun for you. There's a real playfulness in your manipulation of language, and of audience expectations, of plot, of all these things.

SR: It gets to be fun. It gets to be fun when I finally think I know what I'm doing. I mean the problem with writing books like this is that they take a long time to wrestle to the ground, and for most of the period in which one is writing them you feel that they're defeating you rather than the other way round. The book that has been published was effectively written in one year, during the course of last year, in 1987. Before that there was on and off four years of getting it wrong, and that wasn't particularly enjoyable. Bits of it would be got right, you know, I'd get this and that bit right, but there would be big problems in it, and I wouldn't always know how to solve them. And that period is very hard work, I mean that's really the slog. Then finally, in the last draft, I finally managed to start hitting a note which I liked and recognized as being what I wanted for the book, or close enough to what I wanted for the book. And then it did become enjoyable, then I was finally writing sentences that I was enjoying doing, and enjoying the idea of people reading. So that last draft becomes a pleasure, yes, but not the whole thing.

JB: I'd like to end up if I may by asking you about the subject that we've alluded to, and you've probably been talking about more than anything else in the last week: why is your new novel being banned in India?

SR: Well, the point is that there are things in the novel, there are passages in the novel—the dream sequences you mentioned—which are reworkings, in a kind of nightmare way, of incidents from the early life of Islam, or the early history of Islam. Now, within the life of the novel it's quite natural that this should happen, because the character who's doing the dreaming is someone who has lost his Muslim faith, and is then, in his dreams, in a way being punished for that by being given these terrible visions. And those visions, the visions that he would have as a Muslim, would have to be Muslim visions, if you see what I mean. He couldn't have Christian visions because that's not the tradition he knows about. So if he's going to have a nightmare of religion, if he's going to have a nightmare about God and the Devil, it would have to be from the world that he knows about. So that's why it takes the form it does. Now it's possible that, I always knew that, conservative orthodox religious opinion, or people of that type, might not find it to their taste. And that, in my mind, was fair enough. You can't please everyone; as long as you're doing what you're doing seriously, then you accept that some of your readers can't live with it. I do think, sadly, that Islam, the Muslim world at the moment, is in a condition where it finds itself unable to permit discussion of itself in the way that Judaism and Christianity in fact do permit. I was, for example, recently reviewing the new collection of stories from Isaac Bashevis Singer, and I must say my first reaction was one of colossal envy. I mean, there he is with colossal blasphemies, talking about God's mistakes, talking about how Satan's not such a bad person after all, rewriting Bible stories right, left, and centre, and he doesn't get fundamentalists after him, he doesn't get governments banning his books.

JB: Although *The Last Temptation of Christ* has had trouble as a film example . . .

SR: Yes it has, and there is, after all, fundamentalism in more religions than one. Christian fundamentalism is in many ways just as frightening. But I suppose the great difference is that the Scorsese movie in the end was not banned, that it in fact was allowed to be seen, and people could go and make up their own minds about it. So I think what was sad is that really the people who did the banning weren't actually very interested in the book. What's happening is a political struggle inside India in which the book became a football. It was really about whether Rajiv Gandhi would be obliged to do deals with Muslim members of parliament so that he could hope to get, in return for that, Muslim votes at the next election, which he may well lose.

And, you know, you offer a politician a choice between a matter or principle and votes, and it's not surprising that he chooses the votes.

JB: No, literature isn't held in high esteem where one's career is concerned, I suppose, as a politician.

SR: That's right.

JB: Will these changes in India compel you to return to the country as a primary setting for a novel again, do you think?

SR: At the moment I feel, my instincts tell me, not for the moment. But I don't actually have, in my mind, a clearly worked-out plan for what I should write next. So it's rash to commit myself. My instinct is that I should like to look further at the Western experience that I've been living through, after all, for more than a quarter of a century, and have, in a way, only just begun to write about. And I think there are a lot more things there that I think I would be interested to try, but it seems to me inevitable that at some point, whether in short stories, whether in the novel form or whatever form it might be, that I will return to India because it was obviously the place which shaped my imagination more profoundly than anywhere else, and which I carry with me wherever I go.

Salman Rushdie

Ameena Meer / 1989

From *BOMB* 27 (Spring 1989). Rpt. in Bomb Interviews. Ed. Betsy
Sussler. San Francisco: City Lights, 1992. 61–74. Reprinted by permission.

"So, the news of the death threats and bombs is really exaggerated," I say.
As Salman Rushdie nods his head, a car crashes up onto the sidewalk rattling
the huge picture window in front of which we're sitting. It backfires and I
nearly throw myself to the Oriental carpet while terror seems to paralyze
Rushdie. A few seconds later, we're collecting ourselves, trying to look as if
we'd known all along that cars backfire and park on the sidewalks in London.

I am Indian and Muslim so when people found out that I was going to
interview Rushdie, I started to get regular phone calls from relatives. "That
horrible man," said my great uncle, a barrister in England, "how dare he?"

"It's absolute rubbish, Papa can't make head or tails of it," said a cousin.

"Of course it's sacrilegious, he calls the Prophet a liar. He talks about his
sex life."

"Doesn't he have any responsibility to his own people?"

Worse, I like the book. And now I'm sitting in his living room in London,
thinking that I liked all of his books, and a documentary he made for the
BBC that was also banned in India. Something about his chaotic, mystical
style that belongs to the Third World, in the crazy, laid-back streets of Muslim
India: an old man in his kurta pajama, leaning back on a cushion, spitting red
betel juice against the wall, taking another puff of his hookah and contemplat-
ing the nuclear power plant across the road. "Hai baba, this firungi magic is
keeping this country going."

I read *Midnight's Children* on a train trip from Delhi to Hyderabad, a
crashing bus ride from Madras to Trivandrum, and then forty-six hours third-
class unreserved with people lighting little fires to make their tea on the train,
crates of chickens around them, and Michael Jackson's "Thriller" distorted
on someone's radio all the way back to Delhi. The novel melted into the
dusty hours through Deccan plains. It was a book that had entrapped some of
that Indian "magic," in the same way *The Satanic Verses* manages to catch
the spirit of the Asian immigrant in England.

Ameena Meer: You're quite often compared to Gabriel García Márquez. How do you feel about that?

Salman Rushdie: I don't see that much of a similarity myself. When I wrote my first novel, I had never read García Márquez. I think there are clearly certain things, not just García Márquez and me, but a whole group of writers, who, broadly speaking, are thought of as a family.

AM: Magical realists.

SR: Magical realism is a group developed and named of South American writers in the generation around Borges and after. If you talk about it to refer to them, it means something. Surrealism is not really that different from magical realism except that it happened in Paris. It's a kind of writing that there's always been. Always. García Márquez didn't invent fantasy.

The group I feel an affinity with as a writer, not just a modern group, but forever, are the people for whom the processes of naturalism have not been sufficient.

AM: Who are they?

SR: Among present day writers, (Italo) Calvino and [Günter] Grass, [Milan] Kundera—but the older tradition, which is really the one I learned from, are writers like Gogol or Dickens, who have that ability to be on the edge between the surreal and the real. Who understand that the surreal works only when it has very strong roots in the real—in the observed world. Dickens can use very surreal imagery, but set it in a completely known and credible London. If those roots weren't there, then the fantasy wouldn't work. I think that's what I learned from those writers.

I also learned from the store house of Indian stories. And from the *Arabian Nights*. If you look at how this fantastic writing came into Spanish culture, it came when the Arabs took the *Arabian Nights* with them to Spain. And it also came in my direction with the Muslims. In that sense, what you could say about magical realism is that we come from the same source material. But translated through different histories. I was brought up on those stories— flying horses and invisible cloaks—and I loved it all. It seems to me to be the birthplace of stories.

The thing about García Márquez that I admire, that I think is extraordinary, is that his writing is based on a village view of the world. What he does is take reality as it is experienced by the people of Macondo and elevate it above the reality of a city. So that miracles—girls rising to heaven—are commonplace, but he railway car is bizarre. That reversal of his vision is what gives the writing that novel quality.

AM: That's what you do in the story of the girl dressed in butterflies, Ayesha, in the novel.

SR: I think of myself as a completely urban writer. In this novel, it's the first time in my life I've been able to write a passage in a rural Indian setting. That's one of the bits of the novel that I feel very pleased about as a result. For having managed to leave the city.

AM: Tell me about Ayesha, why was she there?

SR: One of the things I wanted to contrast were those views of the world. But something like that really happened. It's different in the novel, in the story of the landowner (whose wife leaves him in order to follow Ayesha). And actually, the girl is different. But there was really an incident in which this girl persuaded a village that they should make a pilgrimage and the waters would open. And they drowned. Lots of people drowned. It was different in that it happened in Pakistan and the village was a Shia village and they were told that they should go to Kerbala. I was trying in the novel, to face up to, not just the nature of revelation, but also the power of belief. If you hear a story like that, where a hundred-odd people, illiterate, impoverished, are willing to, on the say-so of a teenage girl, walk two hundred miles, at all kinds of physical risk to themselves. Leaving their crops, leaving their homes, because they believe that the ocean is going to part so that they can walk to the holy place. Well, the level of belief that requires is astonishing. And I wanted to try to understand it. And the tool I use to understand the world is to write about it. That's why I wanted it in the book. Because it was the most extraordinary image of faith that I'd come across in years. I wanted to see how that works. What is it that drives people?

AM: Don't you think it's a question of the level of education or exposure to the rest of the world?

SR: It happens just as much to the landowner's wife as it happens to the poor. I think it does happen to the educated. Dhiren Bhagat (recently deceased Indian correspondent to the *Guardian*) was a disciple of Satya Sai Baba (a guru). One comes across that all the time in India. People who are completely educated, Westernized, will still have a guru or whoever that they're completely devoted to.

AM: But would they follow them into the sea?

SR: I don't think walking into the sea is that far away. I don't think it's just simple people. I think it's a phenomena of belief and as somebody—I mean, there's nobody who could make me walk into the ocean on the belief that it was going to part, and *I* can swim. One of the reasons for writing books is to try to understand the world other than yourself, and the other is to try to express what it is you see in your position to the world. This book tries to do some of both. But certainly, that section of the book is trying to make a reckoning with the phenomena of religious belief.

AM: It's a kind of magic, isn't it? Like if I run past all the lampposts on my way home, I'll find my lost glasses. It's grown up magic. Like lighting a candle to a saint.

SR: [Saul] Bellow writes that this is an age obsessed with realities. His characters are all "reality instructors," who want to tell you, "It's like this." I didn't set out to be a reality instructor. For example, that section of the novel has a very ambiguous ending. The landowner experiences the truth of the miracle. Which you could explain by saying that he's starving to death and has all kinds of disorders, but you don't have to. You can also take it straight. I wanted to leave that ambiguity. Because I don't want to simply explain it away. It's more interesting that it can't be explained away. It's more interesting that the villagers who survived claimed they saw the miracle.

AM: What about the "Ayatollah in exile" character?

SR: It's another scene from the career of the Archangel Gabriel, isn't it? That's one of the places where this novel really germinated, writing the biography of the Archangel Gabriel. I began to assemble stories in which the Archangel might feature. The question of the Imam, that scene is a description of how what is powerful in religion can turn against the faithful. How religion, which is after all one of the great codifications of good human beings have invented, can become a force for evil. How it can eat its children. Which is certainly how I think about the Khomeini revolution. Which is that it's a genuinely popular revolution. It only could have been organized through the Masjids [mosques], there's no other place through which that could have been done. It united not just the devout, but also the middle classes, the trade unions—and immediately as it won this enormous victory, it ate everybody. It ate most of the people who supported it. It ate the unions, it ate the middle classes, it ate the women's groups, it ate the socialists and left behind only its own bloated members—and that seemed to me quite a proper thing to have in the book, in a book which is about how the nature of good and evil is sometimes very difficult to tell apart. It seems to me that that's an extraordinarily vivid illustration of that fact in the modern world. The Imam is obviously not Khomeini and the opponent is not the Shah; it's fabulated in that sense. But that's because it connects to other sections of the book.

AM: Despite all the exploration of faith in the novel, I really got the feeling that it was more a story of identities—good versus evil, Occidental versus Oriental—or mistaken identities.

SR: Yes, and the upheaval in the self that migration creates, and beyond self, in the community and the culture. That's what it's about, really. It's not what the Mullahs say it's about; it's about that. I think it's obviously a theme that American readers would connect with. But there's a difference between Europe and America. Here, in Europe, you've got an old culture arriving in another old culture, as opposed to arriving in virgin territory, more or less. That makes up a set of completely different tensions and problems. So, in a sense, this is not a novel in the tradition of the American immigrant novels, because the canvas isn't blank here. And there's the frictions between those two cultures—what I wanted to write about was what I had experienced in another way, growing up in a city like Bombay. Because Bombay, much more than Delhi, is a city in which the West is very present. So it's not that I had a sort of pure experience of growing up in India and then came to an entirely other, Western experience. Even as a child, things were mixed up— the kind of relationship between them was different but the mixture existed. And it still exists inside me, I suppose. The nature of that mixture, the hybridity of the self, that's what I wanted to write about. If I do have a kind of moral view of the world, which I suppose I do, I should come clean and admit that I do, it's trying to construct for myself, a sense of the spiritual life of human beings which doesn't rely on outside validation. Which doesn't rely on some moral absolute like a god or a devil or a holy book. But which tries to create—what I'm trying to do for myself is work out a set of spiritual values and a way of thinking about the spiritual life of people which is internal. Which says that we all have that inside us, you don't need to go outside to look for the divine. Nor for the demonic. You don't need to look outside— it's all there—in a shifting relationship. So that a person can be, I mean it's almost banal to say this, a person can be at one moment good and at the next, not so. And especially given what we know about the shifting nature of the self in the twentieth century.

AM: That's what the innkeeper was explaining to Chamcha when he was transformed into the devil/goat, about Lucretius and Ovid.

SR: That's right, you see it's the old debate about whether the soul changes, or whether it doesn't. Whether it's the same thing all along or whether there's a kind of choice to make—about what you think human beings are like—whether social conditions can make such a revolution in the self that there's nothing left of the original self, or whether there is always that irreducible thing. I go more along that line myself. That there is *something*. In another way, that's what the novel's about.

AM: Are you a "lapsed Muslim whose aim is to write your own Koran"?

SR: Yes, I suppose I am a lapsed Muslim. I used to be more religious than I am. "Lapsed" means I don't believe in god. I don't believe in the existence of an external supreme being. But I consider myself to have been shaped by Muslim culture more than any other. I've been a student of it, etc. But I'm not somebody with any formal religious belief. So, in that sense, lapsed. But it certainly wouldn't have occurred to me as I was writing the book, I wouldn't have put it as strongly as that. I never thought that I was writing my own Koran. Centrally, my book is about a dispute between different ideas of the text. Between the sacred and the profane ideas of what a book is. The book whose legitimization comes simply as an act of the imagination—and these other kinds of books that are supposed to be handed down from another place. There is a discussion of the dispute that exists between those kinds of texts. Of the dispute that existed within the life of the Prophet Muhammed between himself and other kinds of writers, which I didn't make up. The argument about the status of the work of the imagination as opposed to so-called revealed texts—it seems to me that that's the real dispute.

In a way, it's rather strange that a book which discusses that dispute, immediately becomes surrounded by exactly that dispute.

The arguments aimed against the book by these Muslim groups are at two levels, with what they seem to be about and what they are about. What they seem to be about is a lot of specific things—like I've called the Prophet's wives prostitutes, which actually I haven't, that I used the name Mahound, which is the perjorative, although it says specifically in the book the reason for doing that is to reclaim the name. The book is full of attempts to reclaim names and phrases. Like the Poet who's writing a poem called "Rivers of Blood," it's a way of reclaiming that phrase from the Right. So the name is explicitly stated as being used as an act of reclamation, but nobody notices that when the Mullahs attack. There are specific answers to almost all the allegations. But the real level of the attack is, I'm not allowed to write about these things at all.

AM: Well, I'm a Muslim myself, but I didn't find the book offensive. First, if you situate it chronologically as a work of literature, it belongs to a certain aesthetic, which I understand. Secondly, I think a discussion of ideas is essential to modern Islam.

SR: I know plenty of Muslims who think like this, who sit around in cafes and have similar discussions to this. I don't pretend to be the first person to ever have these thoughts. I think the real issue is who has power over the story. What these people are saying, the Mullahs and the Saudis, and god knows who, is that they are the only people who have power over the story and that's because they have power: financial power, political power, and the power of the pulpit.

I think that's a very interesting dispute because it's a dispute which goes way beyond Islam. The same dispute is happening in Judaism—look at what happened to Philip Roth when *Goodbye, Columbus* came out. There's a similar dispute in Christian fundamentalism as well, we've seen that. Scorcese's *Last Temptation of Christ* movie is only one example, and not a particularly good example because the status of written text is different. But it happened to Kazantzakis.

You could suggest that as we arrive at the end of the century there's an upsurge of religious belief.

AM: Well, it's also a discussion that hasn't yet happened in Islam, that's going to have to happen if the religion is going to move into the twentieth century. There's never been a Protestant reformation in Islam.

SR: There is a kind of discourse which has become accepted as commonplace in Christianity and Judaism, in spite of the Scorcese fuss. There's a way of discussing principles like, "Did Christ live?" You could have those conversations without being called a blasphemer. Somehow, in that sense, Islam is lagging behind. That skeptical tradition doesn't exist in Islam. People have compared what's happened with this novel to what happened to Naguib Mahfouz—his book is still banned, thirty years later. When the theologians from El Asr in Cairo issued their *fatwa* against this book, they reissued their *fatwa* against Mahfouz—just because he's won the Nobel prize doesn't mean he's allowed to say stuff like this. I do think there's a very obscurantist air around and it's very sad to see this community closing itself off to the processes of the imagination and to the processes of scholarship. All you have is this crazy literalism. And if you go against that, you are called a bad person.

AM: What do you feel about the book ban?

SR: It feels very sad to me. It's hard to talk about. It's easy to talk about the politics of it—and people say it's good for sales and all that, which actually it isn't. I don't think it's at all good for sales, actually. One of the sad things about this is the incredible willingness to receive ideas secondhand. People point and say, "Don't read that, it's full of crap." And immediately, they're willing to repeat that. They're willing to say things about me, although they don't know me, and they're willing to say things about my work which are not based on any reading of the work. The only thing I can think is that it's a short term thing generated by this stink. Gradually what'll happen is that the book will be read. It is being read and it's selling very well and I can't believe there aren't *some* people in the Asian community who are reading it.

AM: But can you understand Rajiv Gandhi's reason for banning it?

SR: It's very easy to come up with sensible reasons for banning books. Everywhere you go in the world, people will give you sensible reasons for censorship. They'll do it to you in Northern Ireland, they'll do it to you in South Africa. South Africa is full of sensible reasons for censoring books. It seems to me that you just have to decide whether that's the world you want to live in. A world in which there can be sensible reasons for not being exposed to ideas. To tell the truth, I'm not surprised that, given the kind of leadership that exists in the Arab world, that this kind of thing could have happened. India's very sad because it shows that it's going down a certain path. Look at the *Last Temptation of Christ*, not banned in any Christian country, but banned in India. That's an even more laughable circumstance. The idea that India's Muslims would be offended by the film and therefore it should be prevented. What would the Indian Muslims do? Burn the country down? It's sad. The country I'm really sad about is India.

AM: There's a very big difference between the way Islam is practiced in India and the way it's practiced, and enforced, in the Arab world.

SR: The form of Islam that developed in the Subcontinent, because of the effect and the juxtaposition of Hinduism and Buddhism—the form that seemed most fitting in that context was basically Sufism. As a result, it was very unlike what the Arabs call Islam. It was a much gentler, more mystical, more pantheistic almost, kind of religion. I think Indian Islam is by far the most attractive manifestation of the animal anywhere. I don't believe Indian Muslims are intolerant and narrow-minded. They're just *not*. I mean I grew up as an Indian Muslim, surrounded by them. It was a very broad-minded, inquisitive community. I think it's very sad that this kind of Wahabi rigorous

Islam—which I don't even *accept* as fundamentalism. I think it's a false term for it. It's not fundamentalism because there are things that it claims as canonical which you don't see in the Koran, which there is only very limited support for. I think it's wrong to pretend that the Koran doesn't have some very harsh remarks about women, but, for example, there's nowhere in the Koran where it says that a woman's legal evidence is only half that of a man's. Or that a woman needs four witnesses to prove rape. It's not there. That's to do with another kind of power. Using the religion to validate itself, passing itself off as the real thing.

AM: There are a lot of practices in Indian/Pakistani Islam that would be considered heresy in Saudi Arabia. Like a milad, for instance, a gathering of women in which they sing songs to the Prophet Muhammed. That wouldn't be allowed in Saudi Arabia.

SR: For example, orthodox Islam says that you should keep no relics of the Prophet. Kashmir is full of them. And Saints, roadside zialeths where people bring flowers and sweets—you're not allowed to have that. So it's sad that those kinds of Muslims are unwilling or unable to speak up for the kind of Islam that they actually enjoy practicing. But nothing is forever.

AM: But Indian Muslims are a rapidly disappearing race. They're either going to Pakistan or getting swallowed up.

SR: I think the situation's going to get a lot worse before it gets any better. I think it's a—the documentary I made was about the heightening of religious tensions. It was banned because the politicians are using it. That's why they attack the film.

AM: Your film, *Midnight's Children* (a BBC documentary about the current views of people born at the time of India's independence) was also banned, wasn't it? My father rented the video from Anand's in Khan market (in New Delhi).

SR: They already have black market editions there, do they? One of the problems in a country in which the broadcast media has been censored, always, very tightly, is that people are entirely unfamiliar with work which is skeptical, caustic, or whatever you want to call it, because they've never seen it. And it's very hard for them to see that kind of work without thinking that the position is hostile. It seems to me that the film is not at all hostile about India. What it is, is critical. I think that's a distinction that people who are completely unused to seeing that kind of work find very hard to make. It's one of the long-term damages that censorship does. There's an attitude that says, "Even if it's true, you shouldn't say it." Television and radio are censored the most. I have seen a lot of what I've said in the English-language press.

AM: In my family, the partition of India and the formation of Pakistan has always been a subtle point of contention: part of the family was for it, and they left; and part of the family was very much against it, and they stayed in India. What do you think about it?

SR: What do I think? It happened. I come, broadly speaking, from a Muslim family which was not in favor of partition. And my father didn't go in 1947. He had no interest. My family, more or less, divided itself down the middle. Sort of half and half. Some of my aunts and uncles went and some of them didn't. My father's parents went to Pakistan, my mother's parents didn't—so it was very divided. And I certainly think there were moments in the independence process in which it could have been avoided. There are key things in the way in which Gandhi alienated Mohammed Ali Jinnah, for example. Instead of being a person who was totally opposed to the partition, which he started out being, he ended up being the person who was the architect of it. There's a lot to do with the power struggle in the Congress that accounts for that. So I think that there were moments in the thirties when it could have gone a different way. But I think by the time you get to the Quit India resolution and the Muslim League starts forming governments after people in the Congress get put in jail—once those kinds of really deep divides happened, it was very difficult to see any other possibility. It seems to me that it was an avoidable thing, and from my point of view, it would have been preferable to have been avoided, but history is history. I can't see a reunification of India, anymore than one can see a reunification of Germany—which is even more plausible.

AM: Or a unification of Israel and Palestine, in the best of all possible worlds, in which both could live peacefully in the country as equal citizens.

SR: It makes a problem like Anton Shammas has been talking about in *Arabesques.* He's writing exactly about that position—being an Israeli Palestinian. And wishing to maintain and express that double self. But I don't believe they'll let that happen. On the other hand, it does seem as if—well, we'll see about the Palestinian homeland. It seems closer than it's been for a while. As everyone says, it's Arafat's last card. If it doesn't work, it's going to be sad. It'll destroy Arafat. It seems to me the cause of Palestine needs

Arafat very badly. As Edward Said says, the point of Arafat is that he's survived. That he's still there means that the subject can't go away. Let's just hope—there is a change.

AM: Do you think Benazir Bhutto is going to make a big change in Pakistan?

SR: No, not really. Maybe in a certain level of society, but she seems to be more concerned with revenging her father's death than with the country.

AM: What do you think about Amitav Ghosh, who wrote *Circle of Reason* and *The Shadow Lines*? He just had an essay in the new issue of *Granta*?

SR: I think Ghosh will get better. There are some good young writers coming out of India right now, like Vikram Seth.

AM: But wouldn't he be an American writer?

SR: I think Seth would consider himself an Indian writer. I know about the *Golden Gate* being written in America, but now he's gone back to Delhi to write this long sequence of family novels set in India. I think he has quite a gift. A big gift.

AM: When I was in India, I did an article on English-language theater in Delhi and I found there was a great dearth of writers writing in English, and not just plays, anything.

SR: I've changed my mind about all this. I used to think that English would remain a very vital artistic language in India. I now have serious doubts about that. You're right, there's very little. When I say that there are one or two writers around, literally there are one or two, and we all notice when they arrive. There's nothing else so you notice a new building because there was an empty space.

AM: Do you consider yourself an Indian writer?

SR: I don't think of myself as an Indian writer anymore because, really, I don't live there. In a way, that experience of belonging to the diaspora is more interesting than trying to pretend that I am what I'm not. That shift in my way of looking at it was this novel. When I wrote *Midnight's Children,* and when I wrote *Shame,* with a slightly greater distance—I'd have been very upset if people reading *Midnight's Children* thought it was an outsider's book. I didn't want it to be. I wanted it to be written from an insider's position.

AM: The character named after you, sort of, in the book ends by going back to India, resolving everything by admitting his origins.

SR: When we are born, we are not automatically human beings. And some of us get there and some of us don't. And in this novel, one of the two main characters makes it and the other one doesn't. And the one who does, does so by facing up to the *big* things. Like facing up to love and death, basically. And the reason why the scene with the father is there, at the end of the novel, is because I think that's the one moment at which he achieves it. Both loving and allowing himself to be loved. And looking in the face of death. And having done those things he becomes a human being or begins to become one. I think that's what does it, rather than the fact that he's returned to Bombay. Because his return home is, anyway, rather ambiguous. You don't know if it's going to last or be permanent. Anyway, the place he's come back to feels very different than the place he left. So it's not some kind of simple, sentimental return. The thing that's important is the recognition of his own humanity. Because it seems to me that up to that point, the book is full of people who have quite a large capacity for love and so forth and never seem to do it successfully. Even Gibreel has it, but he goes down a different path. And Chamcha manages to do it, and in a way, he becomes the hero of the novel, which I hadn't expected. It was one of the valuable things for me about writing the book.

AM: You don't see yourself going back to India?

SR: I love going back to India. Some of my closest friends live there and I feel very joined to it, you know. But the decision I have made for the moment about my life is that I don't want to go and live there. However, then it's very interesting to have a fictional character who makes the opposite decision. You can see what happens. You send him off to do it and you don't have to do it yourself. I think that certainly had a lot of interest for me, in the Chamcha character. Apart from this kind of moral evolution is the fact that in many ways he, at several points in his life, takes the opposite decision from me. For example, his relationship with England is basically an assimila-tionist relationship. A sort of wanting to be the other relationship. It's not one that I really think of as being my position. Although I'm reasonably comfortable in this society, I don't think I have a desperate urge to be a white man. But, to me, it's a completely recognizable need in a migrant, in a settler in a strange land, to want to become the thing you've come to. So I wanted to write about that idea of migration and of the self. So that was one way in which he was not like me. And then, of course, having had that great need to belong that he has, he does the other thing that I didn't do, which is to leave this place which he was very keen to belong to and go back the other way. So, in both senses, he's different. It's much more interesting to write about the other possibilities that you didn't take, than simply to write about who you are.

One of the things that's been slightly irritating about some of the press coverage in this country, which seems to follow me around really, is this kind of assumption of autobiography.

AM: That's inevitable, though. Anytime one writes something, everyone else reads one's life into it.

SR: People assume that because certain things in the character are drawn from your own experience, it just becomes you. In that sense, I've never felt that I've written an autobiographical character.

AM: What are you working on now?

SR: I've been doing some stories, which is rather pleasant after doing something that size which takes that long. I also have a longstanding promise to my son to write a children's book. I have one son who's nine and a half. I more or less made a deal with him that I would write a children's book after I finished this book. So now he keeps asking, he's not letting me off the hook.

I've got the beginnings of another novel, just beginnings, there's nothing really to talk about now. But this book has brought me into a slightly different place as a writer where, what I *think* I think now, I mean, this is obviously going to be disproved by my next book, don't let it fool you. But what I think is that those three books, the last three novels, seem to have completed a kind of project. And there's a certain kind of writing and a certain kind of character that I don't want to do again for a while. I don't actually want any more people with big noses and horns. I think I'm going to have to do without that stuff. I mean, no more magical realism.

AM: No more props?

SR: No, we just have to deal with human beings, straightforwardly. I think I've been doing it anyway. The interesting thing about those two characters is not the horns or the nose, it's to do with their souls. What Saladin Chamcha learns when he's looking at his dying father and what he becomes after that, which is an ordinary human being, is also a lesson for his author. And what interests me as a direction to go in is more of that and less of the magic noses.

An Exclusive Talk with Salman Rushdie

Sarah Crichton and Laura Shapiro / 1990

From *Newsweek* 12 February 1990: 47–49, 51. Copyright © 1990 Newsweek, Inc. All rights reserved. Reprinted by permission.

It was Valentine's Day, of course, which I'm afraid has somewhat changed its meaning for me. It was perhaps the strangest Valentine one could receive. I was in my workroom at home, it was about mid-morning. I was telephoned by a journalist from BBC Radio. I remember her saying, "How does it feel to be sentenced to death by the Ayatollah Khomeini?" It was the first I'd heard of it. She then said, could we have a quote for "World at One," which is a big lunchtime radio program. And somehow, I have no memory at all of what I said, but I actually managed to give them some kind of quote. I then came rushing downstairs to tell Marianne [his wife, writer Marianne Wiggins] and literally our first reaction was to shut the shutters and lock the door. We were both extremely alarmed. I had a longstanding agreement to go on the CBS morning show that day, live; they were sending a car for me. The last thing in the world I wanted to do was go on television, but I just felt I couldn't let them down. These were innocent days: I wasn't at all used to death threats at the time. So I told Marianne I was going to do the interview, and I got in the car and went. The beneficial aspect of this was that I was out of the house when the world media descended. Within ten minutes of my departure there were something like 75 television crews parked outside the house, doing all the extraordinary things that television crews will do— zeroing in on the number of the house on the door, you know, just in order to give everybody the address. Careful things like that. Meanwhile I arrived at the CBS offices, still very shaken. I remember a journalist from CBS saying, I suppose to try and console me, "You don't have to worry about this, Khomeini sentences people to death every day, nothing ever happens. He sentences the president of America to death once a week." I thought, "Oh good, fine, it's just hot air." And then I had to go on air, and that was the last interview I've done until this one.

Salman Rushdie has been in hiding for a year now, protected by Scotland Yard's Special Branch. The fury caused by his novel The Santanic Verses *has*

123

quieted down, but many Muslims still regard the book as criminally blasphe-
mous and the ayatollah's death sentence remains in effect. Last week Rushdie
spoke out for the first time in a 90-minute telephone interview with Newsweek's *Sarah Crichton and Laura Shapiro. He would not discuss any aspect*
of his security arrangements—he called Newsweek *from an undisclosed lo-*
cation at a prearranged time—but talked readily about his state of mind and
his work. He sounded relaxed and reflective, discussing his predicament with
British understatement. In a companion piece he offers his critics an explicit
analysis and defense of The Satanic Verses—*also for the first time—in the*
hope, as he told Newsweek, *of restoring "cool discourse rather than brick-*
throwing."

By the time I came off the air, Marianne had rung the studio and said,
"Don't come home, because everybody and his mother is parked on the
pavement." So I arranged that I would go to my agent's office and she would
meet me there, having packed a bag of stuff. Of course every telephone in
the building was ringing non-stop, and everybody was being told that I wasn't
there. We then had a decision to make, because that afternoon was the memorial service to Bruce Chatwin, who was probably my closest writer friend. It
was very important to me to go to that service, but I had no way of knowing
what I should do or shouldn't do. In the end I just said, "The hell with it,
let's go." I remember Martin Amis sitting behind me and making some supportive, very friendly remark. I remember Paul Theroux attempting black
comedy and saying, "I suppose we'll be here for you next week." It wasn't
the funniest joke I ever heard, but I did write him a letter subsequently saying
that I was glad he's a less good prophet than he is a novelist. One newspaper
man actually came right into the church with his tape recorder running, and
insisted on an interview. I said, "Look, I've come here to my friend's memorial service." He was a very upperclass English gentleman, silver haired, and
he said to me, "You don't understand, you can't talk to me like this; I'm from
the *Daily Telegraph* and I've been to a public [private] school." That was
probably the funniest thing that happened to me. By then it had become
known that I was in the church, so all those people who had been outside my
house were now outside the church. I had not expected that, and therefore
didn't even have a car available. But fortunately a friend of mine was there
with his BBC limousine. He pushed me and Marianne into the back and got
us away.

And then I dived for cover. Marianne had rented a small apartment a few
blocks down the road from where we lived, which she was using as a work

place, and virtually nobody knew about that, so we went there. So there we were, sitting in a hole, with no knowledge of what was going to happen, and actually being quite scared. The local police were keeping an eye on the place. But that was a short term thing. I had no sense of what the long term strategy might have to be. The next day there was apparently a discussion about this in goodness knows what high circles, and I was offered [Special Branch] protection early afternoon of the next day. And we've been following this present structure ever since.

A few days after the ayatollah's death sentence, Rushdie tried to defuse the situation by issuing a statement—"I've always resisted calling it an apology," he told Newsweek—in which he emphasized his regret at all that had happened. Kohmeini was unmoved. "It is incumbent on every Muslim to employ everything he has got, his life and his wealth, to send him to hell." Meanwhile, Iranians had put a price on Rushdie's head, and the bounty quickly shot up to $5.2 million. Thirteen rioters were killed in Bombay, and several bookstores were firebombed.

The first few days were the most off-balance I've ever felt in my life. One of my sisters got an anonymous phone call the day after this all began, where a man's voice just said, "Now is your brother scared?" And the answer is, "Yes he was." [Still], initially everybody thought it was going to be only a couple of weeks. How could something like this last for a long time? It was only gradually that I began to feel that the damage that had been done was so huge that it was going to take an awful lot of undoing. I think one of the problems of unleashing this quantity of hatred is that it's very difficult to put it back in the box. Once you've whipped up crowds in so many countries of the world to march down streets demanding somebody's death, it's very difficult to say, "Well, actually we were wrong, we don't really want to kill him after all."

We would spend extraordinary time in front of a television waiting for each new development; we became television addicts. There was a moment at which I had to quite consciously wean myself from being glued to the TV to find out what would happen next. After three or four weeks I thought, I am not going to spend the rest of my life watching people abuse me on television.

I had walked out literally with the clothes I had on my back and nothing else. Eventually it was possible to send people, with the help of the police, into my house, so I ended up being brought at least a small number of the books I needed, and typewriters and things like that. Many writers have sacred objects that they keep around them to help them work, and I have one or two as well, so I managed to get those out. I have a little inch-high block of silver, Indian silver, engraved with the map of the unpartitioned continent of India and Pakistan, which was given to me as a present by a friend of my father's when I was one day old. It is my oldest possession, so it goes everywhere with me. And I was given, again by a friend, a small, primitive Haitian painting, a very simple little thing of a rural scene, which I've always kept in front of me on the desk where I write. It's only less than a foot tall by eight inches wide. I managed to get that out. So I had a few of my little totems with me.

[But] in the initial weeks, when the heat of the affair was so intense, it was quite impossible to think about any kind of work that I had been doing before. Really all I was doing in those weeks was trying to keep a journal of what was happening to me.

What I decided to do partly as a way of getting back to writing, but also as a way of telling the world that I wasn't finished, was to ring the newspaper for which I'd been doing book reviews, and say, "Look, I'd like to continue doing book reviews." I had to get the discipline back. What I [also] wanted to do was to create a situation where it was normal for me to continue to publish. What I didn't want to do was make people think, "Oh, he's had to dive for cover so he's never going to be able to publish again."

The first three months I don't think I wrote anything, apart from the book reviews and occasional poems and keeping up a journal. And then gradually I did what I was going to do anyway, which was to write a fable for children. This was a book that I've had in my mind to do for three years. It's a long, long story of a very fantastic kind, which I suppose has connections with Arabian Nights stories. It's very pleasurable to write. Once you set the tone of voice and the idea for a fable going, you don't really have to write in any different way than you normally would. You just tell the story, and you make it as interesting as you can because the thing about children is, if they're bored, they tell you. They shut the book.

Rushdie, 42, was one of the pre-eminent writers of his generation even before the ayatollah made The Satanic Verses *a global best seller. His* Midnight's Children, *a dazzling fantasy on India's independence and partition, won Britain's prestigious Booker Prize in 1981; and* Shame, *his third novel, is a rich satire on Pakistan. He was also a familiar figure in London's literary-social scene, out and about with such friends as Harold Pinter, Antonia Fraser, and Fay Weldon.*

I think Marianne is better at solitude than I am. I always had a very high requirement for other people. I can't remember who said that writers need to live in a monastery in the daytime and a whorehouse at night. It was either Faulkner or García Márquez pretending to quote Faulkner. But the point is that a novelist is very used to extended periods of time being by himself. So in that sense I feel very fortunate that that's the kind of writer I am. What I do most of my life is sit in a room by myself. The only difficulty is that this time I can't actually get out of it.

Seeing people is incredibly difficult. I always used to find the telephone a very difficult instrument to use. I wasn't somebody who would have endless telephone conversations; I would have rather brief, businesslike telephone conversations. What's happened in the last year is that I've learned how to become chatty on the telephone. When it's your only means of communication, you develop the gift rather fast. I wouldn't say there are many advantages to the situation, but one of the advantages is that you can choose who you talk to. Nobody can call you, you can just arrive out of the blue. Of course, often people don't believe it's me. People quite often need to be told some piece of evidence—how do you prove that it's you on the telephone? It's really difficult.

What I miss is ordinary life: walking down the street, browsing in a bookshop, going to a grocery store, going to a movie. I've always been a big movie addict, and I haven't been in the cinema for a year. I haven't driven a car for a year. I really love driving, and suddenly I have to sit in the back seat all the time. What I miss is just that, these tiny little things. When you have them you think they're completely unimportant or even chores, like going to do the grocery shopping, but when you can't do them you realize that in fact that's what life is, that's real life. When it's taken away from you, that's the biggest deprivation.

[Not that] my daily life is dissimilar to what it used to be like, in that I get up in the morning and go to work. I spend the day working, and then I find myself watching a lot of bad television and videos. And that's about it, except that instead of being entirely by myself I've got a number of guests around. People with guns.

Last summer Wiggins left their hiding place and returned to public life. For security reasons she no longer knows where he is. Her departure was viewed as a marital separation at the time, but in recent weeks she has told reporters that the marriage survives. "I have become his foreign correspondent, sending dispatches back."

It's always easier when there's somebody else there. I don't really want to say a lot about Marianne, but I do think that I would like to say that of all the people who have offered me support and strength this year, nobody has offered me more than her. Without wanting to go into it any further than that, it should be said that she has actually taken more of the weight of this than any other human being, and in many ways still is. So it's easier in a way being with somebody else, but you do what you have to do.

The British press has reported regular "sightings" of Rushdie ever since his disappearance. According to one widely published account last spring, he attended a dinner at Oxford but had to be hustled away by police when Muslims discovered his presence.

One of the things I've learned this year about the press is that when there's a hot story that they can't find out anything about, they make it up. Without exception, every single sighting of me that I've seen written about has been a complete fantasy. I've never been anywhere near an Oxford college, let alone being *allowed* to have dinner with a group of Oxford dons. And then being attacked by fundamentalist protestors outside—it's the fantasy of bad writers.

For years I had needed to have my lower wisdom teeth pulled, and just before all this happened, the bottom-left wisdom tooth actually broke. That was at the point when I was about to launch, as I thought, on an American promotion tour. So I said to my dentist, "Look, it's an American tour and I don't really want to have a swollen face." And he said, "Well go and do the tour and come back and we'll take it out afterwards." And then instead of having to do an American tour, I had to do this instead. And suddenly I was in a situation where I didn't know how the hell I was going to get these teeth out of me. One of the most impressive of the many impressive things that the police have been able to arrange in the last year was to get me into a hospital, placed under anesthetic—which was scary—have the teeth out, recover from the anesthetic and be taken out of the hospital without anybody knowing I was there. That's what I was doing when I was supposed to be at this Oxford high table.

Rushdie has enjoyed enormous popular support throughout the crisis. At the same time, prominent voices have been raised in sympathy with Muslims

who, while not advocating violence, were deeply offended by The Satanic
Verses. *Several religious figures, including New York's Cardinal John
O'Connor and Britain's chief rabbi, Sir Immanuel Jakobovits; deplored what
they saw as an insult to Islam. Former president Jimmy Carter expressed
similar feelings.*

There have been one or two critics that surprised me. The idea that Jimmy
Carter, of all former presidents of America, should say that he understands
how the Iranians felt about it after having enjoyed as we all know such intimate and *successful* relationships with them—that was almost comic.

I have spent a lot of this year thinking about whether I'm wrong. Which
is, I suspect, not something that the people opposing me have given a great
deal of thought to—whether they're wrong. I've thought about it and thought
about it, and I've spent more time rereading this book than I've ever done
with any book I've previously written—I normally can't bear to read books
after I've written them—but this one I've been obliged to almost learn by
heart. I'm happy to stand by it. If I felt that the novel that I wrote had engendered the kind of offense that people have taken, I would feel very differently
about everything—about what should be done in the future, about whether
one should maintain the present position, everything. The fact is that I genuinely cannot believe that what I wrote has merited the treatment it's been
given.

*Under normal circumstances Viking Penguin, Rushdie's publisher, would
have issued a paperback edition of* The Satanic Verses *this winter. But the
company, which has received numerous threats and reportedly is spending
more than $3 million a year on security, refuses to divulge whether a paper-
back is scheduled. Last October a controversial editorial in* Publishers
Weekly, *the industry's trade journal, urged Viking Penguin to forgo the paperback, asserting that the principle of free expression had been upheld and
that a new edition of the book would only invite more violence from extremists while showing insensitivity to moderate Muslims. Best-selling novelist
John le Carré also spoke out against softcover publication, criticizing Rushdie for his alleged willingness to put booksellers and publishing employees
in danger. Others in the literary community, including most booksellers,
strongly support a paperback. "Treating* The Satanic Verses *differently than
other books would be an act of appeasement and a terrible disservice to free
speech," wrote Michael A. Bamberger of the Media Coalition in a response
to* Publishers Weekly. *Most recently the British press has reported bitter
disagreement on this issue between Rushdie and his publisher.*

There's been a lot of very malicious rumor-mongering on the subject of Penguin and me. I resent attempts to make that relationship seem bad when it isn't. People are running all kinds of extraordinary stories. I felt that Penguin should have published the paperback a year after the hardback, and they took the decision not to. The fact that we have those disagreements doesn't mean that we don't like each other. I still have faith in them as my publisher.

I have always believed a paperback should be published, for a very large number of reasons, of which I should say the commercial reason is the least important. On the other hand, I live by my writing and I see no reason to feel bad about making some money from it. The other reasons are these: Any writer would tell you that paperback publication is the real publication. If you want to keep your book in print for any length of time, you can't do it in hardback. At the moment, *The Satanic Verses* is still an interesting book, it's still well distributed and well stocked in bookstores. Two years from now, five years from now, that's not going to be true. If there is not a paperback edition by that time, then effectively the book will have been suppressed. One of the things I'm very anxious to avoid is to have the book suppressed by this kind of backdoor route.

It seems to me it's very important that this book should be studied, not for reasons of vanity but because a book which has been the center of such an event needs to be very carefully studied. University lecturers have pointed out that if you want a book to be studied, you have to have a paperback edition of it. Books can't go on a syllabus if they're only in hardback.

And there are points of principle. If we do not complete the cycle of publication, we will in some sense have been defeated by the campaign against the book. I see this as an innocent book, wrongly accused and much persecuted. It seems quite wrong for the book to have to be the thing that is removed from the arena in order to end the trouble. *The Satanic Verses* should not just be a book that was in the middle of a scandal for a few years. Years from now, people may wish in the much cooler light of that distance of time to reappraise what the book actually is and is not. If the book is not available in a cheap, enduring edition, that won't be possible.

As for the danger, I'm not an idiot, you know. I know the risks to booksellers and publishers. But I'm not putting the bookstores through it. The people running the terror campaign—they're the ones putting the bookstores through it. It seems to me there's been fantastically disproportionate interest in what le Carré has said, because for every le Carré there's been a hundred people who think that what le Carré said was contemptible. I would hope that John le Carrés's views were not tempered by the fact that I gave his last novel a bad review. I'm sure he's entirely above that.

With no end in sight to his exile, people have wondered whether Rushdie might change his appearance, move to a distant country or take on an entirely new identity.

No, how would that work? It would mean that I would have to cease to be a writer. I would have to cease to be everything that I am. No, that's no life. This is more of a life than that. I simply will not accept that this is going to be the rest of my life—I have to remain an optimist in the sense of believing that solutions are possible. But one of the things that this shows is that there is such a thing as being too famous.

An Interview with Salman Rushdie

Blake Morrison / 1990

From *Granta* 31 (Spring 1990): 113–25. Reprinted by permission.

I met Salman Rushdie at a pre-arranged location on 4 February, the week before he published his essay "In Good Faith" in the *Independent on Sunday* and delivered his lecture "Is Nothing Sacred?" (or rather had it delivered for him by Harold Pinter) at the Institute of Contemporary Arts in London. It was the first interview he had given in person since 14 February last year, when he spoke to CBS News immediately after Ayatollah Khomeini's *fatwa*. In the circumstances, he seemed remarkably relaxed, resilient, even jokey: after a year's silence, broken with his essay, his lecture and this interview, he seemed eager to talk. Outside the curtained window I could hear the rain falling heavily on the street; inside, we drank tea and ate Italian bread and salad. We sat on the sofa next to each other and let the tape run for nearly an hour and a half.

Salman Rushdie: This is a strange experience: I can't remember the last interview I gave, with a journalist sitting in the room.

Blake Morrison: You've chosen to break your silence over *The Satanic Verses* with a long explanatory essay. Why?

Rushdie: It's often said that writers should never explain their work, but perhaps we could agree that these are exceptional circumstances. Normally when you write a novel, it's not a thing that has simply one meaning. Some people will read a scene and find it funny or satirical, others read it and find it sad or spiritual. Usually you don't have to choose between the two versions: the writer can allow both meanings to exist. But I've been put in a position where I have to say "what I really meant." It's a very strange thing to be doing, because, as anyone who writes a novel knows, not all the effects are planned—things happen on a page. It's been a characteristic of this whole affair that you have to talk about *The Satanic Verses* in a language which is really not appropriate to it.

Morrison: You've waited a year. Has it been hard to keep silent?
Rushdie: Yes, it was fantastically difficult being quiet, especially since I

was hearing some quite extraordinary things being said about me and my work: it was very shocking to be the object of so much hostility and falsification. I suppose the reason why I didn't quarrel with all that was that I couldn't see how to do it. There was so much of it, a whole tidal wave coming at me, and I just couldn't shout loud enough to be heard. And I thought that in a way it might be quite eloquent to say nothing: as if to say, here is someone whose business is language who is now unable to speak. But I always knew there'd been a moment when silence would no longer be useful and people would be ready to listen again.

Morrison: And you think that moment has now come?

Rushdie: It's an instinctive judgement. I'm hardly in a position to take a personal feeler on what's happening round the country. But I began to think around Christmas or thereabouts that the moment had come.

Morrison: What do you hope might be achieved by talking?

Rushdie: A number of things. The controversy has departed so much from reality that it needs to be dragged back to reality: the book that people claim I wrote is not the book I did write. I also wanted to explain that in many cases my responses to the events of the last year have been very similar to the responses of the Muslim people who have been attacking me: the attack on the Asian community makes me just as angry as it makes them feel. The idea that the National Front could use my name as a way of taunting Asians is so horrifying and obscene to my mind that I wanted to make it clear: that's not my team, they're not my supporters, they're simply exploiting the situation to their own ends. Most Muslims are reasonably tolerant and decent people, and they've been told a lot of things about my book while also being told by their mosques not to read it. I thought if I could just open up a conversation, I could begin to say that there aren't the grounds here to justify the level of upset and violence.

Morrison: Your article "In Good Faith" seems to address Muslims here in Britain rather than those in Iran.

Rushdie: Well, I don't see how I could talk to those in Iran. It's here that the controversy is happening: it's no longer an issue in the subcontinent or the rest of Europe. This is partly because I live in Britain, of course, but partly too because things have been tolerated here which wouldn't be tolerated in other countries: in France, for instance, the government has made a very strong statement against incitements to violence, and the French imam has said that French Muslims should respect the secular traditions of the country. As for Iran, the problem there has to be dealt with by processes of diplomacy and politics to which I'm not privy: there's not a great deal I can do to influence that situation, other than to express my belief as reasonably as possible that this book does not deserve the treatment it has received.

Morrison: What do you feel about the violence and the threats that have characterized some of the opposition to *The Satanic Verses* in Britain?

Rushdie: I've just read that they're not going to prosecute Kalim* Siddiqui for incitement to murder on the grounds of insufficient evidence. Apparently, it is not sufficient evidence that someone is seen on national television approving of a call for another person's death, joining three hundred other people in a chant of death, and a video of all this exists. Irrespective of the rights and wrongs of the Siddiqui matter, it seems to me as a layman rather puzzling, and as the object of the attack rather upsetting, that it's all right for people to walk around the country calling for my death. I also find it hard to believe that if it were not me, but a government minister, say, the evidence would still be deemed insufficient. The real reason is presumably one of public order—which I can understand, I see the thinking. But I have a rather simple view of the subject: they're asking for me to be murdered, and I think that's a bad idea.

Morrison: What is your position on the possible paperback publication of *The Satanic Verses?*

Rushdie: I've never made any secret of my position. I think the paperback should be published. And actually, contrary to what the newspapers say, I still feel hopeful that Penguin will bring it out. I've certainly never heard from anyone there any serious suggestion that Penguin won't. In many ways this is a whipped-up issue: people have been playing their cards close to their chest, so journalists have had to make things up. The *Observer* reported recently that the paperback would not be published, and since then I've had one hundred per cent assurances from members of the entire management, from Peter Mayer down, that Penguin's position is not what was alleged. It's an incredibly difficult state of affairs, though, and it's very wrong of journalists to drive a wedge between us.

---

*On 21 October 1989, Kalim Siddiqui, Director of the Muslim Institute in London, was filmed on the BBC television news in a chant of "Death to Rushdie" in Manchester Town Hall.

Morrison: You'd not accept that you are "obsessive" about the paper-back?

Rushdie: If I ring my publishers to talk about my book, that's not after all an unusual thing for me as an author to do. That's the basis of our relation-ship. There have been better moments and worse, because people have been under incredible pressure, but given that we get on very well.

I remember a time just after the book came out when I happened to be in the Penguin office and the first anonymous death-threat came through—a voice saying that I was going to be killed. The phone was answered by a secretary, who was very shaken. The level of intimidation in this affair has been extraordinary: hundreds and hundreds of telephone calls making all kinds of menacing suggestions have been received by Penguin here and in America. What has been aimed at the publishers and bookshops has been a very high level scare campaign—I'm resisting the word terrorism only be-cause it has other connotations. But it has certainly been a fear campaign, and one that cannot be justified simply by claiming injury. What about the injury caused to the peace of mind of those on the receiving end of this? I think many Muslims find it an embarrassment to be associated with that behaviour, and I hope that soon they might start saying: we don't like that way of carrying on.

Morrison: Would you consider the suggestion of inserting a prefatory note into the paperback?

Rushdie: I don't have strong feelings about this, but I'm not sure what that prefatory note would be or how it could be written in such a way that it didn't rapidly become outdated. People have said that *The Satanic Verses* should be identified as a work of fiction, not as a study of Islam. Well, it *is* identified as a work of fiction: it says so on the dust-jacket, even if it doesn't say so on the title page, and it's impossible to read the first page and not to be aware it's a novel.

Morrison: What about a consortium publishing the paperback, to reduce the risk to Penguin?

Rushdie: Again, I have no strong feelings about that. It's a matter for the publishers. In some countries publishers have gone down that road, in others not. If Penguin felt they needed a consortium, that would be acceptable to me.

Morrison: Should the paperback be dropped altogether as a peace gesture?

Rushdie: First of all, it's not me waging the war. Should I, therefore, be the one who is asked to make the gesture of peace? In many countries there is no division between the hardback and the paperback. In France and Spain, for instance, the book was originally published in paperback. In England and America everyone except hardback publishers would agree that the major publication of a book is its paperback edition: the real right is the paperback right. And for a simple reason: if you want to keep a book in print for any length of time, and I don't mean huge piles of books but the odd copy, then it has to be a paperback. If the paperback doesn't exist, the book has effectively been suppressed. It's the only way it can receive the judgement of posterity. It's the only way it can be studied in colleges; because hardbacks don't go on the syllabus; and any book that's been involved in a controversy such as this should be studied. Already some Muslim scholars have defended *The Satanic Verses* on the grounds of what they know about the Islamic tradition and how the book fits into it, and it's important that that process continues.

So my main reason for wanting the paperback is to prevent this book from being banned by the back door. Yes, it's sold a large number of copies, but in a few years' time if the paperback doesn't exist, the book simply won't be there for anyone who wants to read it.

Morrison: You've been under enormous psychological pressure. Have you managed to work in an ordinary way?

Rushdie: Well, I'm not working in an ordinary way, but I am working. There have been periods when I've not been able to do very much, but book-reviewing, for instance, has been useful, a way back to writing. At the moment, touch wood, it's going quite well, and there's no doubt that when it is going well it's easier to deal with the situation I'm in. When a writer is writing he feels like himself.

Morrison: This is the children's book?

Rushdie: In the last month, it has been the article "In Good Faith," which has been this thing sitting on my shoulders, unsaid, for a whole year. It has been the most painful and difficult piece of writing I've ever done, if only because when you write as a novelist you're not writing about yourself, whereas here the subject necessarily *was* myself, my motives and personality and so on. When I finished it I felt the sort of exhaustion I would feel if I'd just finished a novel. Literally for three or four days I was completely physically exhausted, which was obviously the release of something very large. I feel much better having said it. As anyone who knows me will tell you, I'm not the kind of person who can zip up his mouth without it being quite an act of will, so it has been a difficult time.

I reckon I've now about two months' work to do on the children's book I've been writing and then it will be finished. I've also put together a selection of my essays and criticism, about ten years' work, something I've wanted to do for some time, and it's now beginning to acquire some coherence. The children's book is a fable . . .

Morrison: And has it, as I've seen suggested, anything to do with your situation now?

Rushdie: Heavens, no, that's the kind of silly thing people invent when they know nothing. I've had the story in my head for at least three years. It'll be a book of about 160 to 170 pages, aimed primarily at children in the twelve-to-fifteen-year-old age group. My ambition is to write a book which children can enjoy but grown-ups will like as well. The great thing about children as an audience is that they tell you when they're bored: you have to make sure every paragraph is interesting. If I get that done, and the book of essays, I can at least feel that I've got something out of the year.

Morrison: And then a novel to follow?

Rushdie: Sure, I've got a novel worked out to the extent that I've written— for my own benefit really—a twenty-five page synopsis. Even if all this hadn't happened I would not have started it: it needed time just to sit in my head and gestate. I hope that when the other two books have been completed, the essays and the children's book, that I can pull the novel out of my head, so to speak, and make a start.

Morrison: Do you foresee any change in the way you will write? Has magical realism come to a sticky end, in view of all that's happened?

Rushdie: I don't think any two of my books are alike, anyway. But the point about *The Satanic Verses* is that it's a novel that begins in a pyrotechnic high-surrealist vein and moves towards a much more emotional, inner writing. That process of putting away the magic noses and cloven hoofs is one the novel itself goes through: *it tells itself,* and by the end it doesn't need that apparatus any more. That was a direction I wanted to move in anyway, so without doubt the next novel will not have cloven hoofs or magic noses.

Morrison: All three of your major novels have been politically contentious in some way. Do you see such contentiousness as unavoidable?

Rushdie: No. It may seem fantastically naïve to say so, but I thought *The*

Satanic Verses a personal, inward and spiritual novel, not a historical or political one as the previous ones had been. It's a novel about whether people can
live without God, about how people change when they move across the
planet. It's about how people come to terms with dying, and how they fail to
learn about love. It's not a novel about religion: the subject is not faith but
the loss of faith. So it seemed to me that I had already in this book moved
away from politics. Obviously, that's not how it turned out [laughs]—some
mistake surely—but that's what I thought I was doing. Writers can sit in a
room for five years and think their processes will be understood, and most of
the time they are, but sometimes, spectacularly, they're not. The idea that I
planned all this is bizarre.

   Morrison: What have you been reading, or watching on television?
   Rushdie: I have been watching a good deal of junk television. Having had
lots of late nights by myself, I've become an addict of American football
over the last year. I watched the Superbowl last week right to the end. I also
became very hooked on a series called *Capital City,* about yuppie bankers
and money, especially as it was on at a time when my other fixes—things
like *thirtysomething, Dynasty* and *Dallas*—were all off the air.
   I have also been reading more poetry over the last few years, and have got
more pleasure out of it than out of novels. The extra attention to language in
poetry, the extra charge: it puts you on your mettle. I always keep Derek
Walcott around, and I've been reading a lot of Miłosz. American poetry, too,
even though Fenton says no American poetry is any good (perhaps even
James Fenton can be wrong). I've also begun to write poetry, which I hadn't
done since I was eighteen. I'm very tentative about this, and "6 March 1989,"
the poem that appeared in *Granta,* was the first one I'd ever published, and I
felt about it like anyone would about seeing their first poem in print. And
then what happens? Because of this weird situation I'm in it's read out on
the *Nine O'Clock News*! I felt very sorry for it—my poor little poem, only
seventeen lines—and it's a front-page story.
   When the *fatwa* came, I had to leave my house in the clothes I stood in—a
classic cliché of fiction—and I've never been home. So a lot of my favourite
books were locked up at first. Since then at various points friends have got
things out for me. I always carry *Moby Dick* around: it's a great, great masterpiece, and transgressive in a way I find very attractive. You have a universe
and this little boat pursuing one kind of devil and being run by another: that's
an extraordinary metaphor—it's not surprising the book didn't do very well

when it came out. I always keep *Ulysses* near me because it's the modern novel that most achieves that charge of poetry, and I read it to be reminded what novels can be.

I've found myself, for fairly obvious reasons, reading various Enlightenment writers. It's very odd, when you think of how much has been written this year about their importance in our culture, to look at what actually happened to those guys at the time. Rousseau's *Confessions* were not published in his lifetime nor *Jacques le fataliste*. Voltaire kept having to skip the country and used to say that he lived close to a frontier because that was very useful. The fact is that, at the time the Enlightenment writers were writing the works that we now think of as the bedrock of European free speech, they were persecuted, banned, reviled and accused of blasphemy. I think it would be as well for Europe to remember that. So yes, I've been reading a lot.

Morrison: There have been consolations, then?

Rushdie: Listen, it's not great. You make the best of the situation. The thing that's worst is the loss of ordinary life: not being able to walk down a street, to browse in a bookshop, to go to a movie—those sorts of trivial things that everyone—including me, once—takes for granted, things you don't value greatly until you don't have them. What they add up to is life. If you can't do them, you have to do what you can, but it doesn't mean it's a positive experience.

Morrison: Have you learned something about yourself?

Rushdie: If you had told me in advance, this and this and this is going to happen to you over the next year, I'd not have been very confident of my ability to stand up to it. You don't find out until you're in the situation whether you can stand up to it or not. Fortunately, so far, I have—but I don't recommend it. As a way of learning about yourself, there must be better ones!

Morrison: The world has changed a lot over the last year. How does it look to you?

Rushdie: In normal circumstances I'd have been on the first plane to Berlin. I envied my friends who did go. I have been to Berlin a few times and always found it a very exciting city, not so much in spite of but because of the Wall, and those images of people dancing on the Wall were quite extraordinary. And to miss the chance of being on it! I felt I'd missed out on one of the great moments of our time. For week after week, all the news seemed to be good: it was very strange for good news to be leading the bulletins.

Those of us who were young in 1968 used to talk of 1968 as the moment when some great shift in power towards the people took place. But actually, nothing happened in 1968: a few kids ran down a street chased by the police. This time it *actually happened.* Eighty-nine does it again: 1689, 1789, and now 1989, the greatest year in European history since the end of the Second World War.

Morrison: Do you take a particular pleasure in seeing Václav Havel as president?

Rushdie: He's clearly an extraordinary writer—apart from his plays, those prison letters to Olga are amazing—so to have a serious writer running a country, quite possibly two serious writers running countries if Vargas Llosa wins the election in Peru, well, it's a sign that perhaps the world is a less hopeless place than I thought it was. Suddenly, intelligent people seem to be in charge. It would be nice if it happened here.

Morrison: Has your attitude to the British state changed as a result of your experience?

Rushdie: Yes. It's very simple: if somebody takes steps to protect you when your life is in great danger, you feel more kindly towards them than you did before. There's no doubt, that at that personal level, my feelings about the British government have changed. And I think that's been assisted by the fact that the party I've supported and voted for all my life, the Labour Party, has been so vocal in the attack on me. There have been people in the Labour Party who have been incredibly supportive, Michael Foot especially, but I felt very shaken by the way in which certain parts of the Labour Party have abandoned positions that are important to hold—such as not playing religious politics, which is a dangerous game. I don't think there's much chance of my becoming a Conservative voter, but maybe I'd use a different kind of language if I was talking about the Conservative government now; maybe I wouldn't be quite as polemical. And I make no apologies for the fact that this is because of personal experience. I dislike this government's policies, and would argue against them, but I'd also argue that a great deal of the Labour Party's policy is mistaken too.

Contrary to public opinion, which always put me down as a raving Lefty, I'm a very bad joiner. I've never in my life belonged to a political party, not even a local constituency party, and I've never been a hard-line zealot. I've always thought that what gave writers a role in these matters was that they couldn't be slotted into a particular category. If what a writer says can be dismissed as Thatcherite nonsense or as the work of a Labour Party stooge, you don't have to think about what he's saying.

Morrison: *The Satanic Verses* is a celebration of doubt. Do you have doubts yourself? Have there been moments of doubt—and even guilt—about the consequences of the book's publication?

Rushdie: Every day, more than once a day, of course. And if I really felt the novel is what it has been called, I wouldn't have been able to sustain my position. I've re-read the book—in a way that writers usually don't, because they hate re-reading their own work—with a view to see if I was wrong. All I can say is that, if I thought I had been, I would have done something about it. I honestly believe there isn't a sentence in this book I can't defend. And if its critics were willing to set aside threats and violence and abuse and actually talk about what's on the page—is it offensive or is it not? Why did you say this in this way and not another?—I'd be quite happy to go through the book with them. That's an open offer. It seems to me, though, that it's very difficult for any acts of conciliation to take place in an atmosphere of violence. And it's not for me to change that. The essay I've written is a way to say, I hope without bitterness or anger: let's talk to one another, not shout at each other. There has been a colossal misunderstanding and it will be a massive effort to unscramble it. What it requires is a moment of good will: that's what I've tried to offer.

Morrison: And if you had your time again and could choose not to have written the book?

Rushdie: I really don't know. As everybody says, I'm not perfect. If somebody had told me, before the book went to the press, what was going to happen, maybe I'd have chickened out; I can't say. I hope I would still have published it, because I think there are very serious reasons why the book takes the shape it does, why it uses the images it does, why it develops the language it develops, and they are reasons I can easily defend. What's very hard is to have to defend your life as well.

Salman Rushdie: A New Chapter

Akbar Ahmed / 1991

From *The Guardian* [Manchester] 17 January 1991. 21–22. Copyright © 1991 by Akbar Ahmed. Reprinted by permission.

Akbar Ahmed: Many Muslims still believe that no Muslim should talk to you. I agreed in a personal capacity because I hoped it would contribute in a small way to creating some harmony. But first, I would like to hear for myself: are you a Muslim?

Salman Rushdie: Yes, certainly.

AA: What prompted you to declare your faith in Islam? Was it triggered by a particular experience, a spiritual event? Has it been building inside you for some time or did you convert under duress as a way out of your predicament?

SR: Certainly not out of duress. No, that would be a foolish and dishonest thing to do. One has to live with it for the rest of one's life and it would be impossible to live with it, because after all one's talking about the deepest spiritual things and if one's being dishonest about those it creates a much longer imprisonment. My books have always drawn their central inspiration out of Muslim culture from my first novel onwards, which drew its themes from Sufism. Even my most recent book, the children's book, takes its inspiration from the greatest classic of Muslim literature, the *Arabian Nights*. Islam is much more interesting than any of the other religions because one can study it not only as a theological event, not only as a spiritual event but also as a historical and as a human event.

AA: You had a Muslim name, you were brought up in a Muslim family. How could you state you were not a Muslim before?

SR: Well, the fact is in my family there was virtually no religious environment. There was no religion to speak of in my house as a child, there was none around to speak of when I was going to school or college in England. So this is a process that I've been engaged in as an adult and not before. I've been slowly, over a long period, moving towards it. There is a thing that Dostoevsky said when he also had a rather close escape from a firing squad and subsequently had a long period of very difficult imprisonment; during this time he wrote in a letter to a friend in which he said—I may misquote—

the spirit thirsts for faith like parched earth and finds it because truth shines brightest in misfortune. Now I think something of the same thing applies to me. And one final thing which was, I suppose, fairly crucially influential on me. Dr. Essawy persuaded me that a person doesn't have to be a perfect Muslim in order to declare that he is a Muslim, because after all most Muslims are imperfect. Indeed, one could say to claim perfection is itself an imperfection.

AA: Although I personally am prepared to accept a declaration of faith on face value, there is a lot of scepticism. This contrasts with the cases of Muhammed Ali, the boxer, or Yusuf Islam, the ex-pop singer, for whom there was an unlimited joy and welcome from the Muslim community. What wrong signals do you think you've been sending out?

SR: Well partly, I think it has simply to do with the bitterness and the hostility that's been around for the last two years. But, as we can discuss in a minute, I'm trying to do a great deal to overcome that bitterness and hostility. I hope that as that process continues the cynicism will diminish. Another thing is perhaps that my natural form of speech is sometimes not simple enough, partly I think, if I may say so, because of my not wishing to claim too much. So if somebody says, you know, are you going to try to be a good Muslim? and I answer, I hope so, and then they say well what do you mean, you hope so? Are you or aren't you? Now all I can say is that everything I've said, I've said straightforwardly, in good faith.

AA: Now that you are a Muslim and are seeing things, in a sense through Muslim eyes, what do you think of the passages of *The Satanic Verses* which have caused so much offence to Muslims?

SR: Well, I think a number of things about them. First of all, one of the things that I have been saying, and which I still say and hope that people will come to accept, is that whatever one may feel about the execution of those passages, their intention was very far from being to defame Islam. The first recent statement on Christmas Eve, was just that I wanted to say very clearly, and again to employ very unambiguous language, that everything that is said in *The Satanic Verses* which is held to be hostile or offensive to Muslim sanctities, is material that I personally do not agree with, and the ideas expressed in those passages, the hostile ideas expressed in those passages, are ideas I absolutely, as a person and as a writer, reject. I feel that had I been a Muslim at the time that I wrote the book I would clearly have written it differently, clearly, and I want to make that point, and let there be no argument about it.

AA: The problem was that any Muslim protest at that stage was seen or dismissed by the popular media as coming from fundamentalists or extremists. In fact, the average ordinary Muslim, a person like me, who normally wouldn't believe in violence, was also very offended.

SR: I accept that it did upset many people who, as you say, were not at all violent or violently inclined people and, I mean, I have many times said that I'm extraordinarily sorry for that and I would say so again. I don't see this as being a quarrel between Western Reason and Eastern Unreason and so forth, and so I've been trying to do my bit to encourage a more sophisticated response from the beginning and I suppose, even now there is a certain element in the Western liberal response which is rather alarmed, almost, by my affirmation of Islam. People say "how can you do it, they are the people who are trying to kill you and how can you say that you are one of them?" My understanding of Islam is that it is a culture of tolerance and compassion and forgiveness and love. And I hope that those statements that I've made will oblige many Western people to adopt a more complex view of Islam and not simply to create these stereotypical black and white oppositions which have embarrassed me in the last two years when they have been used to defend me.

AA: As far as I can see, the majority of Muslims would not be prepared to compromise in terms of the book itself and as long as it is in circulation. So what steps are you taking to convince them?

SR: What I think has been at the bottom of everything I've done has been a desire, first of all to put this behind us; secondly, for me to rebuild my links with the community; thirdly for this crisis to be removed from the community as a problem for it; and fourthly to go into the future in a way which could be more productive. First of all, the cancellation of the paperback edition. The paperback *was* a real possibility and to concede it is a major concession because paperback editions are the way in which a book has a long-term mass life. To give it up is not a small thing for a writer to do. Especially when we are talking about a book which has taken the writer five years of his life. So I think it's important that people in the community understand that this is not just some kind of tokenism but in fact is as large a gesture as any writer could be expected to make. The same holds true of giving up the possibility of further translations. I have already drafted a text which expresses my respect for Islam very forcefully and I am discussing it with Muslims before finalising it and will then arrange for that to be affixed to such copies of the book that remain in shops. In my mind what that does is, first of all, to set the record straight, secondly to form a kind of advertisement for my attitudes and beliefs about Islam.

But, of course, people died and that's the issue: there were demonstrations and there was loss of life. That was a source of absolute horror to me, because nobody who writes a book ever dreams any tragedy on that sort of scale is going to attend the publication of his work. I certainly would want to be part of an attempt to do something on behalf of the families and dependents of the people who died. And I don't mean [by donating] a couple of thousand pounds, I mean very substantially. Beyond that, I have felt that if there's one lesson to learn from the so-called Rushdie Affair it is that in what is a very small world there are these two very, very large cultures which are, broadly speaking, Western culture and Muslim culture which really know very little about each other and which see each other through a series of stereotypical attitudes. I think it's of extreme importance to start a process by which we can improve the mutual understanding of the two cultures. If the Gulf crisis shows anything, it shows that these cultures are not going to get further away in the future, they're going to live in closer proximity and it simply is impossible that such a situation of mutual distrust should persist. So, I've proposed setting up some sort of foundation or trust whose purpose would be to encourage that mutual understanding. I would certainly wish to contribute to that, but I would hope that a large number of bodies and individuals, ranging from Muslim states and organisations to Western religious and secular organisations, might all wish to contribute to that because it's quite clearly going to be of critical importance in the next 50 years.

AA: I would say there is an attempt by the West to dominate the Muslim world in terms of power, which is at the root of the problem, the kind of thing Edward Said talks of.

SR: Well, certainly, the power relationship is there and that needs to be part of what people understand. You know, we're not talking on an equal basis. That most of the money is in one part of the world and so are most of the guns and the rest of the world has to deal with that as a reality and that's frequently an oppressive reality. So I would have thought that this idea of a foundation is not just a constructive one but is an important one. I have to appeal in this matter to the compassion and forgiveness that I know to be at the heart of Islam and I have said throughout this interview and many times before that I regret what happened, that I made mistakes—they were honest mistakes but they were mistakes—and that I ask that we can now go forward in a spirit of friendship. The Koran says that if you take one step towards me I will take ten steps towards you, if you walk towards me I will come running towards you. That spirit of compassion is to my mind the center of Islam. So, I think, that's what I'm trying to say to Muslims. I've taken these steps and I now hope that people will respond as generously as The Koran says that Muslims must and do.

AA: Yes, the two greatest names of God are Rahman and Rahim, the Beneficent, the Merciful. There is one hurdle, however, and that goes back to the book itself. Is your strategy making a dent where it matters for you as a Muslim, in the mainstream Muslim position, for instance, on groups like the UK Action Committee for Islamic Affairs?

SR: Unfortunately, I haven't been able to enter into any dialogue with groups like the UK Action Committee; of course I'm absolutely ready to do so if they should feel that they should. I mean earlier, long before any of the announcements were made I had asked people, intermediaries, to talk to Muslim leaders in Bradford and elsewhere to see if a dialogue was possible. At that stage, sadly, it seemed not to be. The sticking point for the UK Action Committee, as they have said, is the question of complete withdrawal of the book. Now I've thought about this very hard and I want to say a number of things about this which I hope that Muslims will consider very seriously and think about, because they haven't been said for any reason other than trying to come out of this in a good way for all of us, and primarily for the Muslim community here.

One is that actually in the real world the book as an idea, the book as an entity, cannot be withdrawn. It's there as an entity, it's there in many, many people's homes, it circulates freely. The idea of trying to unmake it as an event, somehow trying to turn back the clock is unrealistic.

The second thing is just a technical point but it is an important point which is that, actually, I don't have the ability to withdraw the book. That's one of the things that happens when you sign a contract: it is not in my power to withdraw the book and if we are trying to make a reconciliation between myself and the community of which I am part, it's unreasonable to ask me to do that which is not in my power.

The main point I want to make falls into three categories. What would happen to the book itself?; what would happen to me?; and what would happen to the Muslim community? I'll tell you what would happen to the book itself if it was withdrawn. It would immediately become equivalent to when *Ulysses* was banned or when *Dr. Zhivago* was banned in the Soviet Union. This book which is now an old book, which is fading away, would suddenly become characterised as a martyr, it would be a celebrity, it would become fantastically prominent again. There would almost certainly be illegal, pirated paperback editions which would be impossible to control.

What would happen to me if I were to say that I would withdraw the book is that my reputation would be destroyed, my reputation as a serious person in this country and in this civilisation would be destroyed. Now people may think fine, you know, so what. But, in my view, it's not actually of benefit to the Muslim community to unmake somebody who could be a voice on behalf of its rights, and has been in the past on many issues ranging from Kashmir to Palestine to racism in Britain, who has been a voice on behalf of Muslim concerns—so once again the effect is not productive or constructive.

Then finally, what seems to me in many ways the most important point, what would be the effect of withdrawal on the Muslim community itself? They may think, some of its leaders may think, that this would be a victory. In my view it would be a catastrophic victory if you could call it a victory. The effect would be to unleash against the Muslim community in this country a degree of hostility which would make everything that's happened in the last two years look like nothing. And, it seems to me, that that damage would last not just for a week or two but for decades.

What I would see as a constructive end to this is that the book runs its course without the paperback. The sales of the hardback at the moment are only something like a few hundred copies a month at the most and actually the reason that they're even that high for such an old book is the continuing argument. The more that the argument fades away, the more the book fades away. I am willing to undertake that any remaining income that comes from this dwindling hardback, I will not accept. I will donate that to a charity or whatever. And if the UK Action Committee or anybody else still wishes to dispute or discuss it with me I'm quite ready to talk about it. But I hope we can talk about it in this spirit of what is best for everybody concerned. I'm open to ideas.

AA: Now that you have declared yourself to be a Muslim, and moving from one camp to another you are in the dangerous middle ground between

the West and Islam. Do you feel that you are out of danger or even more
vulnerable?

SR: I've always believed that safety for me means the good opinion of the
Muslim community. The more that we work towards that the safer I feel. And
what I do feel, very much, and what I hope very much, is that as that good
opinion increases that Muslims in this country and abroad will continue, as
they've already begun to do, to speak out themselves against people who
adopt much more threatening attitudes because I don't believe that to be a
Muslim attitude. So to answer your question, I don't think I feel quite able to
walk out into the street, and resume my ordinary life but as this process goes
on, yes, I feel safer and safer. I have stopped living in a box, you know. I
have started doing more.

One of the reasons for reminding people that I am now as a Muslim their
brother is that anybody who attempts to attack me is performing an anti
Muslim act. That is very clear in Islam and the Sheikh of Al-Azhar has
already said that now that I have embraced Islam, whatever happened in the
past must be let go and somebody who attacks me has to answer for that
afterwards at the end of his life and the issue is not so much my life as his.

AA: What about the people who have supported you over the last two
years?

SR: It always happens in any major political event that people come along
for the ride for all kinds of reasons. I have said throughout this two year
period that there have been things said to defend me that I did not wish said
to defend me, you know, the characterisation of Muslims as barbarians. It
has been very offensive to me, and if there are people who now feel that
because of my declarations they can't support me any more, my view is good
riddance. I didn't want them before. For example, the way in which my name
was used by the National Front to taunt Muslims. I have said many times that
that was an insult to me just as much as it was to the Muslims. I do feel that
as far as the bulk of people who campaign on behalf of freedom of speech is
concerned that that was a sincere campaign and that for those people freedom
of conscience is just as important an issue as freedom of speech, if not more
important. I think people accept that if I want to make a declaration of faith,
that is my business, and not theirs, and what I hope it will encourage people
to do is to understand that Muslims as a community are not characterised by
violence.

AA: In a book to be published next month, *Resistance and Control in
Pakistan* (Routledge), I raise the leadership issue in Muslim society. Who

speaks for it, is it the religious functionary, traditional authority, or the government official? Do you find this a problem in dealing with Muslims today?

SR: I think there is a problem that the community here is not well organised politically; that is a fairly standard problem of a new community. I do think that there are many different voices. There is need for work to be done in the years to come to create what might be a coherent voice. In the long-term we do need to think about a structure of representation because in the end if one wants influence in a society one must first have organisation.

AA: We've been talking about many of the negative consequences around the controversy but there's a positive side in the greater general awareness in Britain about the Muslim community. Can this be used to bridge the gap between the two communities, to heal the damage to race relations?

SR: I mean first of all, if we could now, very quickly, agree that this crisis were resolved I think that in itself would have a fantastically beneficial effect on race relations in this country. There's another issue which has to do with the Gulf. Many Muslims are worried and must be worried about the implications for the community in this country. One thinks about what happened with Japanese Americans in the second world war, what happened in Britain to people who had German names in the second world war; there was increasing hostility, there was in some cases internment, there was a kind of general desire to characterise those minorities as a fifth column, or an enemy within. It seems to me that there is a great danger that something of that sort may be aimed at the Muslim community once the temperature gets so high that there's actually a war going on and it's very important in that context that all of us who are able to speak, speak very loudly against that attitude and struggle against it.

AA: What do you think of the situation in the Gulf?

SR: There is a specific historical problem in Saudi Arabia which is the presence of Mecca and Medina. The idea of there being a very large long-term Western military presence there is something which all Muslims from wherever they are in the world, whatever their relation to this specific crisis might be, would find very, very worrying. One of the great fears is that those Holy places may be in danger and that, if nothing else, is one reason why I think there's a legitimate Muslim position in this confrontation which is that one must find an end to it which is not a shooting match.

AA: Your writing is post-modernist, irreverent, ironic, satirical, sceptical. Do you see an internal contradiction developing in your work between this and the Islamic tradition which is rooted in faith?

SR: Not really. For a start I've never called myself a post-modernist. It seems to me that's a term used in scholarship and in study and is useful in that field. It's not particularly useful to me in the act of creation. Also, I think you're making too simple an opposition between a kind of reverential Muslim approach and a kind of irreverential, as you said, post-modernist approach. Islam after all is full of satire and irreverence and fantasy and a kind of mischief in its literature. I mean one has to look no further than the *Arabian Nights* to find it all there. To my mind the *Arabian Nights* was the book which showed me more about writing than anything else. One of the things that one should remember is that what is now called in the West "magic realism" and before that was called "surrealism" and before that was called fantasy or fable etc. is all the same thing. But one very important method by which those techniques entered Western literature was, in fact, when the Arabs entered Spain. They brought with them the *Arabian Nights* and that tradition of literature that took very firm root in Spanish literature and so you know, if García Márquez, now learning from Spanish literature, writes in a certain way that also can be traced back to Arab literature. For example, in the greatest masterpiece in Spanish literature, *Don Quixote*, Cervantes quite deliberately makes his fictional narrator an Arab. Don Quixote clearly comes out of that tradition, clearly telling those sorts of stories, so after all an enormous amount of what would be the Western literature that I identify with derives from the Cervantes-like writing. So it seems to me that one of the things I've felt about my own writing is that it is a way of completing the circle. After all, the *Arabian Nights* went East as well as West, so I found myself imbibing that tradition as a child growing up in India.

AA: I was thinking more in terms of faith, of belief. In a sense this is an age of disbelief, of scepticism, whereas Islam is very clear about these things.

SR: Yes, that's a fair point. But it seems to me the function of a novel is not polemical. A novel which seeks to teach or instruct is almost always a bad novel. A novelist's job is to understand the conflicts and stresses and needs in a society and to seek to reflect those in his writing. Now, clearly we live in an age in which there is an enormous tension between, on the one hand the needs of believing and faith, and on the other the needs of disbelieving and doubt. That tension objectively exists in the world, probably internally exists to a greater or lesser extent inside each one of us and it becomes a function of the writer to reflect that and to portray that and to try to understand it.

AA: I'd like to end by going back to our first question. In terms of your own recent conversion, are you beginning to find out more about Islam?

SR: Well certainly. I do have with me three editions of the Koran with different commentaries and I do read them. Yes, I am trying to understand them. I actually do have with me a number of other books about Muslim culture. It's interesting that in your book, *Discovering Islam,* you talk about the Andalus syndrome and certainly one of the major strands of this novel I've begun a little bit to describe to you, has to do with my having been fascinated for a long time with the Moorish, the Arab period in Spain because it seems to me that there were not just cultures who lived side by side but they actually became the same culture, they actually interpenetrated and became something incredibly rich and one of the great glories of Muslim history. And then what happens is that basically under the pressure of what one might call in simple terms, Christian fundamentalism, was ripped apart so that not only the Muslims but also the Jews were expelled from Spain and that that moment of unity was in a way destroyed forever. Because since that time Islam and Christianity, or Islam and the West, have seen each other as the dark other and a lot of the hostility and stereotyping, misunderstanding and so forth in my mind, can be traced back to the end of that moment. And so I think the end of that moment is crucially important. Because Spain came closer to a kind of terrifying extremism. In faith it made the kind of pluralism that had existed there, impossible. So I think there's a lesson there. I went to Spain. You talked in your book about the effect on you of the Mosque at Cordoba. I also had that feeling when I went to Cordoba when I was 18 years old, a university student. I remember thinking what an extraordinary building it was and how in a way upsetting and pathetic the little Cathedral stuck in the middle looked and I remember also being very struck by the Alhambra in Granada. I felt for a long time that I have some business there because those two cultures that found their richest expression by being fused, are also the two cultures that are fused inside me. So what Arab Spain means to me is the full potential of what can be achieved by these two cultures working together and what the end of Arab Spain means to me is the nightmare of what happens when they become adversarial. So that's something that I've been researching anyway for two or three years now and that certainly is an important strand in the next novel and I think also it partly answers your question about how my new beliefs will enrich the process of writing in the book that's underway already.

An Interview with Salman Rushdie

John Banville / 1993

From *The New York Review of Books* 4 Mar. 1993: 34–36. Reprinted with permission from *The New York Review of Books.* Copyright © 1993 NYREV, Inc.

Under an unknown picture somewhere in India there is hidden a portrait of Salman Rushdie's mother. The story goes like this. An artist, hired by Rushdie's father to paint Disney animals on the walls of the child Salman's nursery, went on to do a portrait of Mrs. Rushdie. When the painting was finished, Rushdie *père* did not like it. The artist stored the picture in the studio of a friend of his, another artist, who, running out of canvases one day, painted a picture of his own over it. Afterward, when both had become famous artists, the friend could not remember which picture he had painted over the other's canvas, or to whom he had sold it.

When Rushdie told me the story recently when I was interviewing him for the *Irish Times* it struck me as peculiarly apt, given both the kind of artist Salman Rushdie is (the painted mother, the harsh father, the Disney creatures poking their anthropomorphic noses through the backdrop) and his present circumstances. He too has disappeared behind a work of art.

We met in the stillness of a post-Christmas bank holiday afternoon. I had not seen him for ten years. He had changed. How would he not? Yet the differences in him were a surprise. I had expected that he would be angry, tense, volubly outraged. However, what I sensed most strongly in him was an immense and somehow sustaining sadness. The confident, exuberant, funny thirty-five-year-old I met ten years ago had taken on a *gravitas* that was at once moving and impressive.

On February 14 Rushdie will have been in hiding for four years. The *fatwa,* or death sentence, imposed on him by Ayatollah Khomeini in retribution for his "blasphemous" novel *The Satanic Verses,* is still in force, backed up by the offer of $2 million in blood money to anyone who should be successful in murdering him. Over the years the world has accommodated itself to this extraordinary situation, but nevertheless it is, as Rushdie himself insists, a scandal.

I began by asking if he could discern any shift in the political situation in Iran that would give him hope that the *fatwa* might be lifted.

"I used to spend a lot of my time trying to keep up with the internal struggles there, but then I thought, to hell with that. It's not my business to understand the internal politics of Iran. The banning of my book and the imposition of the *fatwa* is a terrorist act by the state of Iran, and my business is simply to make sure that the Iranian state is dealt with on that basis, and is obliged to alter its position."

Does he have any contact with people in Iran—people in power? "There have been occasions when so-called intermediaries have popped up out of the woodwork, claiming to have great contacts in Iran. What tends to happen is that I talk to them for a couple of weeks and then they disappear and I never hear from them again.

"The question all these people ask is, What reparations would I be prepared to make? But my view is, who is injuring whom here? It's not for me to say I will withdraw *The Satanic Verses*. The whole issue is that a crime has been committed against the book."

How did the book come to the attention of the mullahs in the first place?

"Well, I think . . ." A hesitation, and a low chuckle; his delight in the rich absurdity of human affairs is one thing that has not changed over the years. ". . . I think it started in Leicester."

So I have my headline: *It Started in Leicester.*

"It does seem the first rumblings against the book started in a mosque or council of mosques there. They circulated selected lines and passages from the book to show how terrible it was. From there, it spread around Britain and out to India and Pakistan and Bangladesh, where there were riots and people were killed." There are a number of legends about how the book came to Khomeini's attention. There is a passage in the novel about an Imam in exile who is not unlike Khomeini, and there is a view that he took exception to it. "I don't find that very convincing because the book did not exist in a Farsi edition, and there were no copies of the book available in Iran at that time anyway. It's since been admitted by quite high-ranking Iranian officials that Khomeini never saw a copy of the book; whatever he did he did on the basis of hearsay."

I ask the only question I have come prepared with: Does he feel the affair has made him into a purely political phenomenon?

"One of the oddest things for me about the business is that while *Midnight's Children* and *Shame* were in some ways quite directly political, or at least they used history as part of their architecture. I thought *The Satanic Verses* was the least political novel I had ever written, a novel whose engine was not public affairs but other kinds of more personal and cultural crises. It was a book written really to make sense of what had happened to me, which was the move from one part of the world to another and what that does to the various aspects of one's being-in-the-world. But there I am thinking I'm writing my most personal novel and I end up writing this political bombshell!

"Certainly it is a big problem that people by and large don't talk to me about my *writing*. Even the novel I wrote after *The Satanic Verses* [*Haroun and the Sea of Stories*], which was a great pleasure for me, and which individual readers responded to warmly, was received on the public level as if it were something to be decoded, an allegory of my predicament. But it's not an allegory; it's a novel.

"All the same I can't avoid the situation; while I don't see myself as this entity that has been constructed with my name on it, at the same time I can't deny my life: this is what has happened to me. It will of course to some extent affect my writing, not directly perhaps but yet in profound ways. I have always to some extent felt unhoused. I feel very much more so now."

Is this not a good, a *necessary* way for an artist to feel?

"We are all in some manner alone on the planet, beyond the community or the language or whatever; we are poor, bare creatures; it's no bad thing to be forced to recognize these things."

An irony of the affair not much remarked on is that *The Satanic Verses* is very sympathetic and tender toward the unhoused, the dispossessed, the deracinated—the very people, in fact, who rioted in the streets and publicly burned what they had been told was a blasphemous book. He nods, smiling, in a kind of hopeless misery. It is deeply painful for him that the people whom he has made his subject, and for whom he has a deep fondness, are the ones who hate him most, or hate at least that image of him fostered by fanatics in the Muslim world.

He is adamant that what is most important here is the integrity of the text. "When at the start of the affair I was able to contact friends and allies and they asked me what I wanted them to do, I said, Defend the text. Simply to make a general defense of free speech doesn't answer the attack; the attack is particularized. If you answer a particularized attack with only a general defense then to some extent you are conceding a point, you're saying, Oh yes, we recognize that it may be an evil book, but even an evil book must be allowed to exist. But it is not an evil book. So I have always been most grateful when people have tried to defend the text for that's at least as important to me as the defense of my life."

What interests me in Rushdie's fiction—in anyone's fiction—is not its public, political aspect, but the way in which in it the objective world is reordered under the pressure of a subjective sensibility. It struck me, rereading *The Satanic Verses* in preparation for this meeting, that the final section, a (relatively) realistic account of a father's death, is perhaps the most significant—and certainly the most moving—passage in the book, the moment toward which the whole work moves, no matter how fantastical what went before. Was this section grounded in personal experience?

"Very much. My father died of the same cancer that killed the character in the book. I was there when he died. He and I had always had a somewhat difficult relationship, and it was important for us to have some time together before the end. I felt a great moral ambiguity about using my father's death in that way, especially as it was so recent, but in the end I thought I would do it because it would be an act of respect. I was afraid that it might appear a stuck-on ending, but as it turned out it seemed to be just what the book needed, had been demanding."

He believes that one of the most important themes in the novel is loss: of parents, country, self, things which to a greater or lesser degree Rushdie himself has lost. Does he feel abandoned by those in the Muslim world who he might have thought would support him?

"Intellectuals in the Muslim community know the size of the crime that has been committed against the book. A few months ago a declaration of unequivocal support for me was signed by seventy or so leading Iranian intellectuals in exile, which was wonderfully courageous; after all, they are not receiving government protection, and in some cases, as a result of their support for me, their lives have been threatened by the Iranians.

"An important part of their statement was that blasphemy cannot be used as a limiting point on thought. If we go back to a world in which religious authorities can set the limits of what it is permissible to say and think, then we shall have reinvented the Inquisition and de-invented the whole modern idea of freedom of speech, which was invented as a struggle against the Church."

We turn to the subject of the book he is working on. "It's about someone who is thrown out of his family because of an unfortunate love affair. It begins with this expulsion from the family, and goes on to recount how he is forced to remake his life from scratch." We are back to the feeling of homelessness that weighs so heavily upon him.

He tells me the story of the lost portrait of his mother. "In my book, about a very different mother and a very different son, there is a similarly lost portrait, and one of the strands of the story is his finding this picture, and in this way the struggle there had been in life between mother and son continues beyond death."

The novel will be called *The Moor's Last Sigh,* which is a translation of the Spanish name of the place from which in 1492 the last Sultan of Granada, driven out of the city by the Catholic armies of Ferdinand and Isabella, looked back for a final time at the Alhambra palace.

"The idea of the fall of Granada is used throughout the book as a metaphor for various kinds of rupture. One can see Moorish Spain as a fusion of cultures—Spanish, Moorish, Jewish, the "Peoples of the Book"—which came apart at the fall of Granada.

"This was the only time in history when there was a fusion of those three cultures. Of course, one should not sentimentalize that entity, for the basis on which it existed was Islamic imperalism; Islam was clearly the boss, and the other religions had to abide by the laws. All the same, there was a fusion of cultures which since then have been to some extent each other's other. In that fusion are ideas which have always appealed to me, particularly now; for instance, the idea of the fundamentalist, totalized explanation of the world as opposed to the complex, relativist, hybrid vision of things."

The last sultan, Boabdil (Muhammad XI, d. 1527), was "weak," that is, he was a "poetic type"—"which means, I suppose, he was someone in whom all the cultures flowed and therefore was unable to take absolutist views; against him there was the absolutist Catholic Queen Isabella, and his own formidable mother, Aisha. As Boabdil paused on that last ridge. Aisha is reputed to have told him, "Yes, you may well weep like a woman for what you could not defend like a man."

"The story is a metaphor for the conflict between the one and the many, between the pure and the impure, the sacred and the profane, and as such is a continuation by other means of the concerns of my previous books. Boabdil's story is merely background—there is no direct 'historical' narrative— and is done rather like Sidney Nolan's series of Ned Kelly paintings.

"The book is grounded in my experiences of these past years, and what makes it particularly interesting for me is that this is true, not fiction; that this obscene thing could happen to me and my book, and could go on and cease to seem scandalous."

Rushdie feels that the reaction to the book was in part a result of the force of the political language of Iran. The Iranians saw the United States as the

Great Satan, and Britain as a satellite of the US, as a Like Satan, whereas the Jews were seen as being responsible for everything that is wrong in the world. "So when, in the mullahs' view, a Jewish American publisher hired a self-hating race-traitor and (British) wog to write a book to attack Islam, the 'conspiracy' was complete.

"The thing I didn't understand—or underestimated the force of—was that whereas in the Judeo-Christian tradition it is accepted that one may at least dispute whether good and evil are external or internal to us—to ask, for instance, Do we need such beings as God and the Devil in order to understand good and evil?—the parts of my book that raised this question represented something that it is still very hard to say publicly in the Islamic world; and to hear it said with all the paraphernalia of contemporary fiction was very upsetting for many people, to which I'm afraid my only answer is, That's tough—because this kind of thing needs to be said."

He was looking forward to going to Ireland, believing that in such a country, with its recent memories of colonialism, and which is still to some extent engaged in nation-building, it would be easier for him to be understood than in many other, more "progressive," countries. "Also, the knowledge that people have who live in countries where God is not dead is very different to that of people who live in countries where religion has died.

"I have always insisted that what happened to me is only the best-known case among fairly widespread, coherent attempts to repress all progressive voices, not just in Iran but throughout the Muslim world. Always the arguments used against these people are the same: always it's insult, offense, blasphemy, heresy—the language of the Inquisition. And you can widen your view and look for the same process beyond the Muslim world, where the same battle is continuing, the battle between the sacred and the profane. And in that war I'm on the side of the profane."

I ask, with some hesitation, if he would like to say something about his public declaration, two years ago, of his espousal of Islam, which he subsequently recanted. He flinched, as at the resurgence of an old pain.

"I feel I've had to undo that; I'll probably be saying that for the rest of my life.

"What happened was this. First of all, I was probably more despairing in that moment than I've ever been. I felt that there was no energy or enthusiasm in the world to do anything about my plight. Secondly, a thing which people sometimes don't understand is how painful it was for me to realize that the

people I had always written about were the very people who were now burning the book. The need in me to heal that rift was very profound—still is.

"Those two things came together—the despair, and the need to heal the
rift—and what I felt was, look, I'd better do something very large in order to
show these people whom I write about that I'm not their enemy; that, yes, I
do have a very profound dispute with the way in which the people who are
in power in Islam attempt to regulate their societies, but that maybe in the
end I could carry on that dispute more effectively from inside the room than
from outside it. I wanted to say, I am not outside the house of Islam throwing
stones at the windows, I'm inside it trying to build it and redecorate it. That
was the way I thought about it to myself at the time, but also I can see that in
that process there was a large effort to rationalize the doing of something I
thought might help.

"All I can say is that, having said what I said I felt sick with myself, for a
very long time, not because so many people who had been supporting me
found it bizarre or whatever—because my response to that was then, and
remains today, that anyone who thinks he can do better is welcome to come
and try.

"The problem for me was not other people's attitudes; the problem for me
was my own sense of having betrayed myself.

"The issue was that the thing that has enabled me to survive in this affair
has been that I have always been able to defend my words and writings and
statements: always I said what I said and wrote what I wrote because it was
what I felt, because it was what came out of me truthfully, and as a result I
could stand by it; but at *that* moment I felt I had done something that I
couldn't defend in that way, that did not represent my real feeling.

"There were good reasons, for it—the attempt at peacemaking and so on—
but it was not a statement I could put my hand on my heart and say I believed
in.

"I found it agonizing that my public statements were at complete odds
with my private feelings. That situation became untenable for me, and so I
had to unsay it; and now I've been unsaying it for two years. I'll probably
have to unsay it to the press in every country in the world.

"After what religion has done to me in the last four years, I feel much
angrier about what it does to people and their lives than I ever did before;
that's the truth. The writer who wrote *The Satanic Verses* was sympathetic to
Islam, was trying very hard to imagine himself into that frame of mind, albeit
from a nonbelieving point of view; I couldn't write that sympathetically now,

because of the very intimate demonstration I have had of the power of religion for evil; that is now my experience, and for me to try to write from some other experience would be false.

"I can still accept at a theoretical level the power of religion for good, the way in which it gives people consolation and the way in which it strengthens people, and the fact that these are very beautiful stories and that they are codifications of human belief and human philosophy, I wouldn't deny any of that—but in my life religion has acted in a very malign way; and in consequence my reactions to it are what you would expect."

I suggest that in the matter of his "conversion" he is likely to be harder on himself than anyone else would be. A great many people do things which they come to be ashamed of, but these actions will never get into the headlines.

"Of course, that's true. Martin Amis very soon after the *fatwa* was imposed said I had 'vanished into the front page,' and I think that it was a very accurate phrase. I have been trying to escape from the front page. What I find now is that the ideas that present themselves as things I want to write about are much less public, much less politically generated than they used to be. I have now had enough politics to last a lifetime. I now want to write about other things."

Have circumstances got easier for him, or has he got used, insofar as one can get used to the kind of life he has been forced to lead?

"They've got easier and more difficult. At the beginning, the first eighteen months, it was very hard for me to emerge from the safe place; it was a very sequestered time." In those early days did he have a garden, somewhere outside, where he could walk?

"Depends where I was; often, no. We had to be very careful because we had no knowledge of what was coming against us. It was a personally difficult time because of my marriage ending. That was the worst time, in terms of physical constraints. It's got a little easier now, even though it does still involve incredible paraphernalia, all this cloak and dagger stuff, but I'm not quite as confined as I was.

"On the other hand, psychologically I find it harder to tolerate now than I did then. When this began, nobody expected it to last very long. I remember the first day when the police came to offer me protection, they said, Let's just go away and lie low for a few days while the governments sort it out. People thought because what had happened was so outrageous it would have to be fixed and would be fixed very soon. This was why I agreed to dive underground, because everyone thought it would be just a matter of days. And here we are almost four years later.

"When it began I could say to myself, It's an emergency, and in such a case you do what is necessary to handle it, so I could accept the need for hiding, etc. Now, four years later, I realize it's not an emergency, it's a scandal. And what's worst about it is that people are behaving as if it were not a scandal."

Does he feel the British government is not doing enough?

"Well, let's face it, they saved my life. They are affording me in, I must say, a very ungrudging way, a level of protection that is equivalent to what the Prime Minister would get, and I'm just some novelist. To that extent they've done a great thing for me. But if we are to get to a position where none of this is needed, it's going to require not just a defensive act, but a positive act.

"As a result of the trips abroad I've been able to make there is a lot of interest in Europe and North America in doing something about the case. And I'm trying to make the government here see that this would be a wonderful moment for it to put itself at the head of that international effort."

Has he met John Major?

"No. I hope that might be rectified. It's a problem. This campaign requires practical acts and symbolic gestures. At that level, the fact the British Prime Minister has never allowed himself to be seen in public shaking my hand is an indication that the affair is being in some way downgraded. It's getting to the point where it's easier for me to meet the heads of other governments than the leaders of my own.

"Things are moving, however. The British government have now formally told the Iranians they will not normalize relations until the *fatwa* is canceled. Also, at the recent Edinburgh Summit the British delegation introduced into the conclusions of the summit a statement that all European nations should continue to pressurize Iran on the *fatwa*."

Was he very frightened at the start? Is he less frightened now?

"It's less now because the situation is less frightening. At first it wasn't a matter really of being frightened. When I first heard the news I thought I was dead. I thought I probably had two or three days at the most to live. That's beyond fear, it was the strangest thing I've ever felt.

"After that it was very shocking and unnerving to see the extent of the hatred that was being hurled at me; that was very disorienting, very bewildering. Then I came to the conclusion that I must not allow myself to be terrified;

the only answer to a terrorist is to say, I'm not scared of you. That was an extraordinary moment. I felt free."

Has the experience of the past four years changed him?

"Yes, it's changed me very much. It has hurt me a great deal. If you are on the receiving end of a great injury you are never the same again; you may not be worse, you may not be better, but you're never the same again. It made me feel everything I thought I knew was false. I was always very impatient— with the exception of writing, where I'm very patient—but now I'm able to take a longer view of things."

The experience must have affected the quality of his life, must have thinned it out. His reply is simple.

"My life has been wrecked."

Homeless Is Where the Art Is

Anonymous / 1994

From *The Bookseller* (UK) 15 July 1994. Reprinted by permission.

Salman Rushdie discusses his work in a remarkably forthcoming way. While some authors have an almost superstitious aversion to talking analytically about the creative process, he appears to be eager to unpick for the interviewer the threads that run through his narratives.

He describes, for instance, the various inspirations for "The Courter," the story that ends his collection *East, West* (Cape, October £9.99, 0 224 04134 7): how he had, like his hero (who is less successful with girls than he was), been joined by his parents in London for a time in the '60s; how his parents had brought over his *ayah* ("nurse," in the sense of the character in *Romeo and Juliet*), who had struck up a friendship with the porter at the flats where they lived; how he had based the porter on a different man, the office boy at the advertising agency where he worked in the '70s.

"The story is about language," Rushdie explains. "There's all sorts of comic business in it about the problems between Indian English and English English, and the ways in which people who seem to be speaking the same language can misunderstand each other. Another thing it's about is two kinds of love: the love of others and the love of home. The *ayah* in the story ends up having to choose between them, and chooses home. The narrator says that he has ropes pulling him in both directions, and he's determined not to choose. In that sense, he is quite like me."

He talks in detail also about "The Free Radio," one of the three stories in the first section ("East") of the book. It is about a young rickshaw driver who dreams of escaping to movie stardom in Bombay. The driver marries, foolishly in the opinion of the narrator, a young widow, and takes on her five children; and he agrees to have a vasectomy because of the promise that the government will give him a free radio as a reward. For months, while he is expecting his prize, he walks around town clutching an imagined radio to his ear.

The story, Rushdie says, is about the space between the driver's hand and his ear: the space in which he imagines. "I liked making real the metaphor of the story: the burden he has to carry, with a wife and five children sitting in the rickshaw. The other thing I liked was the incredibly nasty narrator: here was this sweet boy, having his story told by a sour old retired school- teacher. And yet, despite all the nastiness in him, he actually is very con- cerned about the rickshaw driver—who obviously cares about him too, because he writes him letters when he goes away."

This is a kind of writing that seems to owe more to Narayan than to, say, Márquez, who is more often cited as an influence on Rushdie. Readers com- ing to *East, West* and knowing the author's work only by reputation might be surprised by the human sympathy shown in these stories, their wit and light- ness of touch.

"There has been a kind of cloud hanging over my work for a while—and I'm not talking about the political cloud, I'm talking about the fact that it became rather fashionable to say that my writing was unreadable. Well, I don't think it ever has been. I hope that one of the things these stories might do is blow away that cliché. It would be very nice to have work that's read just as work, without being in the middle of some kind of geopolitical storm."

As he says, the collection shares the concerns of all his work: home, exile and change among them. The first stories in the book were produced at about the time when he was also writing *Midnight's Children* (1981); the last three were written this year. Yet the collection is coherent, with the stories all echoing and commenting on each other. For example, the first—and again Rushdie offers this insight—has a woman apparently petitioning to go to England but aiming to fail; the last has a woman coming to England but wanting to return home.

"I said to people when I started thinking of calling the stories *East, West* that the most important part of the title was the comma. Because it seems to me that I am that comma—or at least that I live in the comma." A slash might have worked too, perhaps. "But I don't feel like a slash. I feel more like a comma."

The examination of this piece of punctuation has been Rushdie's great project. "A lot of writers have a certain amount of baggage which they bring with them, which is the thing that makes them writers. In my case, it had to do with where I came from, and trying to lay claim to it and to understand it in a new way; and also to write about migration, and the metamorphoses implicit in that, or explicit."

This subject has inspired what critics have labelled Rushdie's "magic real- ism." He is wary of the term, believing that it has led people to emphasize the magical elements in his work at the expense of the realistic ones. He says that he is no longer fond of his first novel, *Grimus,* because it was set in a fantastical world, which encouraged his writing to descend into whimsy. But he insists that *Midnight's Children, Shame* and *The Satanic Verses* are realistic novels.

"There is a magic of the real, exposing which is a very important function of literature. In my mind, the use of surrealist techniques was always just a way through to that; it wasn't an end in itself. If Saleem in *Midnight's Children* has a certain sort of nose, it's to allow me to present a certain view of the world, through that nose."

There are no magic noses or flying people in Rushdie's next novel, *The Moor's Last Sigh,* scheduled for publication next autumn. Nor is it, despite having a title referring to the Moors' expulsion from Granada, a historical work. "Most of it takes place in India, and the last 50 or 60 pages are set in Spain, but in the present day. The fall of Granada is used only as a metaphor, as a story people tell, as a subject in a painting by one of the characters.

"I've always written about people who are somewhat outside the central body of society, in India as well as here, and this time I think I've probably found the ultimate fringe character. The central figure is the child of a marriage between an Indian Christian and an Indian Jew—and that makes him part of a very small community indeed."

He has begun to suspect that *The Moor's Last Sigh* will bring to an end the imaginative endeavor that began with *Midnight's Children.* If it does, the completion might be shown to be an effect on his literary career of the *fatwa* issued by Ayatollah Khomeini in February 1989. "I can't go to India at the moment, and that's one of the greatest pieces of damage," Rushdie says.

"This is a book that I conceived, in its essential aspects, long before the *fatwa,* and a lot of the journals and notebooks I'm using for it come out of the time I spent in India 10 years ago. It's very useful to have them.

"I could quite easily go on writing about India and Indian characters for the rest of my life. Exile doesn't defeat a writer in that way: those people continue to be inside you. I'm not saying I won't go on writing about them; what I am saying is that I don't want to become one of those writers for whom writing becomes a form of nostalgia. What I'd like to do is to live in the world that I'm in, and to see what that produces."

Can he, though, continue to feed the part of himself that produces imaginative work while living under a grotesque threat of assassination? "If it were to go on forever, that would be a problem. I have to say, though, that I hate the phrase 'in hiding.' It was a kind of media invention, but I never use it: it sounds so pusillanimous. I've never felt myself that that was what I was doing, and indeed I began immediately after the *fatwa* the process of regaining a life, which I'm slowly managing to do—much to the fury of certain parts of the press.

"No, I don't feel so cut off from the world any more. It's not like it was in the first couple of years, which really were very, very difficult. There are still enormous obstacles in my way, but I don't feel isolated."

He has, however, rarely had a chance in the past few years to talk about his work, except in so far as it deals with Muslim issues. Perhaps this inhibition is why he is so talkative now. "I've had to learn a different language, which is not the language in which books are discussed. I spent almost two and a half years in which I couldn't write, because I was having to engage in a global political campaign. You have no idea how long these things take to organise.

"The meeting with President Clinton, for instance, last October: we started planning that in February. There were ups and downs, yeses and nos, people to persuade: and I don't find it very easy getting on aeroplanes, so even getting there was difficult."

However, even before the *fatwa* it was hard to discuss Rushdie's work without getting involved in other issues, such as his personality, or the size of his advances, or his relationships with publishers and agents. *The Satanic Verses* attracted controversies that had nothing to do with his reference to the verses narrated to the Prophet by the Devil.

"People got irritated that I had been offered some money for my book. People got irritated that I changed publishers, even though what had happened is that my editor at Cape [Liz Calder] had left to start another publishing company. Nobody blamed her. I chose not to follow her; but that's no different, really.

"I know Andrew [Wylie] gets up a lot of people's noses, so there was that too." (Many people in literary London thought that Rushdie had behaved badly in ditching his agent, the much respected Deborah Rogers, to go to Wylie, Aitken & Stone, an agency with a rather more abrasive profile.) "But I have to say—and I think that it's important that I should say it in this interview—that without Gillon Aitken and Andrew Wylie my work would have been completely obliterated in these five years. No human beings have done more for me than those two. That is why this book is dedicated to them."

There were rumours, in the early days of the *fatwa,* of Rushdie spending hours watching television or playing computer games. Now he is working hard again, and has, since the start of the year, completed the first half of a novel, revised six short stories and written three new ones.

"Certainly there were periods when I felt very defeated, and didn't know what to do. *Haroun and the Sea of Stories* really helped me to fight my way past that: writing that book was salvation for me. I feel insanely proud of it, because it wasn't easy to write a happy book at that time."

The relationship of an artist's circumstances to the spirit of his or her work is not always an obvious one. Nevertheless, the reader of the last three stories in *East, West* must admire the poise, sanity and unsentimental depth of feeling of Rushdie's writing. Even the pain that is apparent in the story "The Harmony of the Spheres" is expressed without any trace of sentimentality.

"Pain is probably right: the major experience I've had over the past few years could be summed up as pain. But I would hate to write mawkishly. Somehow you've got to come through it into another kind of comedy.

"I hope the stories have a kind of *earned* lightness. It isn't easy; but then writing is never easy. Plenty of writers have it very tough. This happens to be my version of very tough. I make no special claim for it."

I Am Pessimistic about the Changes Occurring in India

Amrit Dhillon

From *India Today* 30 Sept. 1995: 136–39. Reprinted by permission.

Salman Rushdie has come a long way from the time Ayatollah Khomeini's *fatwa* compelled him to live in strict confinement. These days, Rushdie travels abroad much more, goes out for dinner, shops for his own clothes and has, at least, some semblance of a social life. Now he's back in the news with his new novel *The Moor's Last Sigh*. It's vintage Rushdie: set against the backdrop of contemporary India, the novel is a dazzling mix of satire and sadness, history and humour. And in what has become all too predictable, the applause has been accompanied by the fears of a ban.

At the center of the controversy is the book's unsparing portrayal of right-wing Hindu zealots in Bombay and a brilliantly etched caricature that many believe to be of Shiv Sena chief Bal Thackeray. Even before he had seen the cover, Thackeray gave his verdict. "He has no motherland," he said last fortnight. And, therefore, he had "no business" writing about people he had little knowledge of. As for a ban, Thackeray said he would defer his decision until he had read the book.

Foresight and ill-fortune intervened. The distributors, Rupa & Co., with-held the book's release in Bombay. Said its Delhi manager R. K. Mehra: "In view of the sensitive situation, we are exercising voluntary restraint." The death of Thackeray's wife last fortnight put the Rushdie controversy on the backburner.

Thousands of miles away, the controversy is yet to generate much heat. It's a measure of how much the security straitjacket around Rushdie has been relaxed that all it took for Copy Editor Amrit Dhillon to reach him was to take a short taxi ride from the office of his publishers, Jonathan Cape, to the elegant Halkin Hotel just off London's Hyde Park Corner. Rushdie, smartly attired, was waiting in the room with two policemen in tow.

He spoke on a range of issues: the "controversial" aspects of his latest novel; the future of secularism in India and how it feels to be exiled from his beloved Bombay. Asked what was the first thing he would do if the *fatwa*

167

against him was lifted, Rushdie said: "Catch the first plane to India." Excerpts from the interview:

Q: *It's ironical that first,* The Satanic Verses *was banned to appease Muslim sentiments and now your latest novel has been restricted to appease a section of Hindu sentiments.*

A: As I understand it, there are two kinds of problems. First, I hear this rumour about Sonia Gandhi being upset about the naming of a dog in the novel. And I gather that there is some attempt to have the book banned in the rest of India because there is a dog called Jawaharlal in the novel. I find it a rather ridiculous issue.

This is not a novel that sets out to ridicule the India that Nehru brought into being, but actually to lament the damage done to that vision of India in the succeeding years. Most of the leading characters in the novel are passionately in favour of the Independence movement except for one who is pro-British—an Indian character who is pro-British—and it is this figure, in order to annoy his family who are nationalists, who names his dog Jawaharlal.

It has to be seen in this context. It is the one anti-national character who does this to annoy and all the other major characters in the novel are annoyed by this. Given this background, it would be tragically ironic if people who claim to be protecting the flame of Nehru's memory should see this novel as being hostile to it. This is a point I wanted to make because I think that it is important that this is said in India before people get the wrong end of the stick; before people say, "There is a dog called Jawaharlal in the story, so it must be against him. End of story." Read the book and you will see. I hope that Sonia Gandhi or the Government, or whoever else it may be, understands that this is what is happening in the book.

To come to the Shiv Sena, it is quite plain that I feel that there are forces in Indian society that are transforming it in ways not always beneficial. And if you set a novel in Bombay and you set it in real history, then clearly it is difficult to avoid the events there and the political movements that exist there. In the novel, it's the behaviour and the political interventions of the party called the Mumbai Axis, that's probably more based on the Shiv Sena than the character Raman Fielding is based on Thackeray.

Now there is stuff that is an obvious joke. The cartoonist is fairly obvious in this connection. Although in the novel, the reason why I preserve the idea of a cartoonist is not so much to lampoon Thackeray as because the novel is about artists, and I wanted to make this contrast between the great artist and the cartoonist.

It would be slightly wrong of Thackeray to think that it was only based on him because, of course, his leadership of the Sena is an obvious historical fact. A novel is not a photograph. It does not operate the way in which even a newspaper operates. And so I would say that plenty of people, newspapers, journalists criticise Shiv Sena and Thackeray every day and in language far worse than anything found in my book.

I would have thought that the best thing that the Shiv Sena and Thackeray can do in order to prove their democratic bonafides is to step back. How many people are going to read this, how many votes are they going to lose as a result of this?

I know that there was an attempt to prevent the release of this movie in which Thackeray also believed himself to be portrayed. I know there were some violent attacks in which the director was attacked and the film was censored.

Q: *So there seems to be an increasing culture of intolerance in India.*

A: The India that came into being in 1947 was an India of which the three planks, broadly speaking, were secularism, democracy, and socialism. Now there seems to be a weakening of the democratic impulse, there's more censorship in the country. The growth of Hindu nationalism in the main but also growth of religious extremism of other kinds, both Muslim and Sikh, represent a real threat to the secular principles of this nation.

One can hear people talking about the need to rewrite the Constitution to desecularise it. And then, of course, in the economic sphere, the change in economic structure with the arrival of free-market economics in a very radical way . . . very dramatic. All these things seem to be changing the country so fundamentally that one could say that the country which came into being in 1947 is being transformed into something else.

Q: *The transformation in India that you talk about—are you pessimistic about it? What do you feel about the rise of communalism, the BJP?*

A: I am quite pessimistic. I am anxious not to be too pessimistic because the Indian electorate has repeatedly proved itself to be more sophisticated than most commentators. But broadly speaking, yes, I think I am pessimistic about it because I do not see a strong political force emerging against those ideas. I don't see a strong political force also in the intelligentsia. In large sections of it, there has been an unnerving desire to do business with communalist ideas and that is worrying. I think it is a perfectly proper function of people who care about India and write about it to express their misgivings and their fears and I have those misgivings and fears.

Q: *About three years after the* fatwa, *you announced that you had embraced Islam. Recently, you said that you regretted that decision. Why?*

A: It was the time when I felt very depressed and very abandoned and despairing. It was very easy for everybody to just blame me and not see any other problem. I thought that I must try and do something to say to ordinary Muslims everywhere that, "You have been told that I am this terrible enemy of yours and that I am not and I never was." And I did not know how to say that in a way that anybody would listen and thus it came from that and so it came from perfectly, I suppose, decent motives.

But it was the wrong thing to do because it put me into a place where I couldn't speak honestly about my feelings. The fact is that I am not an enemy of Islam—how could I be when my whole family are Muslims? It would be like being an enemy of my mother. But I am not a believer. I know it is very shocking in India where everybody has some kind of religious belief, but for me, I have never felt the need for that belief to help me explain the world.

Q: *How would you describe your emotional relationship with India?*

A: There is only one place for every human being and always only one place that gives you the feeling of being at home. I was born in Bombay and even now going to Bombay is the only time when I have the feeling of coming home.

By a strange and sad irony, given that I got paid quite a lot of money for *The Satanic Verses*—it was the first time really in my life that I was given a big paycheck—it has always been my idea to use a chunk of that money to buy myself a foothold in Bombay. Just so that I could go there and not have to stay with friends; not to have to stay in hotels. Just have a two-room flat that you could lock up, and when you go back you can open your own front door.

This is the first time in my life that I have ever felt like an exile. Until now, I felt like somebody who chose to live in England as many Indians have but who retained this connection with India. I didn't feel separated from it; I still don't feel separated from it but I have not been able to go there. It's *(The Moor's Last Sigh)* the first book I have written about India without going to India. Fortunately for me, on the many visits I have made before, I have kept very detailed notes, journals, and diaries.

Q: *It must be disappointing for you that India is going through such a rapid change and you are not there to witness it.*

A: It's more than disappointing. It's a great loss, as a writer, and if it were not for circumstances, I would be on the first plane. It's the thing I would most like to do.

Q: *Some years ago, you said that you foresaw the emergence of a new breed of Indian writers who will challenge the political system. This hasn't happened.*

A: I don't remember saying that. What I do remember saying is somewhat different. I mean, leaving aside the political challenge, when I came to India when *Midnight's Children* came out, there were writers who were somewhat older than myself. There was Anita Desai, R. K. Narayan, Raja Rao, all these figures. But in my generation, or younger, at that time I thought they were really very few. What I think is very interesting, in the fifteen years since that time, there is an enormous number of wonderfully gifted Indian writers in English.

Q: *Following the path set by you in* Midnight's Children?

A: Whether they exactly follow my path or not, I think it's probably true that *Midnight's Children* opened a door for some people. Its success encouraged a kind of world audience and big publishers to look towards other Indian writers. Also, it gave permission to people to write their own work. I sometimes felt that some Indian writers have kind of written their *Midnight's Children*-novel and once they've got it out of their system, they go on and write better novels. Rohinton Mistry, for instance, is a very fine writer. Vikram Seth, Amitav Ghosh, lots and lots of people. Mukul Kesavan is a young writer whose book I've said I think has a lot of promise. But I'd like to see the emergence of a really important woman writer. I think there is a kind of lack in that area. I would like to see 'A Suitable Girl.'

Q: *One of your characters says, "Embrace your fate. Rejoice in what gives you grief. That which you would flee, turn, and run towards it with all your heart. Only by becoming your misfortune, will you transcend it." Is this how you have been trying to cope with your ordeal?*

A: Somewhat, yes. I mean, not exactly, because you know you put it in the mouth of other characters and it becomes what other characters would say rather than you yourself. But in some way, it's been necessary to say all I've felt. I think the hardest thing has been for me to find a way of going on being myself. The *fatwa* and the events that followed could quite easily have pushed me, the writer, in different directions. These events could have made me more cautious, more frightened, more conservative as a writer. Or on the other extreme, they could have made me angrier, more bitter, more polemical as a writer. And I felt that the thing was not to be deflected in either direction. Not to allow myself to become defined by the *fatwa*.

Q: *What's your typical day like?*

A: I have a straightforward writer's day. By about half past nine, I'm writing, usually for about four or five hours a day. Then I do whatever I'm supposed to do. These days, it is a little less circumscribed than it used to be, in the sense that, I can get out.

Q: *How often do you go for dinner? Can friends come and see you?*

A: The one thing that is still very abnormal is that the place where I live is kept completely secret.

Q: *Even from closest friends?*

A: Yes. Just because I don't want to burden other people with the knowledge. But, in terms of going out, I don't do it that much—not nearly as much as the tabloid press would have you believe. The difference is that every time I do go out, there is a photographer and it ends up in the newspapers.

Q: *When you go out, what kind of precautions are taken?*

A: I shouldn't talk about it. I'm not really supposed to talk about it. Sufficient precautions are taken. The reason this has worked is that people don't know how it's done. There was an attempt by the Government of this country to imprison me and have the police force of this country become my jailors. Amazing, rather brilliant effort. It is very important to me to demonstrate that that attempt has failed. If there is a picture of me dancing at a party, it is my way of saying that they have not put me in a jail.

Q: *How many times have you moved house?*

A: I haven't counted. I can say it has been much less than people have speculated, but there's still been quite a lot. At least 30 or 40.

Q: *How many of your possessions can you take when you move?*

A: Well, not so many. One of the effects of this is that it taught me to write on a computer since I had to have a way of moving my office. This is the first book I've written on a computer. And I had to teach myself. I wasn't particularly attracted to it, was quite happy with my typewriter. Having switched, I can't understand why I didn't do it before. Just at the level of writing, this is the best piece of writing that I've ever done and I'm sure one of the reasons for this is the removal of the mechanical act of typing. I've been able to revise much more.

Q: *Who does your shopping?*
A: People do. One of the hardest things in the world is to go shopping in your mind. You have a picture of a supermarket in your head that's five years out of date. There used to be the case when I couldn't buy my own clothes. It's just like being a baby because you have to get somebody to buy your clothes. That hasn't happened to me since I got into long trousers. But now if I needed to buy myself a toothbrush, I could. One of my great delights used to be to go and browse in bookstores. But it's true that because I have friends in publishing, people were able to get me books.

Q: *What about your son?*
A: Do you mind if we don't talk about that.

Q: *Have you been able to have relationships with women?*
A: I have.

Q: *At the moment, are you involved in a relationship?*
A: Maybe.

Q: *What do you mean "maybe"? I believe you are.*
A: That may well be. As the character says in *Haroun and the Sea of Stories,* it maybe so or maybe no. I have always been very secretive about my private life and I have more reason now.

Q: *Is she coping well with these circumstances?*
A: Like who would that be?

Q: *It's quite incredible—how you've been able to go on writing. If you had to describe where you get the strength of mind and strength of will to go on writing . . .*
A: It's my job, you know. I think I've been very fortunate in the kind of writer I am in that I'm a prose writer. Suppose I was a playwright. Supposing *The Satanic Verses* was a play. First of all, it would have been taken off; second, no management would have put on a play by me again. Supposing it had been a movie. I would have been unable to make another movie. Writing a book is low-technology form—it doesn't require a high capital investment,

does not require a theatre, doesn't require a film set. Also, I have a stubborn streak. If there's an attempt to silence a writer, the best thing a writer can do is not be silenced. If somebody is trying to stifle your voice, you should try and make sure it speaks louder than before.

Q: *Are you hopeful that the* fatwa *will be lifted?*

A: I always felt that there was a kind of double-track process happening there. One part of it is the political campaign against the *fatwa,* and the other is my own private efforts to regain something like a liveable life.

Earlier on this year, there were a lot of signs that the Iranians were about to relent. When Rafsanjani was in India, he made various statements about how he was not going to send anyone to pursue me; foreign minister Ali Akbar Velayati was interviewed by the BBC and he said similar things. It was all done as a media thing. But five months ago, the European Union asked the Iranians to give this statement formally in writing, but so far it hasn't happened. I believe there is a further meeting on this soon. If we are lucky, they'll produce the statement. If they do not, then it will become necessary to continue the campaign.

Q: *So are you mentally prepared?*

A: I just feel that the campaign has to go on for as long as it has to go on, because there are very important points of principle involved in that: the right of a person to live in his own country without being threatened from abroad.

It would be wonderful if the Indian Government felt able to speak up in this matter. The Indian Government's attitude has been completely silent as far as I know. There have even been very strange events in this country; I've been informed that I am *persona non grata* at Indian institutions, at the cultural center. I asked the director if this was the case. He said while it was nothing to do with him because he was only following orders, it was more or less the case. It's puzzling to me that I should spend my life writing about India and with some success and being so oddly unwelcome.

Q: *Have you thought of making a secret trip to India?*

A: How do you do it? I've got to get a visa.

Playboy Interview: Salman Rushdie

David Sheff / 1995

From *Playboy* magazine (April 1996: 49–62, 165). Copyright © 1996 by Playboy. Reprinted by permission. All rights reserved.

It reads like a scene out of an Ian Fleming novel: First, there's a phone call. "When you arrive in London," the voice at the other end warns, "an agent of the special branch will contact you. He will instruct you where and when the meeting will take place."

Then, in London, there's a second call. It's the special agent from Scotland Yard. "Please be at this address at two P.M. tomorrow," he says, adding with typical British understatement, "We presume you will be alone."

At the designated address, the special agent, dressed in a nondescript gray sports coat, asks for identification and does a quick search for weapons. "I'm sure you understand," he says. "We can't be too careful."

But this isn't fiction. This is real life—Salman Rushdie's real life. For the past seven years, it's been Scotland Yard's job to keep Rushdie alive, as the result of a $5 million bounty that was placed on his head by fanatic Muslims.

Rushdie has been a marked man since the publication of his 1988 novel *The Satanic Verses.* The novel attracted praise and prizes (including Britain's Whitbread award as the year's best novel), but two chapters, in which Rushdie re-creates seminal events in the history of the Muslim religion, incurred the wrath of Islamic leaders around the world. Those chapters involve the prophet Muhammad. Included with the retelling of sacred history are extravagant splashes of sex and fantasy. Pious Muslims believe the Koran to be the word of God as dictated by the archangel Gabriel through Muhammad. It's believed to have been written, perfect and unaltered, by the prophet's scribes. But in the dreams of one of Rushdie's characters, a scribe makes a deliberate mistake in the transcription in order to determine how divine Muhammad is. When the prophet reads over the text, the mistake goes unnoticed. The book was banned in India, Pakistan, Egypt, and South Africa.

In January 1989 an angry Muslim crowd in Bradford, England burned a copy of the book. A month later, six people were killed in anti-Rushdie riots in Islamabad, Pakistan. The British Embassy in Karachi was bombed (and a Pakistani guard killed) and more than 100 were injured during a demonstra-

175

tion in Dacca, Bangladesh. It was on Valentine's Day 1989 that Rushdie learned Iran's Ayatollah Ruholla Khomeini had ordered him killed. The book's publisher tried to diffuse the death sentence (called a *fatwa*) with a statement that the author had not meant to insult the Muslim people. But the ayatollah responded with his own announcement: "It is incumbent on very Muslim to employ everything he has got, his life and his wealth, to send Rushdie to hell." A price was put on his head: $1 million, which has been upped to more than $5 million.

Rushdie went into hiding and the book was pulled from shelves—even, at first, in America. More violence followed. Two bookstores in Berkeley, California were firebombed. An Arab terrorist accidentally blew himself up in a Paddington hotel before he was able to attack Rushdie. There were a series of expulsions from Britain of other Iranians who were suspected of plotting against the author. Finally, Rushdie's Japanese translator was murdered, his Italian translator was injured by a knife-wielding assailant at his Milan apartment and his Norwegian publisher, a close friend, barely survived a shooting.

Scotland Yard, called in to protect him, moved Rushdie from one safe house to another. At first he wasn't allowed to see anyone, including family and friends. His wife, the writer Marianne Wiggins, who had originally gone into hiding with him, left. A year later they were divorced. Rushdie was devastated by his new situation. As a writer, he says he was used to solitude, but he missed his freedom and ordinary life: "walking down a street, browsing in a bookshop, going to a grocery store or a movie." He couldn't leave the house without making elaborate preparations and he couldn't travel. (British Airways and other carriers refused to allow him on their planes because, they claimed, their employees and passengers would be endangered.)

Meanwhile, most writers and many politicians supported him, but some prominent voices dissented, even if they were critical of the death sentence. Novelist John le Carré criticized Rushdie for inviting more bloodshed by his refusal to withdraw the book. Roald Dahl denounced Rushdie as "a dangerous opportunist" and Germaine Greer reportedly called him "a megalomaniac." Wiggins, Rushdie's then estranged wife, told the *Sunday Times,* "All of us who love him, who were devoted to him, who were friends of his, wish that the man had been as great as the event. He's not." (Wiggins later denied the interview ever took place.) New York's John Cardinal O'Connor and Britain's then chief rabbi, Lord Immanuel Jakobovits, deplored what they saw as an insult to Islam. Far more surprising, former president Jimmy Carter wrote in *The New York Times* that, although he condemned the *fatwa,* Western leaders should let the world know that "there is no endorsement of the insult to the sacred belief of our Muslim friends."

Most writers, however, supported Rushdie and his right to free speech. Norman Mailer, Milan Kundera, William Styron, and Czeslaw Milosz were among those who appealed to world leaders to pressure Iran. Even clerks in American bookstores rallied to his defense, insisting that their employers carry *The Satanic Verses* despite the fact that it put them at risk.

Meanwhile, in hiding, Rushdie became desperate. At one point, in 1990, he attempted to make peace by announcing he had become a believing Muslim, but his conversion was short-lived.

When Rushdie made a secret trip to the U.S. in 1992, he was shunned by President George Bush. He fared far better in 1993 when President Bill Clinton hosted him at the White House.

The historic meeting came about after a full-court press by higher-ups in the Clinton administration, including George Stephanopoulos, and pressure from Mailer, Styron, and Arthur Miller. Other advisors felt a meeting would be a mistake, and members of the National Security Council expressed concern that Rushdie's visit could radicalize anti-American sentiment and jeopardize the Middle East peace process. At the final hour, the president was convinced to meet with Rushdie, who was ushered into the White House for a brief huddle.

The fallout began immediately. The head of Iran's judiciary announced that President Clinton had become "the most hated person before all Muslims of the world." Clinton, reportedly surprised by the intensity of the response, attempted to placate his critics, saying he "meant no disrespect" to Muslims.

Regardless, Clinton's support (and support from Britain's John Major) helped Rushdie push other leaders to pressure Iran with sanctions and negotiations. Now the European Union has taken up the cause. Rushdie's case has been brought up at many levels of meetings with Iranian officials, and its peaceful resolution is a condition for normalizing relationships between Western nations and Iran. There have been signs that the *fatwa* may be revoked, though the Iranians have refused to rescind it officially.

After his first two years in hiding, Rushdie began to write again, saying, "If I can't write, then, in a way, the attack has been successful." He has published *East, West,* a book of short stories, and a children's book called *Haroun and the Sea of Stories,* which received excellent reviews. In this fanciful story, imagination is the enemy of authoritarian rulers.

Besides writing, Rushdie began to use his unique position to fight for free speech and to champion other writers who have been targeted because of their ideas. Showing up unannounced at events, he has spoken out about Turkish, Nigerian, Chinese, and Algerian writers who have been imprisoned or otherwise persecuted for their views. He has supported Taslima Nasrin, a Bangladeshi physician, newspaper columnist, and author, who is under death threats from Muslim clerics and faces criminal charges from the government for allegedly criticizing the Koran.

Rushdie began work on an epic new novel set in India. It's a country he knows well—he was born in Bombay in 1947, just a few months before India won its independence and the subcontinent was partitioned into India and Pakistan. Despite that backdrop, Rushdie says he had an uneventful childhood until he reached 14, when he was sent to school in England and first encountered racism.

Like his businessman father, Rushdie attended King's College, Cambridge, where he majored in history and was involved in theater. He graduated in 1968 and joined his parents, who, as Muslims, had emigrated to Karachi, Pakistan. He wrote a teleplay adaptation of Edward Albee's *Zoo Story* for the new government-operated television station, but it was censored for containing the word pork. Feeling stifled, he returned to England.

Back in England he wrote ad copy and dabbled in experimental theater. He completed his first novel, *Grimus,* in 1973. It received good reviews, but it was his next novel that brought him international acclaim. *Midnight's Children* won the 1981 Booker McConnell Prize, Britain's most prestigious literary award. It is an epic story that focuses on the hopes born with Indian independence. That book was followed by *Shame,* a satire based on Pakistan, which further established Rushdie as one of the reigning "world storytellers," as *The New York Times* described him.

Rushdie's first marriage ended in divorce in 1987. He has a son from that marriage, Zafar, now 15. His marriage to Wiggins was reportedly in trouble even before the *fatwa.*

Recently, Rushdie has taken the first steps toward coming out of seclusion with several advertised appearances. "It's been seven years since I have been able to tell my readers where I would be and where they could come to talk to me. It's nice to be back," he says. Still, Scotland yard's presence is always apparent—there are metal detectors, guards and bomb specialists at all of Rushdie's public appearances.

True to Rushdie's history, his latest novel, *The Moor's Last Sigh,* has already caused headlines. This time, members of Shiv Sena, a militant right-wing Hindu group based in Bombay, have called for the book to be banned because of a character who is an obvious parody of their leader, political cartoonist–turned–Hindu nationalist Balasaheb Thackeray. While the book has been withheld in most of India, its publisher has managed to forestall an official ban. None of this has stopped the book from climbing best-seller lists in every country where it has been released (it arrived in bookstores in America in January).

Playboy tapped Contributing Editor David Sheff, who has conducted dozens of "Playboy Interviews," to speak with Rushdie. Here is Sheff's report:

"Despite the cloak-and-dagger routine required to meet him, Rushdie didn't appear the least bit nervous or concerned. He cares deeply about many issues—besides his fiction, he has written essays on many topics—but his foremost concern, for obvious reasons, is the right of writers to express themselves without repression or the fear of reprisals. While we were speaking about these issues, there was a knock on the door. An associate told Rushdie the news that Ken Saro-Wiwa, a Nigerian writer and dissident who had been arrested and sentenced to death for a trumped-up murder charge, had been executed. It was a bitterly sad moment. Rushdie, who had that week written a speech imploring world leaders to do whatever was required to save Saro-Wiwa, was near tears. After some time passed, he spoke with palpable anger. 'What must we do before no writer will be able to be murdered for writing?' he asked. 'What must we do so that this never happens again?' "

Playboy: How have these years in hiding changed you?

Rushdie: When I was younger, I was quite excitable. I waved my arms a lot and talked too much. I was more argumentative. I feel calmer because of a sense of who I am, a sense of what is in my heart. It comes from facing the big stuff—facing the great realities of life and death, and who you are and why you did what you did. You find out what you think about yourself when your innermost core is under attack. The worst moment came in 1990 when I lost who I was.

Playboy: That was the time you announced you had converted to Islam. Had you actually converted or were you trying to placate those who were threatening your life?

Rushdie: Not so much to placate them, but to show to the people who viewed me as some kind of terrible enemy that I wasn't one. It mostly had to do with despair and disorientation. I had lost my strength and felt completely bereft. Many of my friends pointed out that it was the stupidest thing I had ever done in my life. But I had hit bottom, and maybe it was necessary to hit bottom.

Playboy: Was hitting bottom brought on by the fear of being killed?

Rushdie: No. It was brought on by having done something I didn't believe in. I had given up who I was. I could no longer speak if I had been converted. I was supposed to be reverent, but didn't know how to be. I didn't know how to be devout, for God's sake. But by depriving myself of what was, in fact, my nature, I showed myself what my nature was.

Playboy: And so you thereafter recanted your conversation.

Rushdie: Yes. I made strenuous steps to get out of the false position and immediately felt clearer about everything. From that point on, I felt that I would fight for what I believed, and what I believed was what I was.

Playboy: Had you initially been reluctant to fight back against the *fatwa*?

Rushdie: It's hard to exaggerate the extent of the political and public pressure put on me not to fight back. That's one thing that had brought me to such a low point. I had listened to the purveyors of public opinion. Every time I tried to defend my work, I was accused of making trouble again. The only thing I was ever supposed to say in those days was that I was sorry. But I didn't feel sorry. I felt as if the crime was being committed against me, not by me. And so it was. I decided I would speak out and fight, and I decided I would not convince everyone. It was a great liberation to realize you don't have to convince everyone—in fact, you cannot. I decided I would not apologize and would write what I write. If you don't like it, the hell with you.

Playboy: Before the announcement of the death sentence, there was the banning of the book and other protests. Did you feel in danger?

Rushdie: No, but things began to change when the book was burned. Something exploded in my head. I've never been so angry in my life. The image of that burning book enraged me in my deepest places. They nailed it to a post, then set fire to it. They crucified and then burned it. Standing next to the burning book in a famous photograph was this little man looking so proud of himself, so smug, so righteous. I had rarely seen so ugly a photograph. Until that point I felt that my best defense was the normal arguments—to explain the book, to get people to read it. For a long time I took that position: The book—i.e., the work of art—speaks for itself. But when the work of art was nailed to a post and set on fire, it occurred to me that maybe I should speak for the work of art. That is when I began to argue and to confront various Muslims involved in the attack on the book. But although I was angry as hell, I had no sense of danger.

Playboy: When did you first hear about the *fatwa*?

Rushdie: I got a call on my way out the door one morning. I had arranged previously to do an interview on CBS television. Journalists asked me about it and I was bewildered. One journalist said, "Oh, don't worry about this Khomeini character. He condemns people to death all the time. He condemns the president to death every Friday. Forget it." And I thought, Oh well. Maybe that's right. Maybe this is just hot air and it will blow away by tomorrow. But it didn't blow away. It became clear that it wasn't some rhetorical flourish.

Playboy: You quickly issued an apology.

Rushdie: Yes, but I didn't write it. At that point, people involved with the British government—I won't say who—informed me that they were talking with the Iranian government. I was given to understand the situation would be resolved if I would sign a statement they wrote. It was constructed to get a quick fix. At that point everybody desired the quickest fix possible. Remember, I had never been in any position like this before. When the government says to you, "OK, here is the deal: You make this statement and the death sentence will be canceled tomorrow and everything will go back to normal," you do it. Especially if the alternative is that you cannot go home or see your child. You have no idea what the hell is going on. You think you might be dead in a day or two. So this statement was put out in my name.

Playboy: But Khomeini refused to reverse the order and a price was put on your head.

Rushdie: Yes. It's an odd thing to have a price on your head. At the same time, though, the reward has never been a real problem. The real threat has never come from people who are trying to claim the money.

Playboy: Does the real threat come from Muslim fanatics?

Rushdie: Not them, either. The only real threat has come from the Iranian government itself, and it is the Iranian government that remains the danger. It would be foolish not to recognize that there is a small risk from a fanatic. But there has been no evidence, over this whole period, of any real threat from anyone other than the government.

Playboy: Yet Khomeini said that "it is incumbent on every Muslim" to kill you.

Rushdie: Nobody was interested. Iranians have tried to get other Muslim countries involved, but nobody else wants to. Even the hard-line Islamic states such as Sudan are not interested. The Islamic leader there, Turabi, made explicit statements to the general public that the *fatwa* is against Islam. I mean, it's not that they like me, but they don't believe I should be killed.

Playboy: Who in the Iranian government is behind the attacks?

Rushdie: People under the direction of the Iranian intelligence ministry.

Playboy: Why was the *fatwa* continued after the ayatollah died?

Rushdie: It was political. Partly, Iran wanted an easier target after its defeat by Saddam Hussein—though I didn't turn out to be an easy enough target, apparently. Most of all, the Iranian leaders thought they would strengthen their position as leaders of the Muslim world if they killed this enemy of their people. Yet now many Muslim intellectuals and academics have changed their opinions of the book; they no longer view it as blasphemous. The fact is, the reason I did so much arguing in the beginning is because the book, considered properly, would not even have been banned. The book was banned and the *fatwa* was ordered because of rumors.

Playboy: What did you mean when you said, earlier after the *fatwa,* that you wished you had written a book more critical of Islam?

Rushdie: It struck me that a religious leader who arbitrarily condemns people to death and is willing to resort to international terrorism to carry out the sentences probably merits a little criticism.

Playboy: When the death sentence was announced, did you go into complete isolation?

Rushdie: Yes.

Playboy: We read that you became a television addict—watching endless *Dynasty* returns.

Rushdie: You say things to journalists as a joke and they become part of the myth. It's true that it was very difficult to see anybody for the first couple years. Later I was told by people who came into Scotland Yard that the degree to which my freedom was circumscribed at the beginning was completely unnecessary.

Playboy: Why was it unnecessary?

Rushdie: They don't believe that I needed to be so sequestered in order to be kept safe. There is a difference between protecting people and concealing them. For a long time I was offered concealment rather then protection. This has slowly changed, partly because of my argument that if I am seen to have been locked away for the rest of my life, the aggressors have won—the *fatwa* has worked. They didn't have to kill me if they succeeded in silencing me. It was a guarantee that the technique would be used again. Make a threat and get the other side to shut up their own people. That would be dreadful.

Playboy: When you did go out, were you paranoid, looking over your shoulder?

Rushdie: The opposite, really. I have spent a great deal of time reassuring other people. I can't tell you how many newspaper articles there are about me in which the journalist gets very upset when a nearby car backfires. The backfiring car is a kind of motif for these people.

Playboy: Didn't you ever jump when you heard one?

Rushdie: No. In the stories about these backfiring cars, it's always mentioned that I did not twitch. One of the writers called this denial. It was not. It was knowing the sound of a backfiring car. So I spent a lot of my time telling other people that there was nothing to worry about.

Playboy: Yet there was something to worry about.

Rushdie: When you know what there is to worry about, you also know what there isn't to worry about. If you're talking about a professional hit, you know you are safe in certain situations. I came to understand what was risky and what wasn't. It was not risky to be eating in a café, because terrorists know that the risk of being identified and captured is great. We are safe in this room, because even if there were a guy with a submachine gun standing in the street outside, he would not enter this building to attack me, because he doesn't know what he would meet. There is zero risk here.

Playboy: Did you have nightmares?

Rushdie: No. I did think in the beginning that I probably would die quite soon. You live with that. Yet the question of fear was not an issue. There was initially shock, which was followed by bewilderment and by a kind of loss of balance. Then this was replaced by a kind of single-mindedness, resolve and determination. Fear has not been relevant.

Playboy: Did you ever consider changing your identity?

Rushdie: It was never offered and I would not have been interested.

Playboy: Did you ever use a disguise?

Rushdie: There was one ridiculous occasion when they offered me a wig. I looked ridiculous, but I decided to try it out on a London street. I got out of a car in the wig and there were all these stares and comments: "There is Salman Rushdie in a wig." It was so ludicrous that I determined I would never succumb to that kind of thing again. I wore a hat and occasionally dark glasses and I began to venture out a bit more.

Playboy: British Airways and some other airlines would not allow you to fly on their planes. Is that still true?

Rushdie: It's getting better. The fact is, I've flown all over the world on all sorts of airlines and nobody has ever had the faintest bit of trouble as a result.

Playboy: Do you understand their fears that there would perhaps be some nervous passengers?

Rushdie: Well, nothing has happened on the 17 different airlines I've flown, so I don't understand it, no. When people recognize me on airplanes they are incredibly friendly. They have their picture taken with me and ask me to sign their menus. The fact is, airlines are supposed to have good security precautions and either they do or they don't. When I get on a plane, just like when any other person gets on a plane, it is made certain that proper precautions are taken. So actually it's safer on planes.

Playboy: What was your reaction when your translators and publishers were attacked?

Rushdie: I was devastated. It was appalling and tragic. It happened long after the initial declaration of the *fatwa,* too, so there had been a sense that surely it was safe now. These attacks showed that to be untrue. It was terrible and so senseless. In each case, the book was already published. It wasn't that they were going to shoot the translator and stop him from translating the book; it was finished. So what was it for?

Playboy: Did you feel responsible?

Rushdie: I did—I knew I was the one who was meant to be murdered. It was such a tragedy, such a waste. At the same time, when they attacked William Nygaard, my publisher in Norway of 15 years who had become a good friend, I was able to call him in the hospital. The first thing he said was that he didn't want me to feel responsible. He wanted me to know he was extremely proud to be the publisher of *The Satanic Verses* and he would publish it again if given the choice. But you cannot help but feel responsible. He hates to be called heroic, because he says he was just doing his job. So were the other publishers and many other individuals. Immediately after this began, some of the bookstore chains in America pulled the book off their shelves, claiming they were protecting their staffs. But their staffs refused to be protected in that way. That act of heroism got the book back on the shelves. So did the actions of the writer Stephen King, which people don't know about. A lot of literary writers received credit for the way they stood up for me—the Susan Sontags and Don DeLillos and Julian Barneses. But King has not. According to people inside the book chains, he was incensed and did a great deal of arguing on behalf of *The Satanic Verses*. He went so far as to threaten the chains that he would pull his books off their shelves if my book was not on them. He also apparently talked to other best-selling writers to get their support.

Playboy: Was King a friend?
Rushdie: I have never met him. But I certainly owe him one.

Playboy: Amid your many supporters, there were also some surprising critics. How do you respond to them?
Rushdie: Whom are you referring to?

Playboy: John le Carré, Roald Dahl, Germaine Greer.
Rushdie: That's quite a roll call, isn't it? If those people were all together in a room, I'd prefer to be in a different one, OK? But there were so many supporters. It's worth emphasizing that had it not been for their extraordinary campaign and support, I would very possibly not have found the strength to face this thing. People rose to the occasion in extraordinary ways. Some were my friends, but many were not. I didn't know Arthur Miller when he spoke up. I didn't know Don DeLillo. I didn't know Norman Mailer. Some of the ones who were old friends of mine, including Julian Barnes, did more for me personally than I can ever say. So had it not been for this army of people getting it right, I might be more upset about the small handful who got it wrong. It may be wrong to speak ill of the dead, but Roald Dahl, for one, was a bastard. He was a dreadful, horrible old man, a racist somewhere to the right of Hitler. The only thing worse than being attacked by Dahl would be to be his friend.

Playboy: What about le Carré?
Rushdie: Somehow I wasn't upset about le Carré, and I think it's because

he's not a writer I cared enough about. I have a terrible feeling he may have reacted the way he did because of a review I once wrote of one of his books—a bad review.

Playboy: And Germaine Greer?

Rushdie: Well, Greer has made a lifetime habit of stabbing her friends in the back, so why would she stop now? She has since claimed to have been misquoted and misunderstood, but Germaine has spent her life claiming she was misquoted and misunderstood.

Playboy: How do you respond to the attacks from the right-wing English press?

Rushdie: I must say I have been more surprised by the venom in the attacks against me from non-Islamic sources than from Islamic ones. Fanatics behave like fanatics; they are acting in character. But I never expected that other people, even those whose politics were unlike mine, would take this opportunity to kick so hard when I was down. It has been a harsh lesson. I used to get upset, but I learned to take them with a grain of salt. The fact is, despite this extraordinary vendetta, my detractors have failed to convince the British public that I am a bad fellow. Whenever I go anywhere, I am invariably recognized, and people are fantastically supportive.

Playboy: One writer said that it's too bad you weren't a nice guy like John Updike. It would have been much easier to defend you.

Rushdie: But I am a nice guy like John Updike. It was just easier for some people to pretend that I was not. So there was an extraordinary attempt to destroy my character, and like all the other attempts, it didn't work.

Playboy: Among the political leaders who criticized you was Jimmy Carter. Did that surprise you?

Rushdie: I was shocked about Carter. However, he's since sort of made an attempt to back off that stand. I know people who asked him about it. He told them that he's a little sheepish about what was said. I never saw the text, and there is a problem of reporting that gets skewered. In this case, I am disposed to let it slide.

Playboy: Is it true that President Bush and his administration refused to meet with you or take a firm stand in your support?

Rushdie: Yes. I don't know why. Somebody suggested that it might have been because at that stage the Iranians knew where all the bodies were buried in the Iran-Contra business. Maybe people didn't want to upset that too much.

Playboy: Did you expect a change when Clinton became president?

Rushdie: There was a great change. However, it was disappointing that the Republicans viewed this through partisan eyes. Republicans as well as Democrats should be able to agree that we don't kill people because we don't like what they write.

Playboy: How difficult was it to meet Clinton?

Rushdie: It took a lot of lobbying on the part of my supporters in America. John Major also helped pave the way. He believed it would be helpful if I could meet Clinton.

Playboy: Were you disappointed when Clinton seemed to waffle in his support after the meeting, almost apologizing for it?

Rushdie: There was a kind of wobble, yes, but I have to say that the administration has remained very helpful. The meeting with Clinton was of enormous political consequence in Europe. It immediately unlocked all the gates to power here. Because of Clinton, seeing me stopped being uncool. Suddenly they were all queuing up to meet me—all the prime ministers and presidents. There has been a dramatic change in the position of the Iranians.

Playboy: How has it changed?

Rushdie: In continuing conversations between the European Union and Iran, Iran keeps putting up straws in the wind. They have said the *fatwa* will not be carried out, though they refuse to put it in writing. But the tide has changed. They have woken up to the fact that they're broke, they have no friends in the world and they need help. This issue gets in their way wherever they go. Wherever they go for meetings, they spend two thirds of the time being asked about me. And it's a pain in the neck. So they want to end this crisis, but have so far refused to sign a formal agreement.

Playboy: Perhaps they're just trying to get out of this quietly, while saving face.

Rushdie: But the European Union has said that a minimum requirement to end such a large crisis is a formal agreement. I agree, because assurances from Iran mean nothing. We need a document that they can be held account-able to, not something they can deny tomorrow. I have a feeling that we may be only two or three steps away from that. Meanwhile, the situation has changed. I've been much more open recently. I've deliberately tried to prove that the situation has changed by doing ordinary things such as book signings that are announced in advance.

Playboy: There still has been heavy security at such events.

Rushdie: Not by the standards of what it was a year ago. Scotland Yard is still careful, because it has to be until it's actually settled. It is not only my safety that's an issue. If it were, I would dispense with the security precautions at this point. I am tired of being hemmed in. But Scotland Yard continues to respond to what it considers to be the worst possible case, even if the threat has lessened. And now that there have been a few successful events, its attitude has relaxed even more.

Playboy: So you feel your campaign has been successful?

Rushdie: Successful, though if we get a deal with the Iranians tomorrow, I will not feel victorious. I have lost seven years of my life. I have lost the opportunity to share a lot of my son's childhood. I will never get that back. When most fathers were out in the park throwing a ball around with their children, I was not. That time is forever lost. So I won't feel victorious. I feel pleased to have been able to stand up for things I believe in. And I'm pleased this horrendous attack, which attempted to dictate what people can write and read, didn't work.

Playboy: When you were in hiding, how long did it take to begin writing again?

Rushdie: I soon wrote a few book reviews as a way of showing that I'm still here, folks. Then I wrote *Haroun and the Sea of Stories* and then the book of short stories.

Playboy: Was it difficult to begin writing again?

Rushdie: It was difficult to concentrate. There was also a great sadness in me because of what had happened to my book. I spent five years writing in the most serious way, and then had the book reduced to a series of slogans, insulted and vilified, and reduced and burned. I felt, for a while, if this is what you get, it's not worth it. Thank you very much, I'd rather be a plumber. Of course that was simply an expression of misery, nothing else. Eventually I realized that I have to write; it doesn't matter what people think or say.

Playboy: Did you actually write *Haroun* for your son, Zafar?

Rushdie: It's true that I wrote it for him. But, in the end, if you're a writer, you have to find out what your own connection to material is, why you're interested in writing it. So it became for us both—to write again, for me, and to speak to him. There was virtually nothing I could do with him then, but at least I could tell him stories.

Playboy: Was he brought to you in hiding?

Rushdie: He never was. We had to protect him from the knowledge of where I was.

Playboy: At what point did you begin *The Moor's Last Sigh*?

Rushdie: Some aspects of it have been with me for a long time—the setting of Granada, for instance. Also, the character of Aurora, the mother, had gradually grown in my head. The idea of inventing a painter was interesting to me, partly because it has been done so rarely in literature. I came around to Aurora after becoming friendly with a whole bunch of contemporary Indian painters. In them, I found affinities to my own ideas and work. It became easy for me to imagine myself in the skin of such a painter.

Playboy: Do you agree that the central theme in the novel is love—getting it and, most of all, losing it?

Rushdie: Yes, love. The love of nation, love of parents, love of child, erotic love, romantic love. In fact, this is the first time I have ever actually written sex scenes. I've always been shy about them in the past.

Playboy: Why have you been reluctant to write sex scenes?

Rushdie: I think it may have to do with some kind of cultural embarrassment. Sex was something done in private. I found that when I would get to a point in a novel where the next natural moment would be sex, I would tend to have a fade out. It was rather like that wonderful scene in Woody Allen's movie *The Purple Rose of Cairo* where the romantic lead comes off the cinema screen and falls in love with Mia Farrow. They kiss and she wants to proceed, but he becomes increasingly confused. She asks, "What's the matter?" and he says, "There should be a fade-out now." He doesn't know what to do next; he's never had to do it. In the world of the films that he inhabits, there are no sex scenes, only fade-outs. I recognized that problem and I decided I would actually set out to overcome that inhibition, so there are lots of sex scenes.

Playboy: Yet the sex in the book is still fairly oblique.

Rushdie: I wanted to find an interesting way to do it. I find most sex scenes very boring, whether in books or movies, because you know exactly what's going to happen. At least in cinema you can look at beautiful bodies. So here the challenge was to find an interesting way to write about sex. I deliberately wrote the first sex scene comically, about somebody who can't write a sex scene. He's inhibited when he is trying to describe his parents making love, as one might be. He gradually does work his way around to describing it, and so does his author, I guess. At recent appearances, I have read aloud the sequences in which Abraham and Aurora fall in love. I read the scene in which they have sex on the pepper sacks and arrive at church smelling of sex, scandalizing old ladies and perplexing and annoying the priest. I must say that it was a great pleasure to discover that people found it sexy and extremely erotic. Particularly women. To be able to speak to women about lust and sex in a way they find truthful at this moment in history—when the whole area of communication between the sexes is so fucked up—is a particular pleasure.

Playboy: Do you find that love is the central issue in most people's lives?

Rushdie: Love and death. That's not an original thing to say, but yes. I'm enough of an old hippie really to believe that all you need is love. The central story of Aurora and Abraham in the book is a story of what happens when love dies. When it goes away it leaves this dreadful vortex.

Playboy: Does it have to go away?

Rushdie: Passionate love, the sledgehammer love, isn't the one that usually lasts. Then, when it goes, one can be disoriented. That kind of love takes a lot of recovering from and it's easy to tumble out of control.

Playboy: Did you find your marriage to be an object lesson?

Rushdie: Not necessarily my marriage—either marriage—but I have been through it. The most all-consuming love affair I ever had was not with a woman I've married. But like everyone else, I have had my experiences in love gone wrong. It would be very difficult to write about if I hadn't been through it.

Playboy: Of all of those who have attacked you, it was your wife, who had initially gone into hiding with you, who became your most bitter critic. Why?

Rushdie: I think she had to invent me as a person worth leaving. Otherwise there would be a tendency to believe that she should have stood by her man in that old-fashioned way. She tried to create an image of me as being worthless, which then made it possible for her to leave with dignity.

Playboy: Otherwise it would have seemed she was abandoning ship.

Rushdie: Yeah. There are a number of fictions about this period that I haven't talked about before now, but I think I just will say it. First of all, to be strictly accurate, she did not leave me. I asked her to leave. The reason I asked her to leave was that her behavior had become upsetting in ways I don't want to comment on. I preferred to be by myself, which is a mark of how upsetting it was. The idea that Marianne could not live with me because I was unable to live up to history is not true. I asked her to go away because I couldn't stand having her around. There was an enormous amount of dishonesty. There were actions that, in my view, were positively dangerous. So I ended the marriage. Since then she has attempted to construct the view that she decided to leave me, because no doubt it seems nobler. But the fact is that I discovered many things about her that were extraordinarily shocking and distasteful. I'm very glad to have seen the last of her. I feel foolish is all I can say. It is the problem of falling in love with the wrong person. Your friends tell you, but you don't see it until it is too late.

Playboy: Did that experience disenchant you with love?
Rushdie: It certainly shook me. I don't deny it. There was so much dishonesty involved and I'm not a dishonest man.

Playboy: You were in particular bizarre circumstances to be single.
Rushdie: Yes. I remember going on *60 Minutes* shortly after my marriage broke up. Mike Wallace rather courageously asked me what I did for sex.

Playboy: Well?
Rushdie: As I told him, I was rather glad to have a break, actually. He seemed shocked by that answer. But life goes on, and I am not afraid to tell you that my sex life since then has been fine.

Playboy: How do you manage to date and have relationships?
Rushdie: Let's put it like this: People should not feel sorry for me.

Playboy: There was a report that your friends were supplying you with women.
Rushdie: I sued when that was printed. The paper that printed it had to pay and I gave the money to a free-speech organization. It's ludicrous, this idea that my friends were running some kind of pimping service.

Playboy: In your book, the character Aurora needs to express on canvas everything in her life. Is that how you use writing?
Rushdie: It's inevitably the case that when a writer creates another creative artist, something of the writer seeps into that creation. Why do it, otherwise? But I also hope she's more than just a writer in disguise—what Tom

Wolfe called a painted word. I hope she's not just a series of painted words, because I was genuinely interested in the kind of painter she was. By the time I came to write the book, I actually knew her pictures very well—I had a clear sense of what they looked like. I just can't paint them.

Playboy: How religious was your family?

Rushdie: Not very. I was brought up more or less without God. Although we were Muslim, religion was worn very lightly. I think my father would take me to the mosque twice a year, the equivalent of going to church at Christmas. We did not eat the flesh of swine, but that was about it.

Playboy: The religious people in your books are not very admirable. Conversely, secularists are generally the more moral. Is that your view?

Rushdie: It is. I object particularly to fundamentalism, whether it's Hindu, Muslim, or Christian. It's completely barren on any intellectual level. Fundamentalism purports to defend culture, but it doesn't know about the culture that it's defending. If religion is supposed to be a repository of a certain kind of truth, fundamentalism seems to me to be a denial of the truth. It is about the creation of falsehoods and goes after the worst sides of people. I'm alarmed by what's happening wherever fundamentalists rise—such as the rise of the American religious right. It is at least as dangerous as anything happening in the Third World—with more weapons, probably. I don't think Americans can afford any longer to see this as something happening to other people. It's important to understand that fundamentalism does not even pretend to be a religious movement. It is a political movement. It's about power. So watch out.

Playboy: Do you view all religion as dangerous, even the less extremist forms?

Rushdie: No. I'm perfectly able to see the ability of religious systems to provide identity, a sense of community and belonging, a sense of hope and comfort and even a kind of moral structure in people's lives. But these past years I've been given an object lesson in the ability of religion to do some other things, which are not so likable. I've experienced the capacity of religion to do harm. So while I am completely fascinated, even mesmerized by the history of religion and religious myths, I can't stand the system of rules. This inevitably filters into my books, though I have never seen myself as a religious novelist. There are others for whom religion is the central issue. I am instead a writer of memories, a playful writer, a writer who tries to look at history, a writer with some kind of central linguistic ambition. And I see myself as one who wrestles with his times and tries to make sense of them. Even *The Satanic Verses* isn't a novel about religion, but about migration.

Playboy: What do you remember most about being sent to England at the age of 14? You've said it was the first time you were aware of being Indian.

Rushdie: Yes. Before that, speaking English and knowing the culture quite well, I never expected to feel foreign in England. When I arrived, however, I couldn't quite work out why I was meant to feel foreign. There was racism from some of the boys, though not from the staff at the school. I had three things against me, as far as the students were concerned: I was foreign, intelligent, and bad at games. It was a triple whammy.

Playboy: Did you know you wanted to be a writer by then?

Rushdie: I knew I wanted to write when I was very young.

Playboy: After college, while writing your first novels, you worked as an ad copywriter. What were some of your advertisements?

Rushdie: The slogan that people hang most around my neck is one used for cream cakes: naughty but nice. There was also a campaign for a chocolate bar called Aero, which is full of bubbles, for which I invented a whole series of bubble words: Adorabubble, delectabubble, incredibubble, etc.

Playboy: From the outset, did you plan to write political novels?

Rushdie: Only indirectly. The thing that made me a writer was the fact that I came from over there—that is, India—and I ended up over here, in England, and I had to make sense of that. I had a bundle of stories I brought with me, my literary baggage, and I wanted to tell those stories, and have those stories lead to other stories. Part of the stories is the way history and people's lives rub up together. We find ourselves in a position in which public life often determines our fates in ways that have nothing to do with what sort of people we are. Economics is destiny, politics is destiny, terrorism is destiny.

Playboy: What's it like to write about India from exile?

Rushdie: There's no doubt that one of the great losses in my life was having to stay away. It's the only passage of seven years in my life in which I have not been in India. It feels like losing a limb. So writing the new book was a journey home, the only way of going. Writing from exile is emotionally charged, however. I was conscious of the trap, which is sentimentalization on the one hand, or exaggeration on the other. I was desperately anxious not to commit those crimes. The consequence of being removed from India allowed or released in me the flood of feelings that shapes this novel. There is also a sense of personal loss. And sadness, which I think is a constant of what happened.

Playboy: Is it just too dangerous for you to travel to India?

Rushdie: India is not Iran. It's not a fundamentalist country. I'm quite popular in India. If I just turned up in Bombay, more people would be pleased than not pleased. The reason I haven't been back has to do with my worries about being politically exploited. There are a small number of Muslim politicians who might see it as a way to get some more mileage out of the situation. Frankly, speaking as a political football, I've been kicked around enough. I just couldn't bear going there and suddenly encountering a new round of demonstrations, etc. Any Indian politician can create a demonstration on the street in five minutes.

Playboy: Are you convinced they would?

Rushdie: They would. Perhaps when the dust settles after the election year, we'll see. I feel quite optimistic about going back to India.

Playboy: But not to Iran, we imagine.

Rushdie: I've been to Iran. I don't need to go again.

Playboy: Did you find it difficult to write about modern India while being away?

Rushdie: I carry India around with me. I can't escape India. I know how people think and talk and feel. If I read in the newspaper about a political event, I know how people will react. I know how all different classes of the country, all different communities, will react. In that sense I don't feel disconnected, because I can immediately play the scenario in my head. At least so far I've felt that.

Playboy: Are you optimistic about the current state of India?

Rushdie: There were three pillars of independent India. The first was democracy—the commitment to a democratic political system despite the incredible difficulties of having a democracy in a country of that size. The second was the protectionist economy—the government nationalizing everything in sight and putting up tariff barriers against the imported rival goods, and so on. The third pillar was secularism, which grew out of the great violence of the partition period. It was quite clear to the founding generation of politicians that, in order to prevent a repetition of the violence, it was important to separate church and state so that no religion, no matter how numerically superior it might be, could have a constitutional advantage over others. Broadly speaking, that is the India that people of my generation, the generation of independence, were sold. We grew up buying that India and liking it and feeling its air free to breathe. But now I feel that all those pillars are tottering. The secularist principle is being strongly opposed by increasingly powerful political parties that talk about rewriting the constitution. The second pillar is gone—the socialist—protectionist economic pillar has been replaced by a free-market economy, which is transporting India at a most extraordinary speed. Now the pillar of democracy itself has been shaken. There has been an arrival of political leaders who overtly act democratic but who set themselves up as more or less absolute fascistic leaders in their states. People are disillusioned with public life. This has become so extreme that there seems to be an appeal of more authoritarian forms of leadership, which seem to promise more discipline, less crookery and so on. So this is the historical climate that has replaced the India I grew up in. Let's say I'm worried.

Playboy: Is your latest book banned in India?

Rushdie: What has happened is something more Indian than a straightforward ban. A couple of members of the right in Bombay got annoyed on behalf of Bal Thackeray, the leader of the Shiv Sena Party. He himself hasn't uttered a word other than to allege that he has not read it. As a result of it all, however, some parts of customs apparently have imposed a block on importing further copies. They say they're doing this because a ban is being considered, though they don't say by whom. When they're asked why it's under consideration, they don't answer the letters. At the moment this is an informal stoppage, which is not being called a ban. This is the Indian technique, to wrap things up in red tape. But we are cutting through this. The Indian publishers, along with the booksellers' association, have taken the government to court. The government must show cause why it is doing this. If it cannot, and the general view is that it cannot, it will have to lift the blockade. India is still enough of a free society that it has an independent judiciary that is impatient with government bans on novels. Especially when the only reason for the blockade is that an opposition politician doesn't like it.

Playboy: You were, of course, satirizing Thackeray, right?

Rushdie: If you are going to write about a Bombay-based Hindu extremist party, then inevitably the Shiv Sena comes to mind, and Thackeray is the leader of that party, so obviously the character in the book has something to do with Thackeray. But it's not all Thackeray. Another model for the character was Russia's Vladimir Zhirinovsky. If I had wanted to write about Thackeray specifically, I would have included him in the book. In *Midnight's Children,* when I wanted to criticize some deeds of Indira Gandhi's, I introduced character called Indira Gandhi in the book.

Playboy: And, indeed, Gandhi sued you for it.

Rushdie: Yes. There was one sentence in the book where I repeated something that was often repeated about her: that she was responsible for her father's death She sued about that sentence. But then she died and the suit became moot.

Playboy: In *Moor's,* you have Aurora, though she loathes Indira Gandhi, very upset when she died.

Rushdie: I was upset. Since the Emergency I was a strong opponent of Mrs. Gandhi, but on the day she was shot, I was bereft. It was such a hideous thing to have happened. In a piece I wrote about it, I said that everybody who loved India would be in mourning that day. And Mrs. Gandhi was a remarkable individual with great personal charm, great political and personal courage. It so happened that she went down a political road that I objected to. Like Margaret Thatcher—I've been a lifelong political opponent of hers in a passionate way, but that doesn't mean that I can't respect her. And, clearly, no matter how you feel about someone's politics, you must be horrified in the face of an assassination.

Playboy: How were you affected when you heard about the assassination of Yitzhak Rabin?

Rushdie: It reminded me of what my parents had told me about learning the news of the assassination of Mahatma Gandhi. At the time there was a very heightened tension between Hindu and Muslim communities in India. They said that the instant fear was learning the name of the assassin. By learning the name, you would know which community the person came from. They would know if it were a Muslim name. If it were, the consequences would be absolutely horrible. So they went home and locked the doors and waited. And when the name of the killer was released, and it was a Hindu name, their first reaction was a sense of relief. It didn't lessen their sense of the tragedy, but they were relieved that it wasn't a Muslim. Similarly, when

I heard that Rabin had been shot, as horrified as I was, my first thought was, What's the name of the killer? Had it been an Arab name, goodness knows what would have happened. When we heard it was a Jewish name, that, of course, unleashed another kind of horror. But I can't deny that my first reaction was relief, because it would have harmed the peace process immeasurably if the murderer had been an Arab.

Playboy: How do you feel about having become a symbol of freedom of speech?

Rushdie: I have no interest in being a symbol. I want to be a writer, and that's all. I do want to be a good writer and one who engages in public themes, as well as private ones. I wanted to have my say—to be part of that conversation. But I didn't want to become some kind of statue.

Playboy: But isn't there, in your work, an intent to stir up trouble, to incite?

Rushdie: It depends on what you mean. I think all good art is provocative. I don't particularly like the idea of demonstrations in foreign cities—that wasn't something I wanted—but I do want art to stir you up, to make you think and feel. I think the reason for being a creative artist of any sort is that you want to be a part of the conversation: I see this. What do you think? Here's how I feel. Do you feel it? That's what the work of art does to you. If it doesn't, it's inert. If it does, it's provocative. Certainly I would hope that everything I wrote provoked people. But that doesn't mean provoke them to anger or violence. It can mean provoke their sense of duty or their sense of horror or their sense of justice or injustice or their sense of humor. It's true that I have a fairly emphatic view of the world and I express it. Inevitably it means a lot of people don't like it. That just comes with the territory. *Midnight's Children* was written in the aftermath of the Bangladesh war, in which mass genocide was committed by the Pakistani army. Immediately afterward, everybody denied the genocide had taken place. It also came in the aftermath of the emergency rule of Mrs. Gandhi, when there were all kinds of atrocities. Once again, afterward a lot of the evidence was destroyed and the experience was denied. If I'm trying to offer a truthful picture of what happened in those times, remembering what happened inevitably becomes politicized. Just writing down the story of the mass graves found in Bangladesh by the liberating army or the people who got their testicles cut off in various prisons around north India brings you into conflict with the authority figures who denied that those things happened.

[*The interview is interrupted with news that Nigerian writer Ken Saro-Wiwa has been executed. Rushdie is silent, near tears, for ten minutes. He then begins speaking again.*]

Writers have been wiped out all over the place, and it is horrifying the way in which nothing much happens as a result. I will be interested to see what happens to Nigeria as a result of this. I suspect a three-letter word that begins with O and ends in L—with I in the middle—might prevent anybody from being too harsh. Yet here is a man who has been killed because he set himself up against the interests of oil. A very brave man, because he didn't write from exile. He wrote from inside the belly of the beast and it was dangerous. Then the gave up his writing to put himself at the head of the democracy movement. He knew the rest of the world was getting to be wishy-washy and nobody was willing to do anything. [*He stops again, collects himself.*] You know, I feel that so much attention has been paid to me while so many other writers have been in danger. I have spoken about other writers because it would be obscene to use this attention and not talk about those others. I wish people would listen more to this.

There were great writers in the Soviet gulag whom we fought for. We smuggled out their work and published it, and gave them voices and fought for them. Now another group of writers is fighting against equivalent tyranny and equivalent injustice, in the Muslim world or out. Because our interests do not dictate it, we ignore them, we let them die, we let them go to jail and rot. We must stop a situation in which writers are getting wiped out every five minutes, in which writers are being exiled, in which Saro-Wiwa can be murdered. China continues to persecute its writers. All over the world, writers are being thrown in jail. They mysteriously die in police custody and they are falsely accused of committing crimes. It is open season on writers and it must stop.

The Moor's Last Sigh

Charlie Rose / 1996

From *The Charlie Rose Show* 18 January 1996. *Charlie Rose* transcripts re-printed courtesy of Rose Communications, Inc.

Charlie Rose: Salman Rushdie is here. His latest book is called *The Moor's Last Sigh.* It is third in a cycle that began with *Midnight's Children* and *The Satanic Verses.* And I am pleased to have him back on this program for a conversation about this book, about the themes, and about his life, which could not have been easy over the last number of years. But it's a pleasure to have him back.

Welcome.

Salman Rushdie, Author. Thank you. It's nice to be back.

Charlie Rose: It was a little bit easier to arrange this than it was the last time that we came together, with a series of things that we had to do in the interest of security.

Salman Rushdie. Yes. I think that's a kind of indication of the fact that I'm just trying to get things back on the road here.

Charlie Rose: How close are you to some sense of feeling—

Salman Rushdie: Well, I'm pretty close. I feel most of the time as if I can get things done now in a way that was previously very difficult, and actually, having the novel come out has in some way, in *some* mysterious way, it's changed the air. Suddenly *Satanic Verses* feels really like a long time ago, and people want to talk about books again, and it just seems to have cleared up something.

Charlie Rose: So you can move on to the subjects. Do you think—I want to come to all of the themes here. Did it take a toll on you, other than the obvious? You have to live that way looking over your shoulder and making sure that you're doing whatever you can to maintain security for life, does it take some other toll in terms of that creative thing which are the assets of a writer?

Salman Rushdie? I think it did. I can't avoid thinking that, yes, there was damage, and there was a long period when I could not fire on all cylinders. And I was very conscious of the fact that at the time that I wrote the children's book, *Haroun and the Sea of Stories.* I was pleased with the way it turned out, but it was a small project, you know. Because it was for children, there were other simplifications involved. I felt at that time, "That's as much as I can do." I could not at that stage have embarked on a big adult book like this. And so it's been a hard road back for me.

Charlie Rose: And it completes a cycle for you.

Salman Rushdie: It does, I feel. I certainly felt when I finished this that kind of excitement that writers feel when the hairs on the back of your neck stand up.

I thought it was all right, this book, when I finished it. I also thought that it finished something,—a kind of project which really I've been embarked on for 20 years, ever since I started writing *Midnight's Children.*

Charlie Rose: Define the project for me and where does this fit in that evolution?

Salman Rushdie: I suppose, broadly speaking, it's the project to try and describe the world I came from and the world I came to and how those two collided. A lot of people are saying to me—and it's interesting because I didn't think of it at the time—that *Midnight's Children,* which is now 15 years old, and this book, act like kind of bookends. Because they've been saying it, I've been trying to think what they meant. And the way I've come to understand it is that *Midnight's Children* was a novel which I wrote out of—really out of childhood, out of the experience of being a child in Bombay. The narrator of that novel, even though he grows up, retains a kind of childlike view of the world. And it's a novel about beginning, it's a novel about something being born in the country and a person and so on. One of the things I like about the way this book turned out is I feel that it is not a child's view of India. It's not a child's view of Bombay. I feel that the Bombay in this book, the world of this book comes out of the grownup knowledge that I have of India and of this world.

Charlie Rose: It's interesting you say "grownup knowledge" because it is not coming out of a memory of an India that you have seen or a Bombay that you have seen recently.

Salman Rushdie: Well, not for a while, no. I haven't been there for almost eight years, and that also is very strange for me because it's the first time in my life that I've spent that long without going to India. In 48 years, this is the only eight-year period in which that's true. And so I find myself in the odd position of an exile, which I never expected to be. It's seven or eight months since I finished it, and it's been out a while. I look at it and it seems to me as if that condition of exile gave the book an extra emotional gear because I really needed India. I really needed it badly. I felt the loss of it very keenly. I missed it. I missed my friends, and I missed the place, and this was the only way I could go there—by creating it for myself. I think that need, that neediness in me has given a kind of emotional charge to this book.

Charlie Rose: Was it difficult because it was an India that had to come from memory and not from recent experience?

Salman Rushdie: It's difficult anyway. I think in that sense, I discovered a truth (which many exiled writers have said before) which is that you carry it around with you. The fact that you are not there, it doesn't mean that you don't have it, you know. I still feel that I possess India and can easily inhabit it. But I was very keen not to be told that I was out of touch. If my Indian friends had got in touch and said, "Listen, Salman, you know, it's not like that anymore."

Charlie Rose: India has passed you by.

Salman Rushdie: Or "It's wrong. That was once true. It's not like that now. It's like this." I would have been deeply mortified. And so the fact that in India the critics and the first readers of the book have *really* been eulogistically happy about the fact that the book depicts a world that they feel they live in, that's a matter of great pride for me.

Charlie Rose: What is its publication status in India?

Salman Rushdie: Well, it's a strange thing. I mean, as you know, there was an objection raised by one extremist politician, who believed himself to be satirized, which, to be truthful, in part he's right. What's true is that the character is based on a number of people. It is not just a portrait of him.

Charlie Rose: He can find parts of himself in that character.

Salman Rushdie: Sure. Satire, after all, is something he should well know about since he started life as a satirist himself as a political cartoonist. Any way, because of this man's irritation with the book, the Indian government has done a very odd thing. They haven't done anything as extreme as ban the book. What they've done is to create a customs blockage. They say we can't bring any more copies in. And when we say, "Why not?" they say they're considering the advisability of allowing more copies in. And then we say, "How long will it take them to consider?" and they don't answer our letters.

So this is a very Indian technique to kind of just tie something up in red tape and hope everybody forgets it.

Charlie Rose: And are you without endeavor? Are you without resources to change that?

Salman Rushdie: No, no. We can do something about it. I think already there's a kind of stink in India about it, and there's a legal procedure which the publishers of the book have embarked on to demand that the government shows cause why it's behaving like . . . the general view is that the government can't show cause, and we have also been given a number of nudges and winks from the government to suggest that actually the government would be rather pleased if the courts unbanned the book.

Charlie Rose: But this man's political party now is in control of the state where Bombay lies.

Salman Rushdie: Well, you see, it's a coalition partner in the government. And what's interesting is that their partners, the other sort of big Hindu party, the National Party, the BJP, has said that it would not support a ban even in Bombay. And without the BJP, they can't do it. So, we just have to solve the problem of this curious, very Indian, blockage, which you can't call a ban. See, if it was a ban, you could challenge it in court more easily. So it's a piece of Machiavellian behavior.

Charlie Rose: Explain the title, *The Moor's Last Sigh.*

Salman Rushdie: The title, actually, is a translation of a phrase in Spanish, *el ultimo suspiro del Moor,* which is a tag attached to the story of the fall of Granada at the end of the Arab period in Spain. It is said that the last sultan of Granada, on surrendering the Alhambra to Ferdinand and Isabella, the reconquering Catholic monarchs, sighed and wept as he departed into exile. And this moment, the end of Arab Spain and the weeping of the last sultan is known as the Moor's last sigh. So the story enters this novel, if you like, as a kind of metaphor for modern India and for the ruptures of cultures not only in India but in the modern world.

Charlie Rose: And that's what I want to explore. Help me understand in what way it is a metaphor for modern India.

Salman Rushdie: Well, what happened in the Arab period in southern Spain, in Andalusia, was that a kind of composite culture grew up. Although the Muslim sultans were the rulers, there were Christians and Jews and Muslims living side by side for hundreds of years, and their cultures affected each other. So the Muslims were no longer completely Muslim and likewise the others. And this composite culture of Andalusia is something which certainly in Spain and people who know about it have always found very attractive. Out of it came great poetry and great architecture and so on. And then this was destroyed by what you might call Christian fundamentalism, by the reconquering Catholic kings. Now, it seemed to me that the world I come from, India, the world this book comes out of, is also a composite culture. It's also a place where there's a Hindu majority, but there are many different cultures—Hindu, Christian, Muslim, Jewish, et cetera—forming this kind of mélange, this kind of composite entity, which is the world I grew up in and which I find very rich and pleasurable, and which I enjoy. There is a kind of threat to that composite culture now coming from a new kind of fundamentalism, which is basically Hindu fundamentalism, the fundamentalism of the majority.

Charlie Rose: And that's why they're upset at you.

Salman Rushdie: And that's why they're upset because I'm pointing this out. But I have to say that it is not, as it were, most Hindus who are upset about this. It is the fanatic fringe. The book, actually, has had in India the best critical response and the best readers' response of any book I've written since *Midnight's Children,* and in many cases, surpasses that.

Charlie Rose: Some might ask did you have to write this?
Salman Rushdie: I had to write this.

Charlie Rose: Did you have to take on more extremists?
Salman Rushdie: I'm afraid I did. The truth is that, for me, I've always only written the books I had to write. I've always had the view that there are enough books.

Charlie Rose: And so you should only write if you have something you have to write and something you have to say, and something that you think makes a point.
Salman Rushdie: Yes. If you can't avoid writing that's a reason for writing. If something drives you, impels you to give birth to it, that . . .

Charlie Rose: So your answer to why did you take on the Hindu extremists, your answer is "I had no choice because I had something that was important to say about that culture that I love."
Salman Rushdie: That's right. I had no choice.

Charlie Rose: And what might be happening to it.
Salman Rushdie: Yes, and also, let me just say that the theme in this novel

is not even the primary theme. I mean, I set out to write what you could loosely describe as a sex comedy.

Charlie Rose: A sex comedy?

Salman Rushdie: This is a novel which, I think and I'm happy to say that the people who read it seem to agree, is probably the funniest book I wrote.

Charlie Rose: They do say that.

Salman Rushdie: One of the tasks I set myself was that I had always been very shy about sex in my writing. You tend to find in my books that when the characters get to bed together, that there's a kind of fade out.

Charlie Rose: And why is that?

Salman Rushdie: Well, I think it actually is something about coming from India. People feel that it's difficult to talk openly about this stuff. And I think I've always been delicate about depictions of physical love. I thought this time, "Go for it." This time you've got to find a way of doing it. It has also to do with the fact that the character that came to me of Aurora, the main character in the novel, the painter, is a sexy lady. I mean, she's a very sensual woman. And I thought in order to represent her sensuality, in order to give that life to the novel, I couldn't duck it. I couldn't have dot, dot, dots and fadeouts. I had to talk about it.

Charlie Rose: Are you hopeful that you will be able to return?

Salman Rushdie: To Bombay? To India? Yes. I'm hopeful. I wouldn't like to put a date on it because the worry I have about India is not a question of my personal safety because India is not Iran. It's a different kind of place. The worry I have is that in the way that happened at the beginning of this, of this whole crisis, one or two extremist politicians might seek to use my presence there to make political capital for themselves, and frankly, I've just had . . .

Charlie Rose: To create a conflict that is beyond you but benefits them politically.

Salman Rushdie: Yes. I've had it up to here with being a political football. I just could not bear to become the tool of some politician again. And my worry about going back to India is that that would happen. Now, particularly, I think this year there's a problem because this is a general election year in India, so I think at the moment it would be stupid to go because everybody's looking for angles. My feeling is that I will let the election happen, which will be sort of some time between now and the middle of the year, and I'll see how that pans out and let the dust settle and then maybe.

Charlie Rose: What are you saying about religious fanaticism?
Salman Rushdie: Well, I'm saying it's a growing force.

Charlie Rose: Throughout this world.
Salman Rushdie: Throughout the world, and the novel's about India, but it's not only about India. I hope that people who read it here will feel that there are echoes in their own experience that they can feed into what's happening in this book. There's religious fanaticism here. I've often thought that although America and India are so unlike—so far apart; one is so rich; the other is so poor, et cetera—the cultures in many ways could counter-recognize each other.

Charlie Rose: Because?
Salman Rushdie: Well, because they're both cultures made up of mixtures. They're both cultures made up of people who come from elsewhere, and who kind of transform themselves and make themselves again here. They're both mixed up people.

Charlie Rose: They're both cultures with a connection to England.
Salman Rushdie: They are both ex-colonial cultures. Yes, there's that, too. And they both have these great rotting cities that populate my books.

Charlie Rose: They both have extremes of poverty and wealth.
Salman Rushdie: That's right. I would have hoped that an American reader coming to this, even if they don't know anything about India, can say, "Oh, well, that's not so unlike my own neighborhood."

Charlie Rose: What is it—and this is not part of this, but I have friends who have traveled to the Middle East, both as journalists and as observers of people, just going because they wanted to soak up, learn, experience a culture. They come away with something that I can't describe any more than saying the magic of India. What is it?
Salman Rushdie: Well, I think India is an assault on your senses. When you go to India, India is not a low key country. India is a country with a volume control turned up to maximum, with the smell control turned up to maximum. Everything is excess. It's that thing that India overwhelms you—the sights of it, the sounds of it, the smells of it, the taste of it, the touch, the feel of it. People who are not Indian who go there—they either loathe it, they

either have a really strong revulsion against it, it's too much for them, or they fall in love and they can never see the world the same way again.

Charlie Rose: You're right. What about violence in the culture?

Salman Rushdie: Well, it's there. It's there. And I think one of the things that I tried to face in this book was the nature of that violence. I hope this is a very comic novel, but underneath it, there is—there's no question—a layer of darkness. And that darkness has to do with what you say about the violence in the culture because every so often in India there are outbreaks of extraordinary—I mean, extraordinary, hyperbolic acts of violence. And if you come from there and you define yourself in part as being from there, you want to say, "Where does that come from in us?" And I think it's not enough to say, "Oh, it's just those violent guys over there who did that," because I think you have to say that we are capable of this, too, and where in us does this come from? And in this novel, what happens to the narrator, who is not a violent person, is that he becomes at one point a very violent person, and that happens in the novel because I wanted to face that fact, that the violence is in us, too.

Charlie Rose: How much of this story—and some will make this point in reviews—is your story, your experiences in some translatable way over the last few years?

Salman Rushdie: I would say it's not, really. And what I'd say is that if every time you use a first person narrator, as I've done in this book, then inevitably a chunk of your experience and your attitudes and your feelings and passions will come out through his mouth and will come out through his experience. That's true. I do not deny that. That is true about this book. However, he ain't me. And I think it's often the case when writers have used point of view characters in a very intimate way that there is an attempt to associate them, and yet Bellow is not Herzog.

Charlie Rose: But at the same time, it is possible—and you touched on this—that he's more you than you realize.

Salman Rushdie: It's entirely possible. But I would say he's not the only person in this book who's a bit me because I think the character of Aurora, the painter, even though she is a girl, has some of my ideas.

Charlie Rose: Like what?

Salman Rushdie: Well, the kind of painter she is is a little bit the kind of writer I would like to be—that's to say she's an encyclopedic painter. She tries to put the world on her canvas.

Charlie Rose: And so do you here and in everything you write. In a sense, you're trying to put almost everything you have learned and your own intellectual voyage in this. Right?
Salman Rushdie: Yes.

Charlie Rose: And the genius people attribute to you are the best skills. You do it with a certain verbal dexterity that defines you as a great writer.
Salman Rushdie: I am very happy with the language in this book. I've always tried to find a very fluid language, which can, amongst other things, make very quick transition from comedy to tragedy, from danger to comfort, so that the reader is kept a little off balance as to whether he should laugh or cry. And I feel in this book the language does work well for me.

Charlie Rose: What are the lessons—for the lack of a better word—since you received that death sentence? What have been the lessons that might even in part be here, but certainly are part of you here in your head and in your soul and in your heart?
Salman Rushdie: Well, there's quite a few, I guess. It's true to say that some of them are in this book. There's an idea about fear, for instance, which the narrator expresses, where he says "With fear, it's all or nothing." You know that you either surrender to it, in which case you sit in a corner and gibber, or else you simply put it away, and then you get on with your life.

Charlie Rose: You can't go halfway on that equation?
Salman Rushdie: No. It's either/or with fear. And that's clearly something that I learned. There are other things I've learned, which is that some of the values that I've always most cared about, the values of pluralism and multiplicity and being many things and not being narrow, not defining yourself or your culture narrowly. That can also lead to great weakness of purpose. So that one way of interpreting the story we were talking about, the story of the fall of Granada, is that here is this wonderful, pluralist, civilized culture. When it's faced with this narrow spectrum, obsessive, very focused fundamentalist attack, it disintegrates, gives up without a fight, doesn't have a chance. And I think if these are the ideas that we care about—freedom, tolerance, living side by side with difference and so on—we must also understand how they can create weakness, and therefore, you know, by understanding that, may give us a way of guarding against that attack, that intolerant, narrow spectrum, vicious attack.

Charlie Rose: Someone made this point so I can't take credit for it. It is that somehow by probing the depths, what you have seen is the most humane aspects, also.

Salman Rushdie: I think it's true that I've tried to say it whenever I could, that the upside, if you like of what happened to me is that people behave incredibly well towards me and around me; that as well as all the evil and darkness and anger and et cetera that was aimed at me, the other thing that was aimed at me was affection and love and commitment and solidarity and support and courage and unflinching and unwavering determination to confront this thing. And that wasn't just my friends. That was people I didn't know. It was people who came together to form campaigns and to defend the values that they felt were threatened in this case. And I think an awful lot of people behaved heroically. Ordinary men and women in bookshops, who had to be on the front line of the threat, continued in the most determined way to say, "We will not get scared about this."

Charlie Rose: And some paid with their lives, too.

Salman Rushdie: Absolutely. And there were attacks on people.

Charlie Rose: Two or three that I know of.

Salman Rushdie: Yeah. There were bombs, et cetera. And yet, an enormous community of people stood up against this threat, and I think that's very admirable.

Charlie Rose: How do you appraise how you behaved?

Salman Rushdie: I think what I would say is that initially I was very off-balance. I think it took me a long time to blunder around and do the wrong things and bump into the furniture and fall over and hit my nose against the wall until I learned how to deal—how to face this thing. I think very few of us would be familiar with how to confront a threat such as this, and certainly I was not. And I would say the first couple of years of this thing were years that I would describe in this way: that they were full of false starts and confusions and bewilderments.

Charlie Rose: Some combination of being paralyzed and unable to find your footing?

Salman Rushdie: Yeah. I think what happens in a situation as extreme as this is that your picture of the world is broken. And when that happens, you don't quite know how to act for the best. You don't know what is a right act and what is a wrong act: Should you mollify people? Should you defy people? Should you appease people? Should you fight back against people? And everybody's giving you advice. Everybody has their point of view and knows exactly what you should do, and it's confusing. It's confusing.

Charlie Rose: Is there a right point to find between—I mean, I think of somebody like Natan Sharansky. You remember when he was released and having been in the gulag at the time, he walked back, and he deliberately zigzagged as a last act of defiance because the KGB had said to him, "You will walk right over there," and he wanted to say "One last time, I shall defy you."
Salman Rushdie: Yeah. Well, good for him.

Charlie Rose: Good for him, but it is that act of somehow—
Salman Rushdie: I think I found my way to clarity in this matter. The trouble is, one wants to be liked. You write a book. A lot of people say, "We hate you." And there's an immediate tendency to say, "But you're wrong, guys, and if I could just explain it to you. If you'll just listen to me for a minute, I'll explain it to you. You will realize that you're just wrong. I'm not a bad guy. I'm a good guy." And you have that desire to do that. And one of the things I had to learn was that that was a mistake. That actually what was aimed against me was not something to appease. It was not something to try and befriend. And I learned that the hard way by making the mistakes.

Charlie Rose: And for other reasons, it had an irrationality that you couldn't even deal with.
Salman Rushdie: Yes. You couldn't face it because they were not listening. Eventually, I thought, "Okay, I accept the fact that there are people out there who don't like me, but the issue here is not to make them my friends, but to win this fight." And at that point, I became a lot clearer about what had to be done.

Charlie Rose: You became a kind of poster person—poster boy, poster child—for artistic freedom. Yes?
Salman Rushdie: Yeah. I guess so.

Charlie Rose: You did.
Salman Rushdie: Yeah.

Charlie Rose: Does your case become so consuming that every other issue is less significant?
Salman Rushdie: No, no. That's again a thing that I found my way to,

that I felt more and more that the importance of this issue included everybody else who was engaged in this. It was not just that it was me and my book, but that it was, as you say, representative of a large conflict. I began more and more to find out about that larger conflict and to become involved with these other cases and other fights. For instance, in Europe, I'm now the head of a writers' organization which exists specifically in order to help out other persecuted writers and actually find them safe havens if they need it and so on. I felt that one of the things that was incumbent on me to do because so much was done for me is to put some of that back, if possible, and I have been trying to do that.

Charlie Rose: I think Martin Amis said that what had been stolen from you is a writer's most important asset: the purity of a response to your work. Your work, at least now, will be judged in a context, not just for what's in this book.

Salman Rushdie: Martin did say that, and I think it was a shrewd remark, like many of his remarks. I remember he used the wonderful phrase, when *fatwa* first happened, as having vanished into the front page. And I have been trying to emerge from that front page ever since, to become visible again. And you're right. People have tended to try and find in my work echoes of this or that aspect of my life. But I must say that—and it's one of the greatest thrills to me—the way in which this book has been published and has been received is that in the end, actually, this is not what people have done to this book. The book has somehow imposed itself on people's imaginations so that in the end, they can say, hey, there's something to do with Rushdie in here. But in the end, what they like about the book is itself. And I feel that something important has been gained, and I do feel that as a kind of victory in this matter.

Charlie Rose: So you think, in a sense, you have been able to overcome—or the critics have been able to overcome all of the contexts that this could be placed in and judge it.

Salman Rushdie: For the most part. And I think readers, too, which is more important than critics, are beginning to do that. I felt that the thing that happened to me with the *fatwa* was that it actually seriously damaged my reputation as a writer. In spite of all the sort of symbolic aspects that you mentioned, it made many people think that I must be, as I was accused of being, a bad, arrogant, unreadable, turgid, theological, polemical, who-needs-it writer.

In spite of this colossal fame that came my way, this was negative fame. It was bad fame. It did not make people more anxious to go out and read my work. It made them less anxious to go out and read my work, and I have had to overcome that.

Charlie Rose: So for anybody who wants to step forward and say, "Boy, if I could draw that much attention to my book, I'd be prepared to walk in his moccasins," you're prepared to say, "Don't even think a second."
Salman Rushdie: "Don't even think about it."

Charlie Rose: "There is no benefit."
Salman Rushdie: There was not. If there had been, I would say so; actually it was the opposite. It's as if the characteristics of the people who attacked me—their humorlessness, their bigotry, and so on—were dumped on me. I must be like that, too, if they're so angry with me, was the sort of general view. And one of the great things about the reception of this novel is that it's as if it has rejoined me to my previous self as a writer.

Charlie Rose: Someone said—and I'll give credit—I think maybe *The Washington Post,* and I may be wrong—said in the opening line, "We tend to forget that Salman Rushdie, because of all this, is one of our greater writers," or something to that effect.
Salman Rushdie: Yeah, something very nice.

Charlie Rose: Very nice like that, but it is this context question, which you think, in a sense, you may be beginning to overcome.
Salman Rushdie: The only way I can fight it is to go on writing my books. And if they are good books and if they please their readers, then gradually, *The Satanic Verses* will just be one amongst many. If you think about it, *The Satanic Verses* was the fifth book I published. This was the tenth book.

Charlie Rose: Yes.
Salman Rushdie: Gradually, it's that novel that is being set in a larger context.

Charlie Rose: A couple of things about that experience there. Did you become a Muslim?
Salman Rushdie: No, no. This is what we're talking about, blundering around into the furniture. At one point, when I tried to appease this thing that was coming at me, I flirted with that and immediately felt sick with myself. I think it is the worst mistake I ever made, and it's over five years ago now,

and I'm still, as it were, explaining why it happened. But it was something I rather rapidly realized was a bad blunder born of desperation and so on, and not true, which is the worst thing.

Charlie Rose: When were you the most fearful?
Salman Rushdie: I think right at the beginning.

Charlie Rose: At the beginning because you didn't know if you would even survive it. There's nobody you could go to and say, "What is it like to live in this horror?"
Salman Rushdie: I have to tell you I did not expect to survive it.

Charlie Rose: You did not.
Salman Rushdie: No.

Charlie Rose. You knew that one day, somewhere, somebody was laying in wait.
Salman Rushdie: Well, I thought it might not even be some day. At the time that I first heard about the threat, it did instill in me the thought that I might not have more than a few days left to live.

Charlie Rose: So what did you do?
Salman Rushdie: Well, I didn't feel very good about it. But what I did, actually, was—on that day—go to my friend Bruce Chatwin's memorial service, and I remember Paul Theroux sitting in the chair behind me and saying, "I guess we will be here for you next week," and he was making a joke. It's his characteristic black comedy, but I thought it just slightly missed the mark of the tone of the day. But I think I genuinely felt at that time that there is not much time left.

Charlie Rose: Where do you think it is today?
Salman Rushdie: It's very hard to judge. What I feel is that there is a colossal change in the atmosphere, and one part of that is that I think as far as the mass of Muslims and the Muslim community in different countries is concerned, I really think this is not a problem anymore. One of the reasons why I began to do advertised and open public events again in England when the book came out, around Europe, is because I had this very strong sense, very strong belief that that aspect really was not a problem. And so it was proved. That's to say, there were no protests. Indeed, many of the audiences contained large numbers of Muslim readers, and they were very keen to meet me. So something was healed there. Some rift in the world was healed. And

so what remains is the issue of the government of Iran. Now, for the last year, the Iranians have been making very mollifying noises about this. They've been endlessly saying, "No. We're not going to do anything about it. We don't want to kill him. We're not going to. We haven't tried to. But we will not, so far, cancel the *fatwa*." And so this is clearly not an acceptable situation. One has to say that it is a major shift in their language, because until a year ago, they were saying, yes, they would go on and kill me.

Charlie Rose: What was the impact of your meeting with the President? Do you think that did any good?
Salman Rushdie: Yeah.

Charlie Rose: Did it send a message that might not have been as total as the message you'd like to have sent, which would be picking up the phone and saying, "Would you please—"
Salman Rushdie: "Stop this."

Charlie Rose: "—stop this."
Salman Rushdie: I think it made quite a difference in a number of ways. First of all, it was a very clear demonstration of policy and feeling by the most powerful man in the world and the leader of the most powerful nation in the world, and I think that really is significant. It's significant if only because it really stiffened the sinews and the spines of the European countries. Once President Clinton met with me, suddenly it was cool to meet me. I mean, there was a point at which it had been uncool to meet me, and it suddenly became cool. Suddenly, they were queuing up to have their picture taken with me.

Charlie Rose: Just to say "I've been on your side all the time."
Salman Rushdie: Exactly.

Charlie Rose: "I was there with you," and—
Salman Rushdie: And since then, the European Union's policy in this matter has toughened considerably, and they are now engaged in a campaign of pressurizing Iran into coming to a solution of the matter, and that has happened, if you like, in the wake of the meeting that I had in the White House, not only with the President, but also with Warren Christopher and Anthony Lake, and I do feel that that was helpful.

Charlie Rose: Do you think on some journey between zero and 100, where are you, do you think?

Salman Rushdie: Well, my mood shifts about this, but I think on the whole, I would have said we may be 80. I think there are some steps that need to be taken. . . .

Charlie Rose: By you or by others or in combination?

Salman Rushdie: Well, you see, I've always thought there's two roads in this, and one of them is the steps that I take and the other is the kind of political process. Now, the political process is really not any longer for me to do much about except to go on pressurizing. But that, of course, must end up, in the end, with Iran renouncing these threats, and that's the goal, and we're not there yet. At the same time, I've embarked on a road back into the world, and the biggest step in that to date has been to step back into the public. It is not endlessly to be a surprise or unannounced guest, but to say, "I'm doing a reading next Thursday. Would you like to come? Come and buy some tickets, and I'll read to you from my book." Now, the fact that I've done that a lot in England and in Europe, that feels like a very significant shift to me.

Charlie Rose: So you would have no fear—or at least you would have no reservation about appearing for a public reading at a bookstore in New York City.

Salman Rushdie: I would not.

Charlie Rose: You would do that if the opportunity was offered to do that?

Salman Rushdie: Absolutely. Oh, certainly. Yes.

Charlie Rose: Because my impression was not that somehow there was still a kind of level of "We've got to be very careful about this, and we don't want to be somewhere where somebody will have time if they know."

Salman Rushdie: "Well, all I can say is we've done it in England and Europe, and so there is a precedent for it. Now, in fact, very recently— because I've just been more or less around the world, I went to South America and Australia and so on. In South America, Carlos Fuentes and I did a kind of event at the big Guadalajara book fair and that was well-known. I was on TV the night before talking about it. I was in the newspapers on the morning of the thing. Fifteen hundred people were there. It was fine.

Charlie Rose: One last question about that. Do you know if anybody tried and failed?

Salman Rushdie: I know that they didn't get close, but I know that in the first three years, let's say, that yes, there were a number of attempts. I have this on the say-so of the British authorities, who told me that there had been, on various occasions in their view, attempts in earnest. The last time I heard seriously about an attempt was around the time of the Gulf war. At that point, there was apparently a very serious attempt. A contract had been put out and accepted. In these years, quite a large number of Iranians—I can't remember exactly how many, but over a couple of dozen—have been expelled from Britain from time to time on a national security basis, and I've been told several times that many of those people who were expelled were, in the opinion of the government, in the country for reasons connected with the Iranian *fatwā*.

Charlie Rose: What's next for you?
Salman Rushdie: Well, more books I hope.

Charlie Rose: But is there one underway that—
Salman Rushdie: There's one just beginning. My own feeling has been for some time, as I said, that this was the sort of culmination and completion of a project of work. I'd quite like to go somewhere really different next time. Somewhere really surprising. I might even write a novel about America. You never know.

Charlie Rose: All right. Thank you very much. Salman Rushdie's novel, *The Moor's Last Sigh,* in which he touches on many subjects and brings them together in his unique style. Thank you very much. A pleasure to have you here.
Salman Rushdie: Thank you.

Salman Speaks
Peter Kadzis / 1999

From *The Boston Phoenix,* 7 May 1999. 28–31. Reprinted by permission.

As a young man, Salman Rushdie considered becoming an actor. But he stayed true to a more primal ambition and became a writer. Today the world is his stage, and—although he may have wished otherwise—he has become perhaps the most famous writer in the world. That distinction was thrust upon him 10 years ago, when the Iranian government placed a bounty—a *fatwa*—on his head after the publication of his novel *The Satanic Verses.*

Although some Islamic fundamentalist groups would still like to see him dead, the Iranian government backed away from its *fatwa* last fall. In the wake of that decision, life for Rushdie has become more relaxed, yet hardly casual. He still travels with armed guards. But even though his movements are still cloaked in a degree of secrecy, he moves more freely than he has in years.

In recent weeks Rushdie has indeed been on the move, publicizing his most recent novel, *The Ground Beneath Her Feet,* which was simultaneously published in 12 nations—an act of creative (not to mention commercial) affirmation that clearly pleases Rushdie.

Even for this most protean of talents, *The Ground Beneath Her Feet* is a startling and sprawling novel. To simplify: it is a rock-and-roll story. To amplify: it is a retelling of the ancient myth of Orpheus and Eurydice. To sum up: its ambition is epic.

Perhaps the most succinct summary of the story comes from *Publishers Weekly*: "Ormus Cama, a supernaturally gifted musician, and his beloved, Vina Apsara, a half-Indian woman with a soul-thrilling voice, meet in Bombay in the late '50s, discover rock and roll, and form a band that goes on to become the world's most popular musical act. Narrator Rai Merchant, their life-long friend, is a world-famous photographer and Vina's 'back-door man.' Rai tells the story of their great abiding love (both are named for love gods: Cama as in Kama Sutra, and Vina for Venus)."

Rushdie's fame as a controversialist is, as he explains below, unwarranted and unwelcome. Before the publication of *The Satanic Verses,* he already

216

enjoyed an international reputation as the man who, said the *New York Times,* "rewdrew the literary map of India" with the publication of his 1981 novel *Midnight's Children.*

Before Rushdie, the tone of Anglo-Indian literature was decidedly cool. There was, for example, the sensitive reserve of E. M. Forster and the stiff upper lip of Rudyard Kipling. Rushdie's prose is more pungent, his range of reference more polyglot, and his world-view playful to the point of daring.

Although I suspect that Rushdie—who exhibits a sort of muscular diffidence—might shiver at the suggestion, he comes as close as anyone in public life to matching Hemingway's ideal of courage: grace under pressure.

Q: *Let's talk first about growing up in Bombay. In* Midnight's Children, *you wrote, if I recall the line correctly, that you were "floating in the amniotic fluid of the past."*

A: The thing to say about the Bombay of the 1950s and the 1960s is that it was a very different place than the city that now exists. I suppose it's true that, to a certain extent, there's a kind of golden glow of childhood about it in my memory. But it's also the case that the people who were of an older generation thought of that city as going through a particularly beautiful and sort of memorable phase. It does seem to have been Bombay's great moment. How to describe it? I mean, as a child, it was a very exciting town to grow up in. It was a very cosmopolitan town, much more so than most other Indian towns. Like any great city, it acted as a magnet, and so people came to Bombay from all over India. It had a greater diversity of Indians than other Indian cities. And it was the commercial center, so it attracted a large population of non-Indians. When I grew up, the kids I played with were by no means all Indian kids. They were American kids, Australian, Japanese, Europeans, and so on. It felt like a very cosmopolitan, big-city upbringing.

Q: *So you were multicultural before your time?*

A: Well, we all were. I think this idea of a separation of cultures between the East and the West was certainly never the idea I grew up with. They were all mixed in together from the beginning.

Q: *Your parents were Muslims. Was your family religious?*

A: Not really, as far as I can remember. I think that's one reason why, although it was technically an Indian-Muslim family, my parents—at the independence of India and at the division of India into India and Pakistan— never considered going to Pakistan. They certainly felt more like Indians than

Muslims. And my father's family was an old Delhi family from the old Muslim neighborhoods of Old Delhi, and that's where my parents lived when they first got married. They decided to move to Bombay about nine months before I was born, I guess. They, like many other people, were nervous about the trouble that everybody could see coming at the partition. And my father felt that Bombay would be a safer place. Bombay has always had—until recently, anyway—a reputation of being a more tolerant environment than the rest of India. So they moved to Bombay to get out of the firing line. When the terrible events of the partition happened, the riots and the massacres and so on, almost nothing happened in Bombay. And so they stayed there, and that's where I was born and raised.

Q: *Can you recall your extended family?*
A: I can't remember my father's father, who died before I was born, but he was, by all accounts, one of my few literary antecedents, in that he was an essayist and a patron of young writers and so on—and he also made a fortune, which my father then spent most of his life losing.

Q: *How about your mother's father?*
A: Yes, my mother's father I remember very well. He was a huge figure in my childhood. Unlike my parents, he was really quite a religious man. He was a practicing Muslim. He said his prayers five times a day. He performed the pilgrimage to Mecca. But at the same time, he was one of the most tolerant and open-minded men I've ever known. For myself, my sisters, my many cousins, he was a huge figure in all our lives because he loved children and was never happier than when he was amongst us.

Q: *How did his wonder manifest itself?*
A: I remember—not when I was a very small child, but when I was more grown up—we would needle him by claiming not to believe in God and so on. You'd say, in your 10- or 11-year-old self, "I don't believe in God, Granddad." And he'd say, "Oh really? Come and sit down here and tell me all about it." And so you'd sit down next to him and he would very seriously listen and probe as you offered your 11-year-old reasons for not believing in God. And then, instead of contradicting you, he'd say, "Yes, well, that's a lot to think about, I think you've given me a lot to think about, I'll have to think about it." And then, a couple of days later, he'd come back and he'd say, "I just did have a couple of thoughts about what you were saying, and let me just talk to you about them." And he'd then offer you, in a very gentle way,

his rebuttals to your childish atheism. And when you'd say, "No, no, Grand-dad, that's just complete nonsense, it's completely wrong," he'd say, "Yes, well, you're probably right, but I just think we should go on talking about it." So certainly, the atmosphere around him was that anything could be said, anything could be discussed, and that's how we all grew up.

Q: *What was the first rock-and-roll record you ever bought?*

A: Oh, I think *Heartbreak Hotel.* It was very difficult in India in those days to buy rock-and-roll records, because they were not locally produced. You had to rely on occasional imports and then run to the record shop when the bush telegraph told you that there were some there. And these were old-style 78 rpm discs that I'm talking about—fragile, you know? They were often damaged in transit or scratched because they were secondhand and being sold off by somebody whose family was going home. So it wasn't easy to come by these things. There was a particular record store in Bombay, called Rhythm House, which used to occasionally have these imports.

Q: *Did you listen to rock and roll on the radio?*

A: Yes, but not, oddly, on Indian radio, which was state controlled and didn't permit the playing of Western music. I think in that post-colonial mo-ment, it was thought to be culturally unsound. Radio Ceylon, as it was then called—it's Sri Lanka now—had a rather more tolerant policy, and, yes, at the weekends, it would play a few hours of a Western hit-parade kind of program. That's where we first heard a lot of these songs. But also, because the city was so international, we had access. I often heard this music in my friends' houses, listening to their records. It wasn't easy for that music to arrive, given these constraints. And yet it did arrive, and we all heard. So, in a way, it became the first globalized cultural phenomenon.

Q: *As a former colonial, what was it like going to Rugby and Cambridge? Was it a tough transition?*

A: Rugby was tough. Cambridge I had a very good time at, but coming to Rugby was really quite brutal. I was not quite 14 and taken aback to be made to feel like a foreigner, which, until that point, I had never thought of myself as. I did experience certain amounts of racial discrimination—not from the staff, from some of the other boys. And that was shocking and depressing. And so I remember my school days as not being particularly happy. I was bad at games. I think it was the triple whammy: foreign, clever, bad at games. [*Laughs*] I think if I'd been any two of those three, I might have been able to get away with it. Foreign, clever, good at games—that would have been all right. I mean, there were some boys there with Indian or Pakistani or, indeed, African backgrounds, but who were excellent sportsmen, and they seemed to have a perfectly nice time at school.

Q: *How was Cambridge different?*

A: Well, for a start, there were girls. That helped. But also, I didn't feel any oppression. I didn't feel any racism aimed toward me. I didn't feel excluded. And then, also, I was at Cambridge at quite a good time to be young. I went there in 1965 and graduated in 1968 and, you know, of all the years in the last 50 years to have been at university, those were probably the years.

Q: *Did you always know you wanted to be a writer?*

A: I did, really. My parents tell me that great deal of my life trying to understand and write about the world from which I came originally, I find myself turning away from that, feeling that I've done enough, if you like, or enough for the moment—and I find myself more and more interested in the world to which I came, about which I first wrote in *The Satanic Verses*. That's the aspect of *The Satanic Verses* that really got blotted out by the storm that surrounded that book.

Q: *One critic pointed out that* The Satanic Verses *is a book in which a novelist named Salman moves not only westward, but also increasingly inward, searching for yet another way to describe a world that is increasingly connected, but in no way yet whole.*

A: It's not at all a bad description of the way that I felt at the time that I wrote *The Satanic Verses*. I felt that I'd written one novel, broadly speaking, about India [*Midnight's Children*] and one novel, broadly speaking, about a kind of version of Pakistan [*Shame*, published in 1983], and I thought it was time that my writing made the same movement that I'd made—that's to say, migrate into the West. And I felt, first of all, that I wanted to write a novel about the act of migration and, secondly, a novel about the internal effect of migration. It's so ridiculous in light of what happened, but I did think about *The Satanic Verses* that it was the least political novel I'd ever written. I thought it was a novel of introspection and a novel which tried to make sense of the kind of life experience that people like me had had. And then, boom. It turned into the most public novel I'd ever written.

Q: *In a time when so many people seem to doubt the potency of literature, did this experience scare you? What was it like to find out that fiction could matter so much?*

A: Well, of course, it was an extraordinary discovery that it should be my book that ended up mattering so much. Particularly when it was written as an introspective book, not as a book designed to shake the world. I suppose *Uncle Tom's Cabin* was designed to have a certain public impact and did have it. But in this case, it really caught me unawares. But I do think that, as somebody once said, you can judge the importance of literature by the apparatus that tyrants set up to repress it. And the more repressive the society that exists in the world, the more tightly literature is censored and the more danger writers are in. I was in the unusual position of living in a free country and being attacked across the world from a much more censorious and closed society, but it happens to writers around the world all the time. And in that sense, what happened to me is not unusual at all.

Q: *What did it feel like when you found out that* The Satanic Verses *was being burned in England?*
A: Well, all I can say is, it was the most shocking moment of my life. And I think the moment when I actually saw television images and, afterwards, photographs of my book being burned was the moment that engendered in me the kind of fury that I can't remember otherwise feeling. This was, after all, a month before Khomeini imposed the *fatwa*. And in that month, what I did was to more or less go on the warpath and try to make sure that this act was seen as—I can't think of a word other than barbaric. I also wanted to make sure that I was fighting this with all my strength. And then, a month later, there was the escalation from Iran, which changed the argument again.

Q: *Artists and performers long for fame. What's your reaction to being perhaps the most famous writer in the world?*
A: Well, I don't know. The main reaction is one of disappointment. It's a terrible thing to be famous for the wrong thing. I'd always hoped that people would respond to and like my work, and that's all I'd ever wanted, really—to write books that did well and that were well thought of. I'd begun to do that with *Midnight's Children* and *Shame*. It's easy to overlook this now, but they were books which had quite a considerable international reputation. The road I was going along was the only life I'd ever wanted, and I was delighted that I was beginning to have it. And to have this other reputation hasn't at all been beneficial to me as a writer. I think in many ways, for people who didn't know my writing or don't know my writing, it's often been something that put them off because they felt that this dark, theological cloud that descended over my work must in some way be representative of the world itself. And, I

think, it made them think I must be an arcane writer, with these dark, theological inclinations. And I think it made a lot of people less likely to pick up a book by me as well as, of course, making some people more likely, even if only out of curiosity.

Q: *How much energy did it take to keep going in those days?*
A: It took a lot. It was terribly bewildering. I had to find my feet again. I had to learn how to fight back. I had to find the strength to get back to writing, and I had to then set about the task of going on being a writer in fairly difficult circumstances. But you discover things about yourself under extreme pressure, and I guess one of the things I discovered about myself was that I was able to find that equilibrium again, and I was able to find ways of fighting back, and I was able to go on with my work. So I guess I'm tougher than I thought.

Q: *Did this experience change your concept of liberty or your feeling toward freedom?*
A: Well, it made me think a lot more about it. I think one of the things about living in a free society—which, broadly speaking, I've done all my life, first in India and then in England—is that you don't have to examine the idea of freedom too much because it's simply there. You've got it, you don't need to make great speeches about it because you already have it, and it would seem unnecessary to bang on about the importance of free speech when everybody has free speech. I guess what happened in my case is that somebody tried to turn off the tap. Somebody tried to deprive me of those basic freedoms and, as a result, drew my attention to the importance of them—not just the importance, but the importance of articulating the case for these fundamental freedoms. I became much more involved in that battle than I ever had been before. I mean, one is always asked to sign things. I'd probably sign my share of petitions on behalf of this or that. But it suddenly became to me, for obvious reasons, a very central issue of my life, and I think it will remain so even though the bad days have come to an end.

Q: *Why a rock-and-roll novel? You've said rock is a universal, an international language?*
A: Yeah, that had something to do with it, but that wasn't the starting point. I mean, that was one of the valuable things about rock and roll. It meant that there was a language of cultural reference that I could use which people all around the world would easily get, just in the same way that people

once might have got a range of classical or mythological reference. Rock is the mythology of our time. It was interesting to contrast it in the novel with that older mythology, which now requires more explanation than it used to. I wanted to write about rock and roll partly because it's the music of my life. When I was young, it was young. We've more or less grown up and grown old together. It feels as if rock music is the soundtrack of my life. As if I could associate all kinds of moments in my life with songs, and songs would evoke memories that otherwise might have been lost.

Q: *Could you sketch that soundtrack?*

A: Well, I suppose it starts with Elvis, Little Richard, Jerry Lee Lewis, Bill Haley—all that takes me right back to the late 1950s and early 1960s, even before I'd come to England. Many of those songs can evoke moments of my childhood. Then I came to England at the time when the music was in the process of transforming into what became the Beatles and the Rolling Stones. And that music, the music of the Beatles and the Stones and the other bands, that period seems to have been the background to most of my teenage years. Bob Dylan was very, very important for me. I remember one of the boys at Rugby, in the boarding house where I lived, first introducing me to an early Bob Dylan album. And actually, I have to say, at that time, he made a bigger impression on me than the Beatles or the Rolling Stones. I'd never heard this noise before, you know, the nasal intonation, the strange phrasing, the —oh, you know, the harmonica, the extraordinary surrealism of his lyrics. And I became a Dylan fan at that point, and I have never ceased to be one. So yes, it was very important.

Then what I've always considered to be my political awakening was the protest against the war in Vietnam, which took place in England because the British government so strongly supported the American presence in Vietnam, even though no actual troops were sent. That protest seemed also to be very closely wrapped up with the music. Traditionally the music of war is there in order to instill, in soldiers and civilians, patriotic feelings. But this was music which was much more—I'd say, much more dissident than that. And music which was simply affirming love during a time of death.

Q: The Ground Beneath Her Feet, *for all its range of reference and mythological underpinnings, is a very American novel.*

A: The country that has mattered the most to me with this book has been the U.S. It should be well received here, and I'm happy to say that it has been, if only because it's my first American novel. I mean, not just because a lot of it happens in America, but because rock and roll is a thing that came from America. And so one of the things that I was writing about was how the rest of the world had responded to American culture, and how America has responded to the rest of the world. That's one of the kind of—the under-themes of this novel.

Q: *It seems like a logical step in your westward progression that we alluded to earlier. If I were to try to boil 575 pages down to a sentence, it would be this: you can kill the musician, but you can't kill the music.*

A: Yes, I mean, I think of the end of the Orpheus myth, in which the head of Orpheus, having been torn from his body, is thrown into the river and goes on singing. That's the meaning of that story. You can destroy the singer, but you can't stop the song. And I think for fairly obvious reasons, that's an important thought for me to have and to hold on to. The durability of art and the paradoxical fragility—that was the message, that was the thing that I wanted people to take away from the book.

Q: *In* Midnight's Children, *your hero is born at the inception of India's independence.* The Ground Beneath Her Feet *begins on Valentine's Day 1989, as did your exile. Surely there is a message here?*

A: It's really a very simple thing, and what I should say is that, of all the things in this novel, it was the thing I was most uncertain of. I vacillated a great deal about whether to leave that date in or not. There was a bit of me that thought it was digging the reader in the ribs too hard to leave it in. In the end I did, simply because I thought, well, one of the reasons I'm writing a novel about cataclysms in people's lives, about earthquakes, about the fact that the world is provisional and the life that you think is yours can be removed from you at any moment—one of the reasons I'm having these ideas and writing this book is because of what happened in my life, and I may as well just acknowledge the fact.

Q: *Let's talk about twins for a second. Vina Apsara is the surviving sibling of a dead baby twin, as was Elvis. Is this a coincidence?*

A: No, not at all. I think where it comes from in my writing, all this business with twins, is that I've always been very conscious of the choices that I didn't make in my life. That's to say, when I left university at the age of 21 I decided that I would make a life in the West and not back in the East. And I've always wondered about what would have happened if I'd gone down the other road. So I've always had this strong sense of the path not traveled, the road not taken, and of that shadow self, of the person that I might have been but chose not to become. And that kind of doubling and splitting in myself is the reason why it keeps happening in my books and is the reason why, in this novel, the character has a shadow self running down the corridors of his mind. But I think this time I may have done it. I may have pushed it to the limit with two sets of twins and, indeed, a twin world, an entirely parallel world as well as the real world. So I think maybe that's enough twins.

Q: *Apsara becomes the inspiration for a posthumous cult. This reminds me of Princess Diana.*
A: Yeah.

Q: *Coincidence?*
A: Well, in a way it is a coincidence, in that I'd actually devised the book and, indeed, written an earlier version of what happens after Vina's death before Princess Diana's accident. It was obviously essential to the idea of the book that Vina dies— indeed, she dies in the first sentence, and by this time she's one of the most popular singers in the world. That she would be much mourned was obviously always a part of the design, but then the real-life event happened, which was on a scale so much greater than anything I'd envisaged. It shocked me because it seemed as if it jumped off my pages into the real world. It made me think again about what I'd written and actually rewrite it on a bigger scale, and with a dimension to it that it certainly couldn't have had without that real-life occurrence. So yes, in the end the book is affected by what happened, both what happened to Princess Diana and what happened after her death. But it is one of the most bizarre things about writing this book, that I'd actually already written it before it happened.

Q: *Well, I suppose no more bizarre than our fighting in the name of ethnic Albanians after the movie* Wag the Dog.
A: Yeah, this is true. Well, *Wag the Dog* does seem to have become the text of our times.

Q: *There's a religious aspect to celebrity culture. Was that part of its imaginative appeal for you?*
A: You don't actually worship the celebrities, you just watch them and obsess about them.

Q: *It's very mythic.*
A: I think I'm interested in the way in which we as a culture use celebrities.

In that respect they are quite like the old pantheons of gods, who, you know, behaved very badly. Ancient gods were not model examples, but simply instances of human beings enlarged to divine proportions. It was about how humans might behave if you removed all restraints and gave them great power. In that sense, celebrity is a kind of recurrence of that theme: we take this group of people and we shine on them a very bright light and give them, if not great power, then certainly great influence. We ask how they behave when we remove all controls and restraints, and we enjoy watching the answer to that question. Sometimes they behave very well, and sometimes they're destroyed by it.

Q: *Why did you choose to have a photographer as the narrator? And why is he tone deaf?*

A: Well, he can't sing because I can't sing. That's very simple. He's a photographer because I thought, if you look to the left of a rock star, you'll find the photographer. And if you want a point-of-view character, a slightly voyeuristic point-of-view character, it seemed a perfectly appropriate choice of profession. And then again, mentioning Princess Diana, in the aftermath of her death, I discovered—having already chosen a photographer for my narrator—that for a moment there, photography became the most unpopular profession in the world. All photographers, even artists like Richard Avedon, suddenly began to be thought of as paparazzi, and the profession began to be something that people scorned. There'd be boos when photographers took cameras out at public events. And I thought how strange that was, and it made me even more interested to write about the business of representation, the business of image-making, about what it is to take a picture of the world, what it is to walk up, walk up to the world and take its photograph. So it became doubly interesting to me. And I've always been interested in photography. I'm not particularly a good photographer, but I've got great heaps of photography books.

Q: *You've said, I forget exactly where, that you're proud to have avoided two traps set by the* fatwa—*writing timid novels and writing bitter ones. How did you manage that?*

A: Well, just by great bloody-mindedness. [*Laughs*] I love literature. I think of it as a great privilege to be able to do this thing that I admire so much, the art of the novel. And it just struck me that lots and lots of writers have had a hard time. I'm not the first one. And many wonderful books have been made by writers who have gone through or are going through very bad times. And I just thought I could not use my particular bad time as an excuse. "Just get on with it and do your work," I thought. So, I've always gained something—I've said this before, but I do think it sums my feelings. If somebody's trying to shut you up, sing louder and, if possible, better. My experience just made me all the more determined to write the very best books I could find it in myself to write.

Q: *What's next?*

A: Wish I knew. I like to find new things to do. And in this book, I found quite a lot of new things to do, both in terms of rock-and-roll music and in terms of being able to write about the West in a way that I'd not written before. And also, I felt that I found a new and very liberating and rich language to write in. I hope that I just find another new step to take, because otherwise I'd bore myself.

Q: *Could that someday mean moving to America? At least for a while?*

A: Well, I'd like to spend time in America, and I hope—I hope that I will spend more time here. I have a two-year-old son, and I'm not sure whether I want to send him to school in America just yet. It seems to be too many people getting killed in schools in America just now.

I think certainly my wife would not be very keen on it, on educating a child over here, but the truth is, I've always loved coming to America. I hope things are loosening up a bit so that I will be able to spend more and more time here.

Index